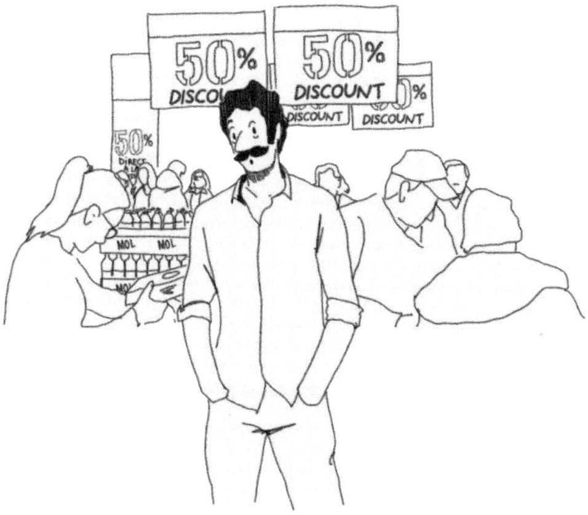
50%
DISCOUNT
50%
DISCOUNT
DISCOUNT
MOL
MOL

First published in English in 2020
by SelfMadeHero
139–141 Pancras Road
London NW1 1UN
www.selfmadehero.com

English translation © 2020 SelfMadeHero

Written and illustrated by Cédric Taling
Translated from French by Edward Gauvin
Cover design by Cédric Taling and Thierry Sestier

Publishing Director: Emma Hayley
Editorial & Production Director: Guillaume Rater
Sales & Marketing Manager: Steve Turner
Designer: Txabi Jones
UK Publicist: Paul Smith
With thanks to: Dan Lockwood

© Rue de l'Échiquier, 2019

This book is printed on FSC certified 140g woodfree offset paper.
The cover is printed on FSC certified 300g Tintoretto Neve.

A CIP record for this book is available from the British Library

ISBN: 978-1-910593-83-7

10 9 8 7 6 5 4 3 2 1

Printed and bound in Slovenia

THOREAU AND ME

CÉDRIC TALING

TRANSLATED BY
EDWARD GAUVIN

SELF MADE HERO

AUTHOR'S NOTE

SPEECH BALLOONS
THAT LOOK LIKE THIS

INDICATE EXCERPTS OR PARAPHRASES
FROM *WALDEN; OR, LIFE IN THE
WOODS* BY HENRY DAVID THOREAU,
FIRST PUBLISHED IN 1854, OR FROM
HIS *JOURNAL*, FIRST PUBLISHED IN 1906.

I. Definitions

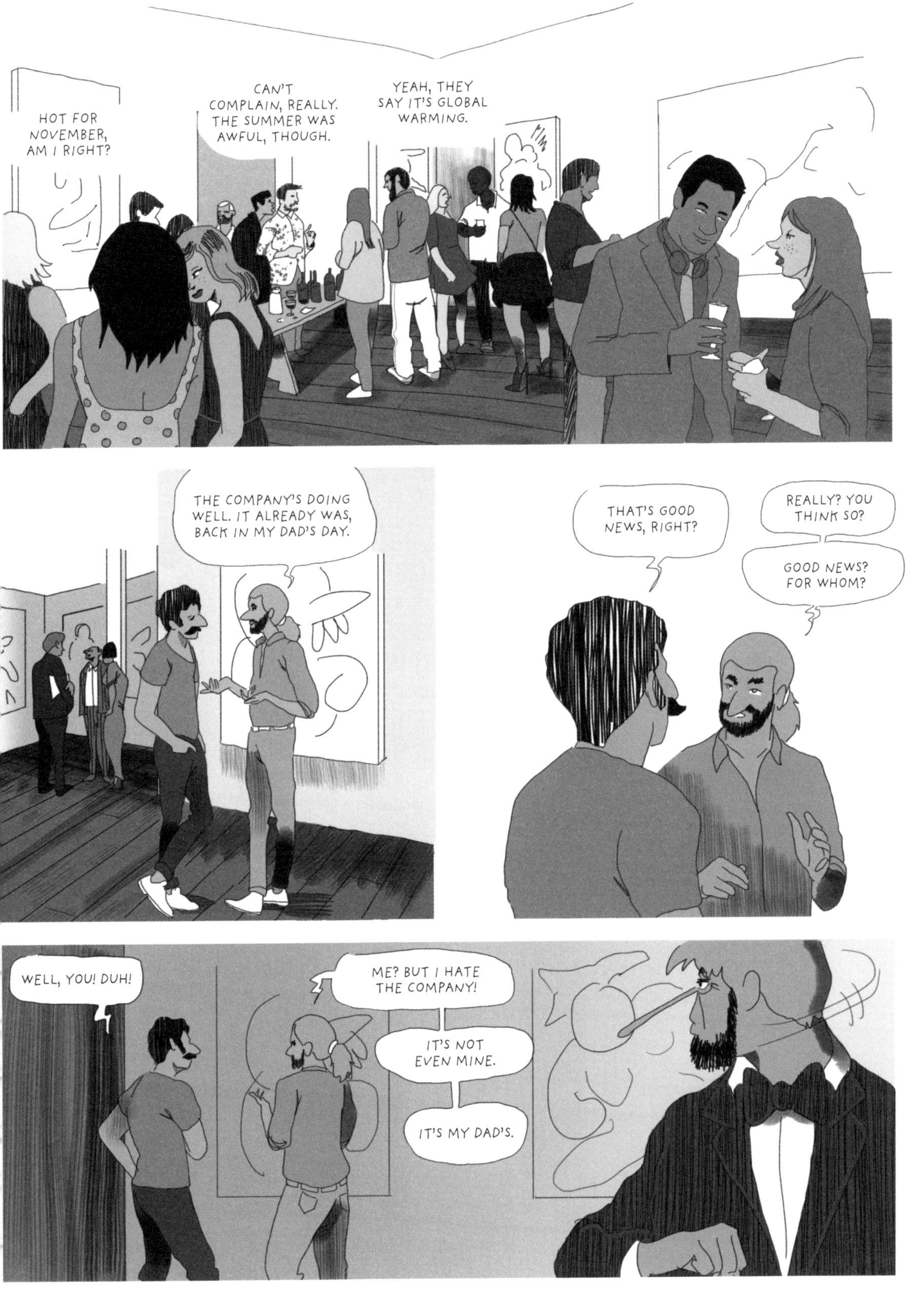
HOT FOR NOVEMBER, AM I RIGHT?
CAN'T COMPLAIN, REALLY. THE SUMMER WAS AWFUL, THOUGH.
YEAH, THEY SAY IT'S GLOBAL WARMING.
THE COMPANY'S DOING WELL. IT ALREADY WAS, BACK IN MY DAD'S DAY.
THAT'S GOOD NEWS, RIGHT?
REALLY? YOU THINK SO?
GOOD NEWS? FOR WHOM?
WELL, YOU! DUH!
ME? BUT I HATE THE COMPANY!
IT'S NOT EVEN MINE.
IT'S MY DAD'S.

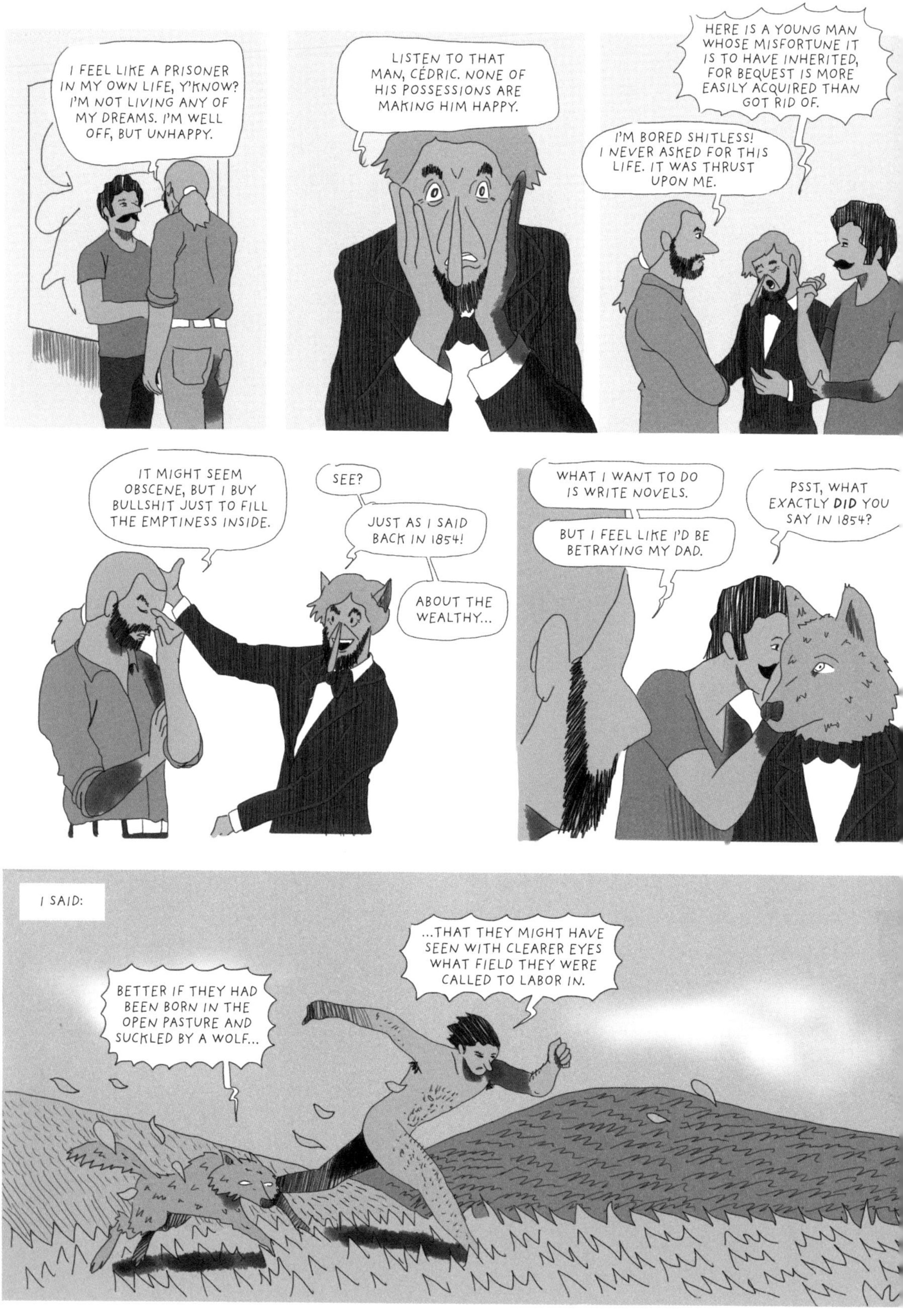
I FEEL LIKE A PRISONER IN MY OWN LIFE, Y'KNOW? I'M NOT LIVING ANY OF MY DREAMS. I'M WELL OFF, BUT UNHAPPY.
LISTEN TO THAT MAN, CÉDRIC. NONE OF HIS POSSESSIONS ARE MAKING HIM HAPPY.
HERE IS A YOUNG MAN WHOSE MISFORTUNE IT IS TO HAVE INHERITED, FOR BEQUEST IS MORE EASILY ACQUIRED THAN GOT RID OF.
I'M BORED SHITLESS! I NEVER ASKED FOR THIS LIFE. IT WAS THRUST UPON ME.
IT MIGHT SEEM OBSCENE, BUT I BUY BULLSHIT JUST TO FILL THE EMPTINESS INSIDE.
SEE?
JUST AS I SAID BACK IN 1854!
ABOUT THE WEALTHY...
WHAT I WANT TO DO IS WRITE NOVELS.
BUT I FEEL LIKE I'D BE BETRAYING MY DAD.
PSST, WHAT EXACTLY **DID** YOU SAY IN 1854?
I SAID:
BETTER IF THEY HAD BEEN BORN IN THE OPEN PASTURE AND SUCKLED BY A WOLF...
...THAT THEY MIGHT HAVE SEEN WITH CLEARER EYES WHAT FIELD THEY WERE CALLED TO LABOR IN.

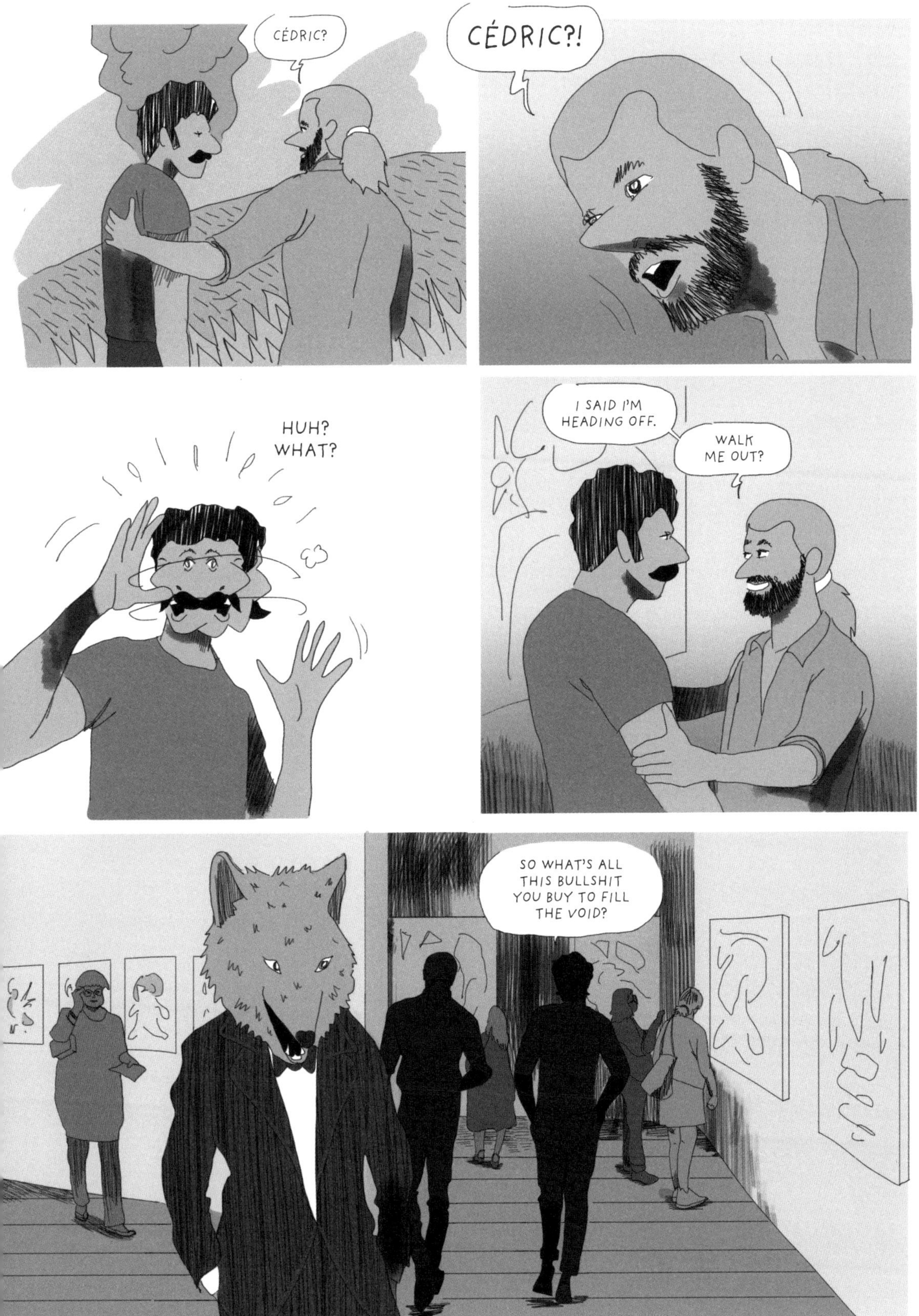
CÉDRIC?
CÉDRIC?!
HUH? WHAT?
I SAID I'M HEADING OFF.
WALK ME OUT?
SO WHAT'S ALL THIS BULLSHIT YOU BUY TO FILL THE VOID?

HOW TO SPEND YOUR MONEY

WITH CORDIAL ASSISTANCE FROM MEN'S

VOGUE

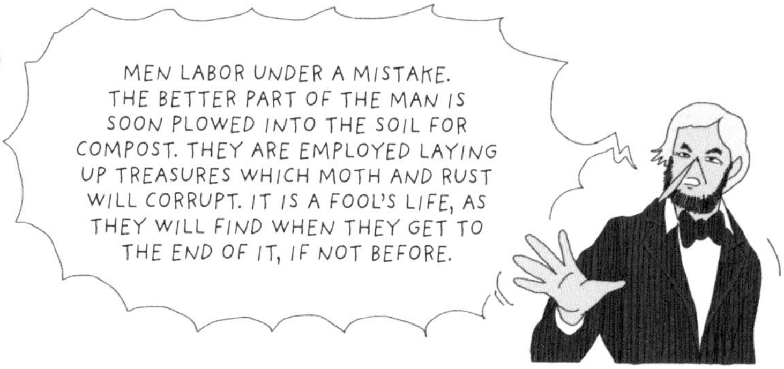
MEN LABOR UNDER A MISTAKE. THE BETTER PART OF THE MAN IS SOON PLOWED INTO THE SOIL FOR COMPOST. THEY ARE EMPLOYED LAYING UP TREASURES WHICH MOTH AND RUST WILL CORRUPT. IT IS A FOOL'S LIFE, AS THEY WILL FIND WHEN THEY GET TO THE END OF IT, IF NOT BEFORE.

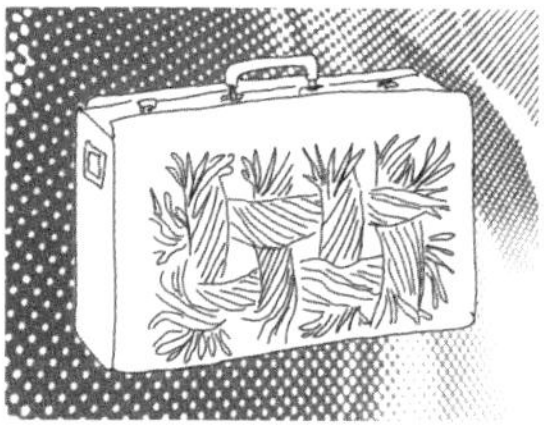

LOUIS VUITTON MADE-TO-ORDER
LAMBSKIN WEEKENDER
$33,226 / £25,248 / €30,000

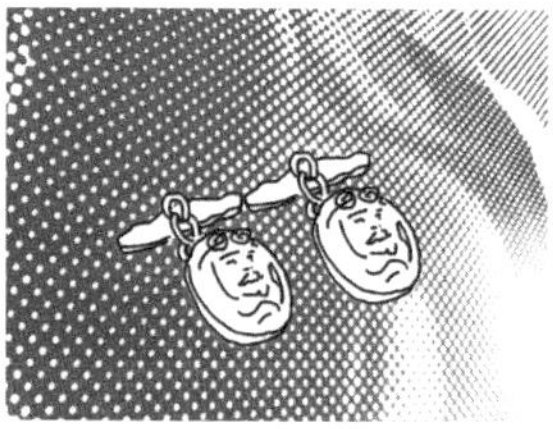

FOUNDWELL VINTAGE SOLID GOLD
AND DIAMOND CUFFLINKS
$4,425 / £3,362 / €3,995

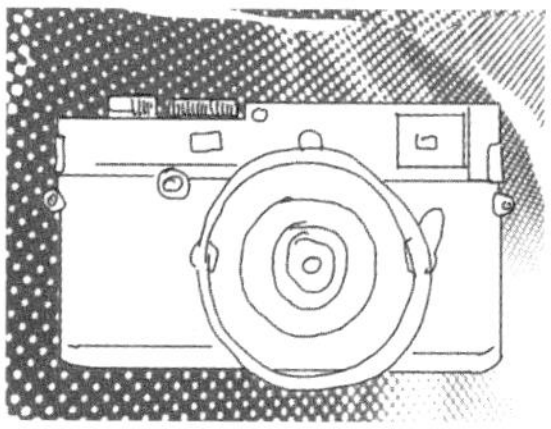

"SAFARI" EDITION
LEICA CAMERA
$15,508 / £11,782 / €14,000

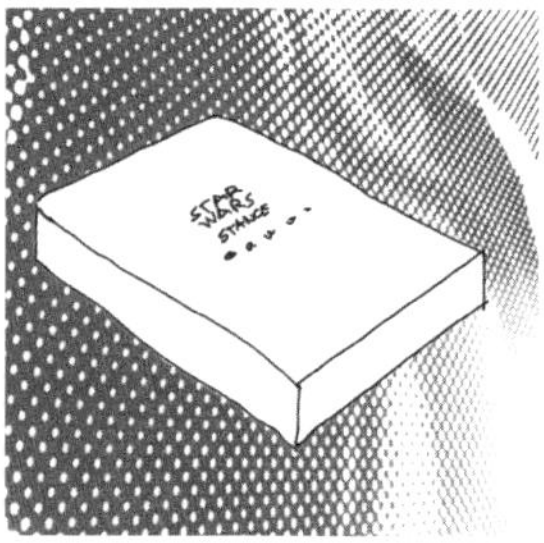
STAR WARS STANCE

BAKER'S DOZEN SET OF *STAR WARS: THE FORCE* SOCKS
FROM STANCE
$227 / £172 / €205

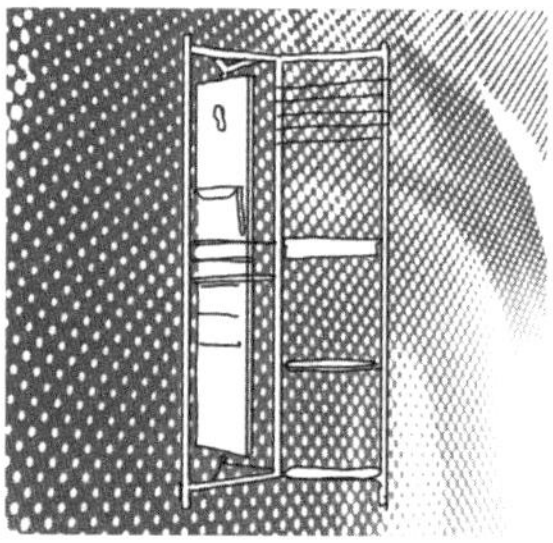

HERMÈS VALET IN LEATHER
AND SOLID WALNUT
$40,760 / £30,965 / €36,800

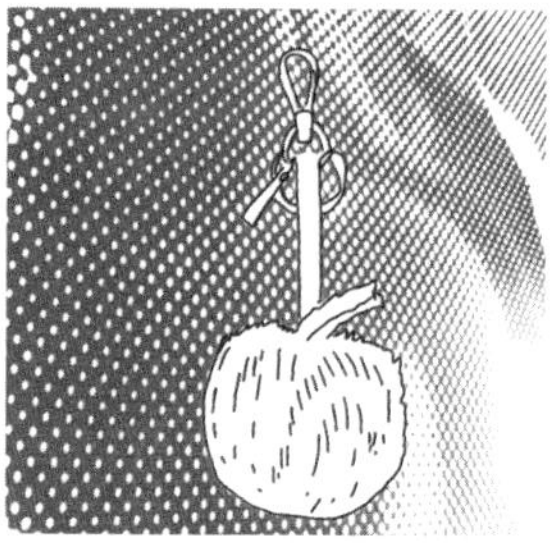

FENDI APPLE KEYCHAIN CHARM,
ETCHED LEATHER
$626 / £475 / €565

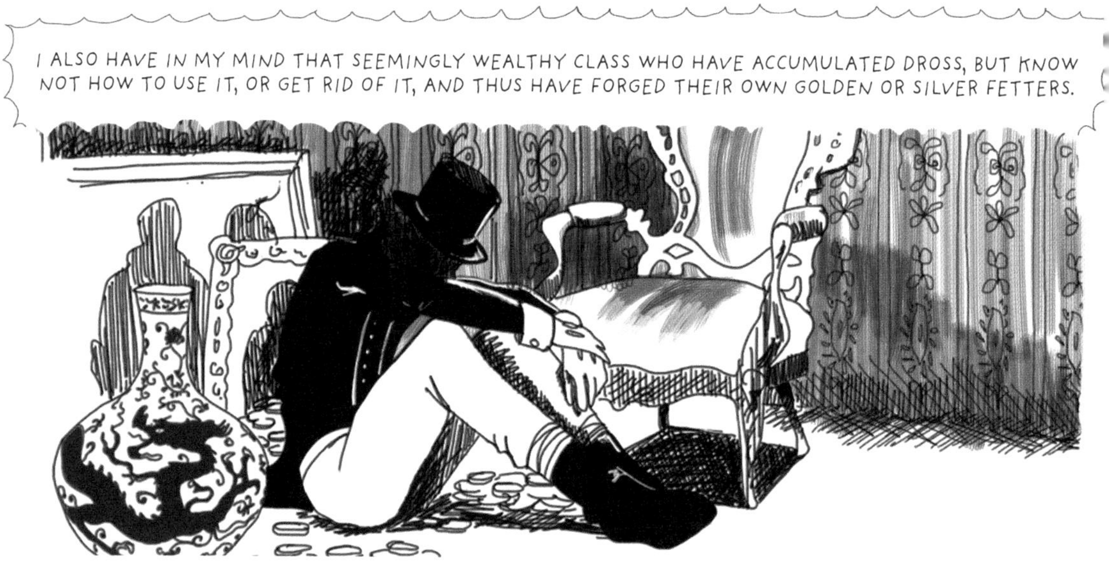
I ALSO HAVE IN MY MIND THAT SEEMINGLY WEALTHY CLASS WHO HAVE ACCUMULATED DROSS, BUT KNOW NOT HOW TO USE IT, OR GET RID OF IT, AND THUS HAVE FORGED THEIR OWN GOLDEN OR SILVER FETTERS.

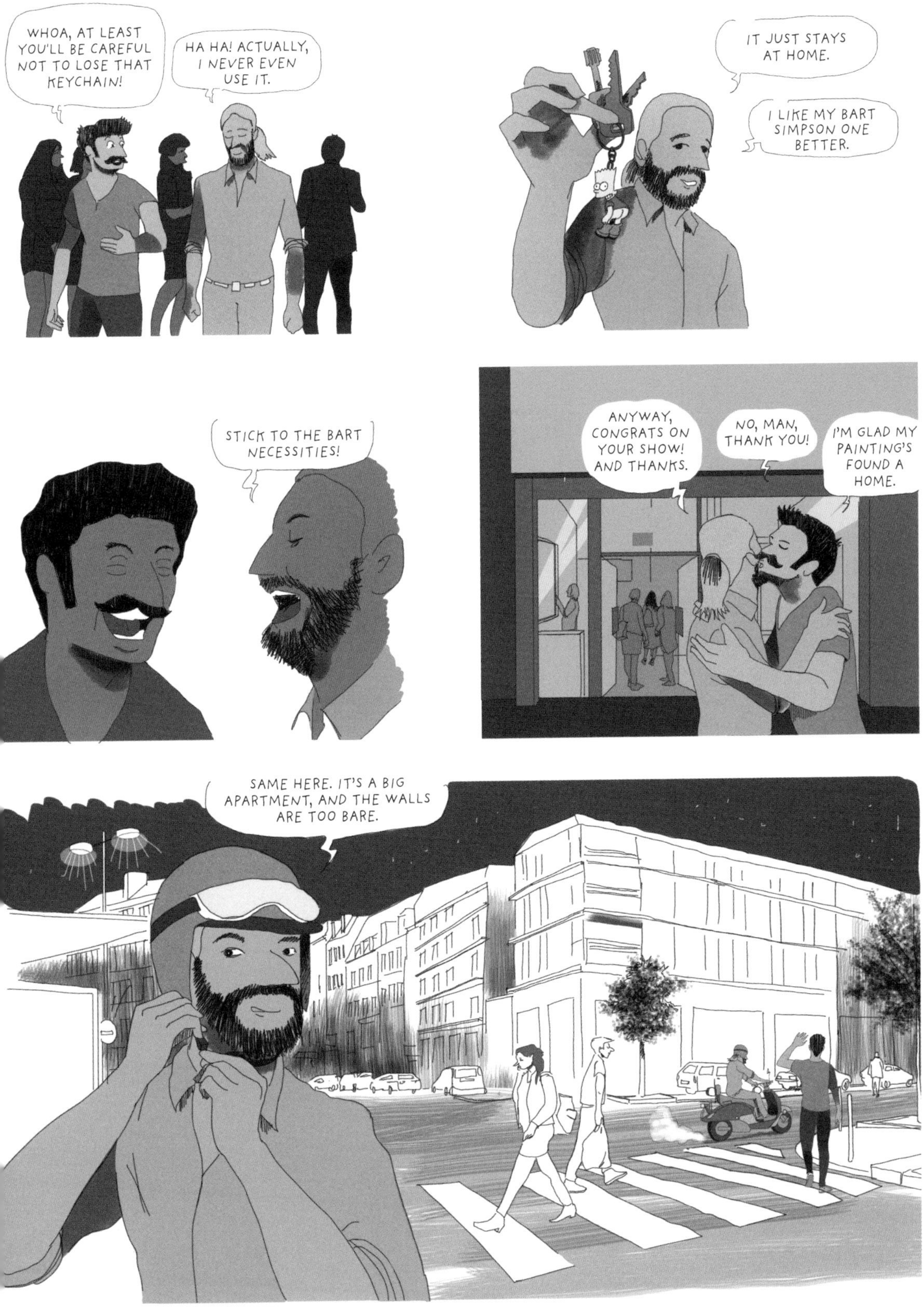
WHOA, AT LEAST YOU'LL BE CAREFUL NOT TO LOSE THAT KEYCHAIN!
HA HA! ACTUALLY, I NEVER EVEN USE IT.
IT JUST STAYS AT HOME.
I LIKE MY BART SIMPSON ONE BETTER.
STICK TO THE BART NECESSITIES!
ANYWAY, CONGRATS ON YOUR SHOW! AND THANKS.
NO, MAN, THANK YOU!
I'M GLAD MY PAINTING'S FOUND A HOME.
SAME HERE. IT'S A BIG APARTMENT, AND THE WALLS ARE TOO BARE.

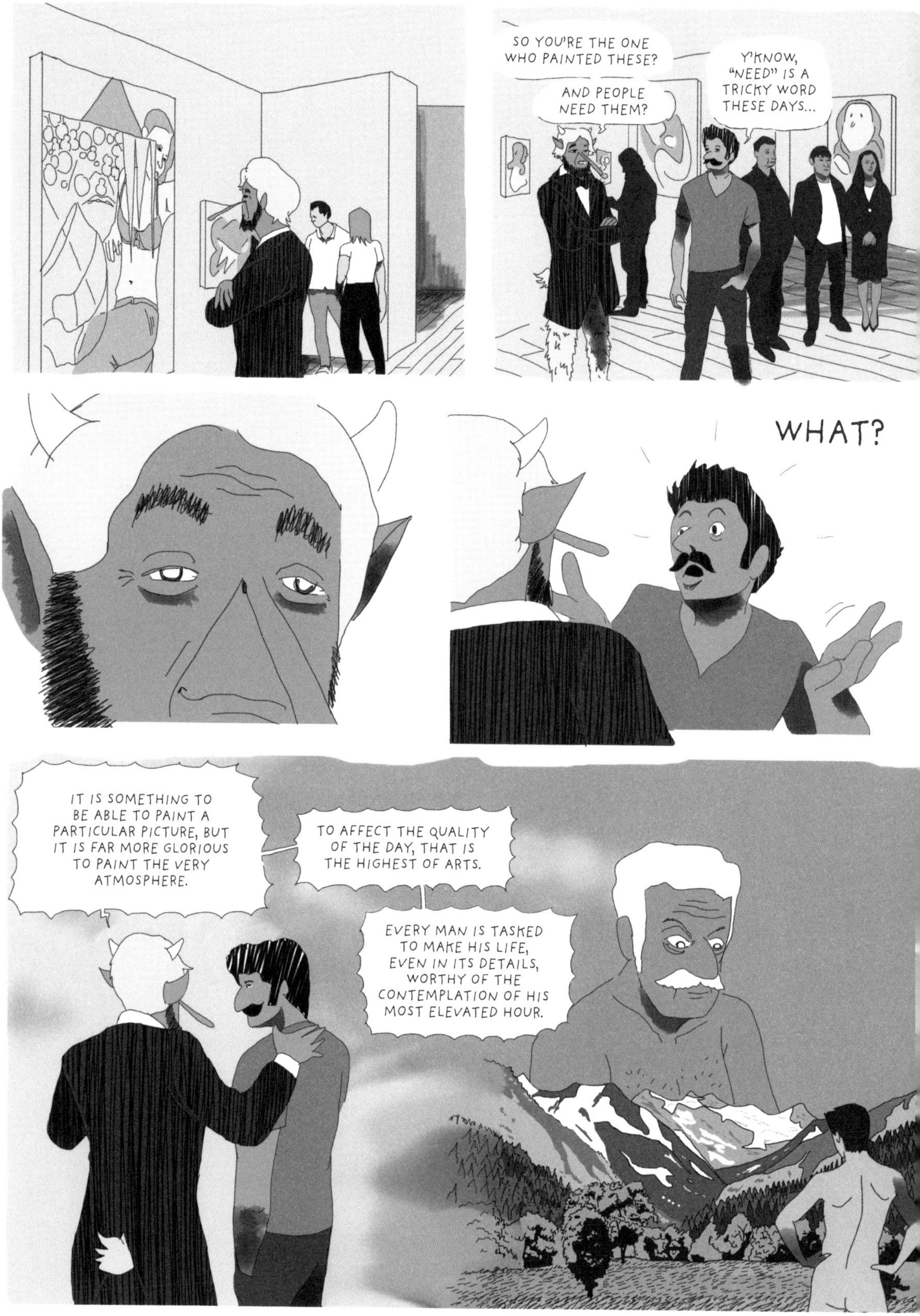
SO YOU'RE THE ONE WHO PAINTED THESE?
AND PEOPLE NEED THEM?
Y'KNOW, "NEED" IS A TRICKY WORD THESE DAYS...
WHAT?
IT IS SOMETHING TO BE ABLE TO PAINT A PARTICULAR PICTURE, BUT IT IS FAR MORE GLORIOUS TO PAINT THE VERY ATMOSPHERE.
TO AFFECT THE QUALITY OF THE DAY, THAT IS THE HIGHEST OF ARTS.
EVERY MAN IS TASKED TO MAKE HIS LIFE, EVEN IN ITS DETAILS, WORTHY OF THE CONTEMPLATION OF HIS MOST ELEVATED HOUR.

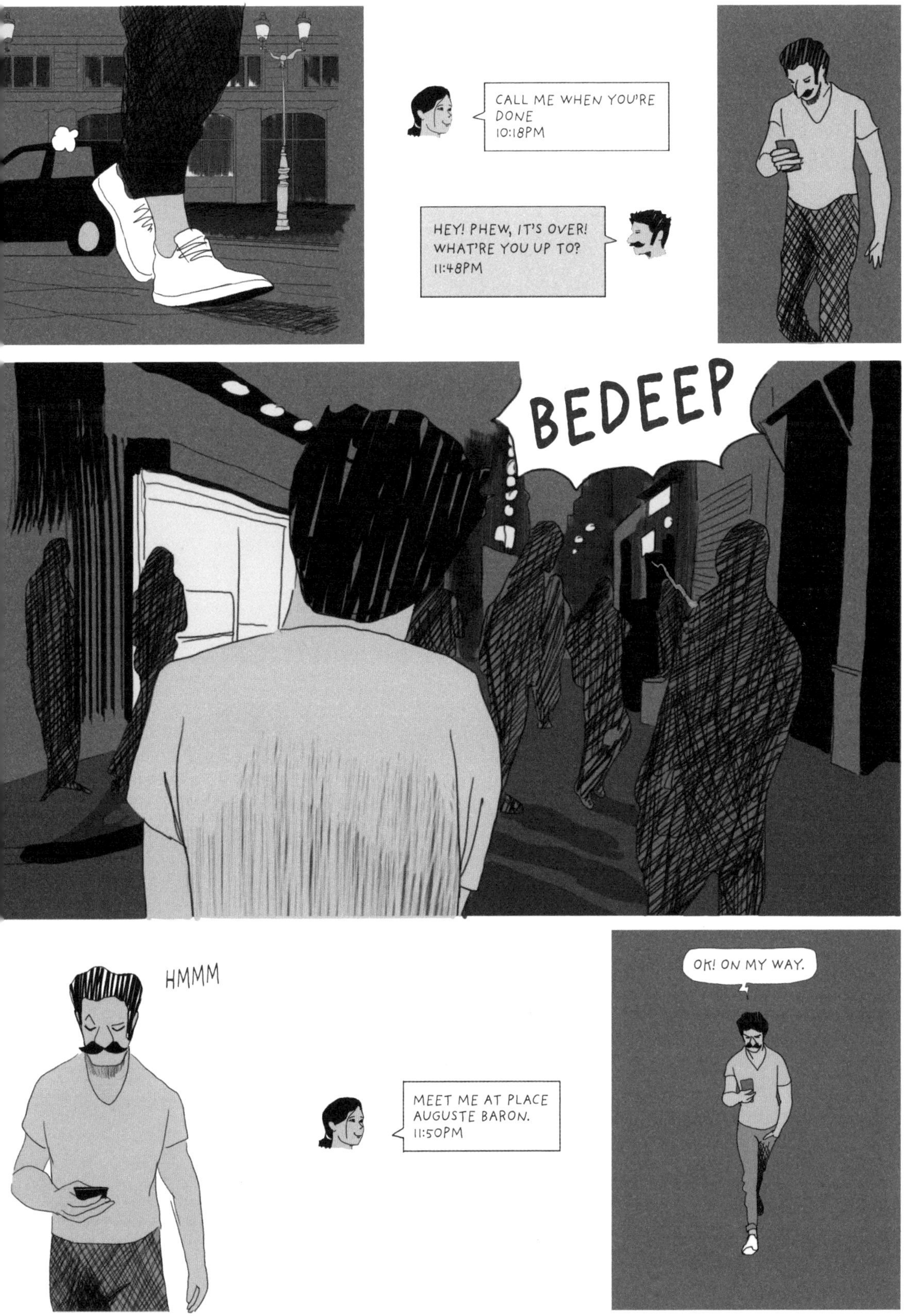
CALL ME WHEN YOU'RE DONE
10:18PM
HEY! PHEW, IT'S OVER! WHAT'RE YOU UP TO?
11:48PM
BEDEEP
HMMM
MEET ME AT PLACE AUGUSTE BARON.
11:50PM
OK! ON MY WAY.

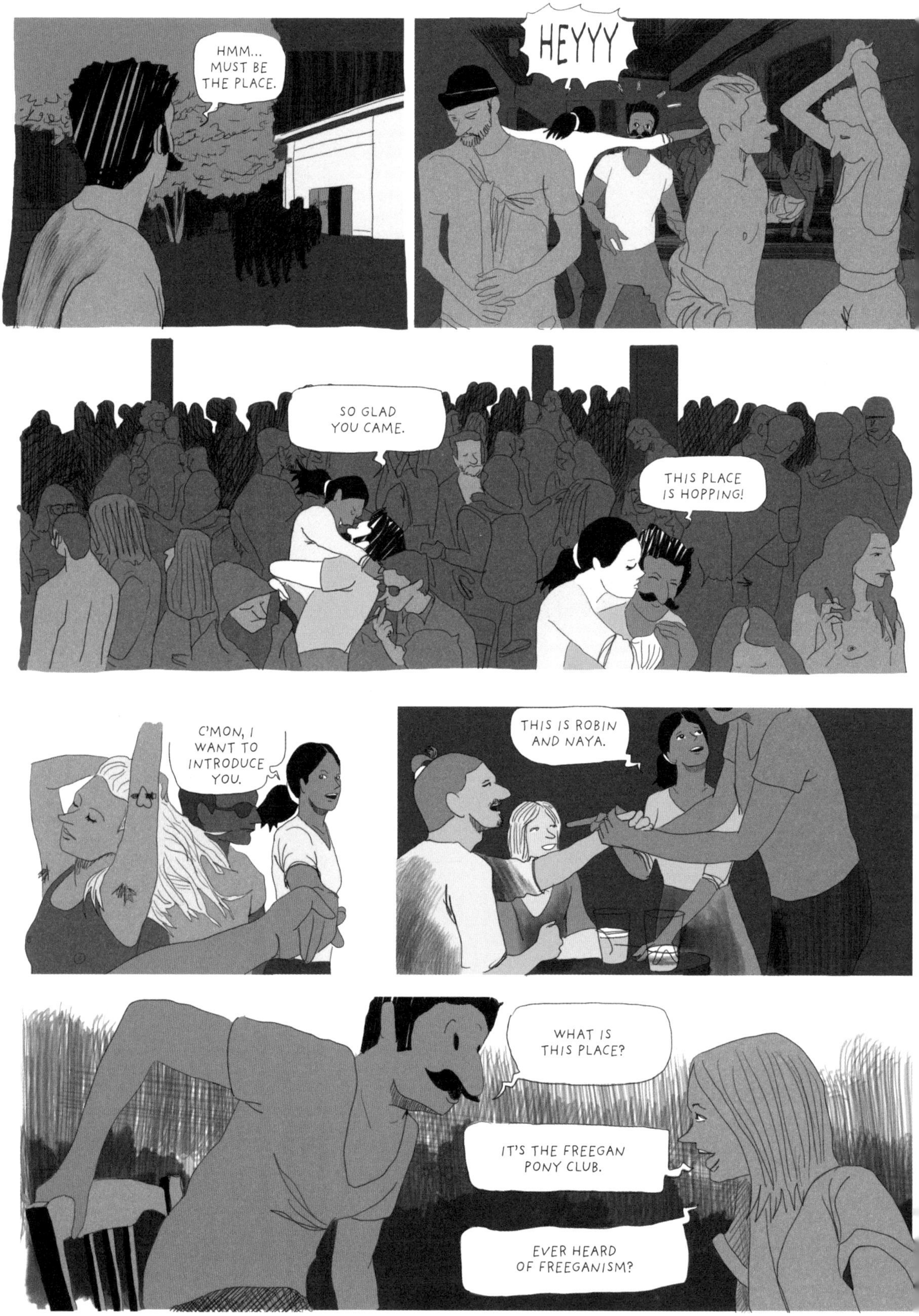
HMM... MUST BE THE PLACE.
HEYYY
SO GLAD YOU CAME.
THIS PLACE IS HOPPING!
C'MON, I WANT TO INTRODUCE YOU.
THIS IS ROBIN AND NAYA.
WHAT IS THIS PLACE?
IT'S THE FREEGAN PONY CLUB.
EVER HEARD OF FREEGANISM?

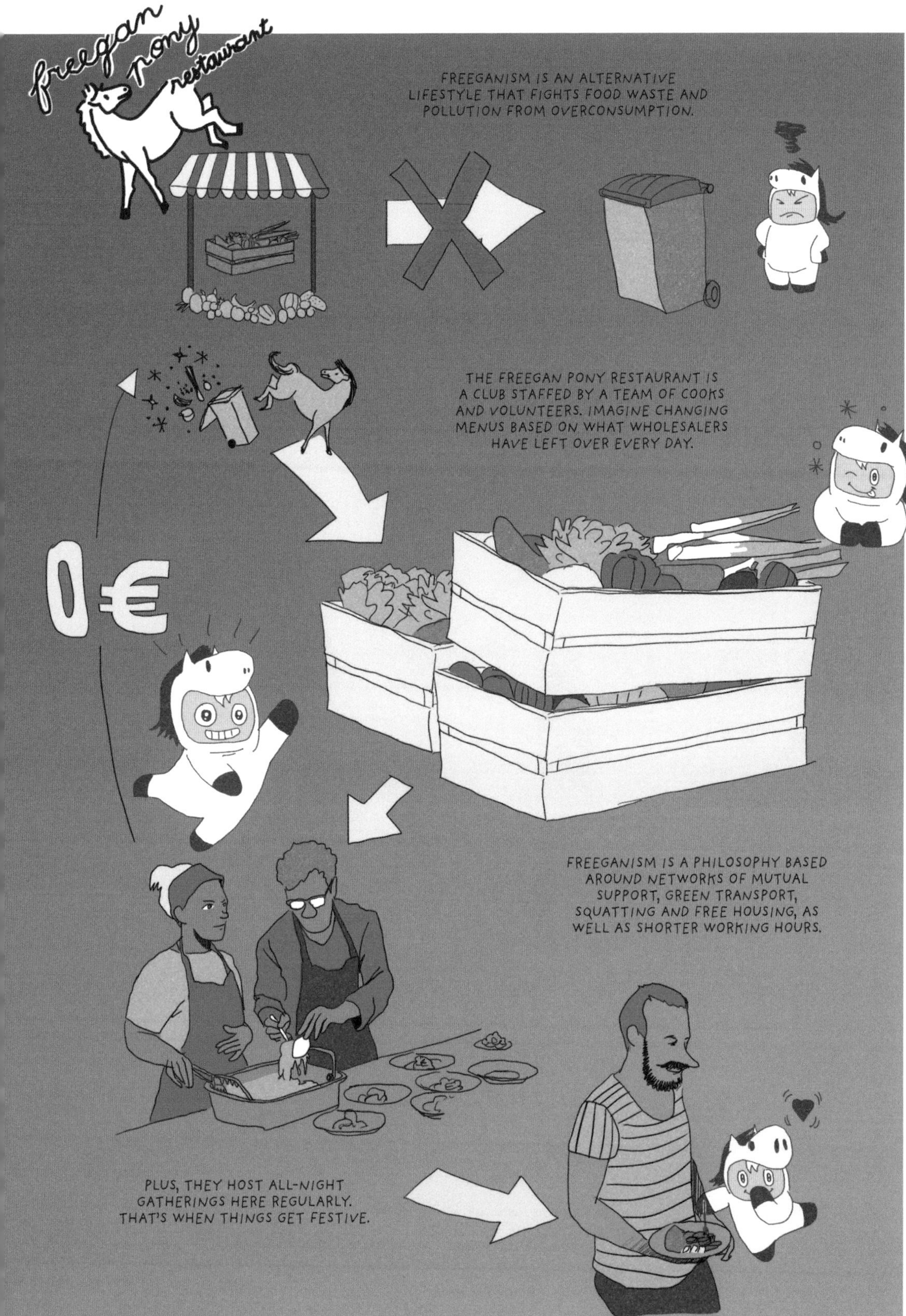
freegan pony restaurant
FREEGANISM IS AN ALTERNATIVE LIFESTYLE THAT FIGHTS FOOD WASTE AND POLLUTION FROM OVERCONSUMPTION.
THE FREEGAN PONY RESTAURANT IS A CLUB STAFFED BY A TEAM OF COOKS AND VOLUNTEERS. IMAGINE CHANGING MENUS BASED ON WHAT WHOLESALERS HAVE LEFT OVER EVERY DAY.
0€
FREEGANISM IS A PHILOSOPHY BASED AROUND NETWORKS OF MUTUAL SUPPORT, GREEN TRANSPORT, SQUATTING AND FREE HOUSING, AS WELL AS SHORTER WORKING HOURS.
PLUS, THEY HOST ALL-NIGHT GATHERINGS HERE REGULARLY. THAT'S WHEN THINGS GET FESTIVE.

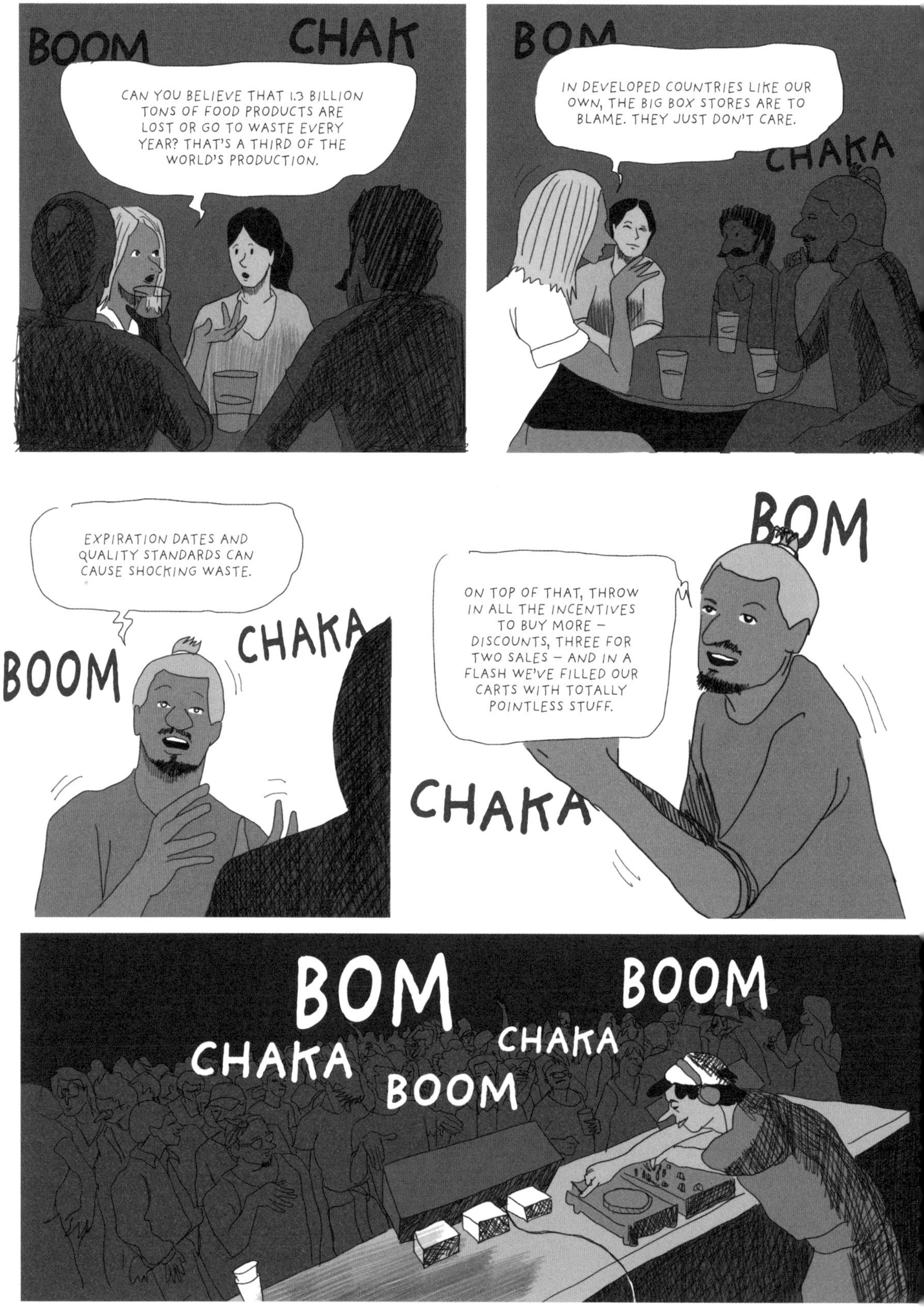
BOOM
CHAK
CAN YOU BELIEVE THAT 1.3 BILLION TONS OF FOOD PRODUCTS ARE LOST OR GO TO WASTE EVERY YEAR? THAT'S A THIRD OF THE WORLD'S PRODUCTION.
BOM
IN DEVELOPED COUNTRIES LIKE OUR OWN, THE BIG BOX STORES ARE TO BLAME. THEY JUST DON'T CARE.
CHAKA
EXPIRATION DATES AND QUALITY STANDARDS CAN CAUSE SHOCKING WASTE.
BOOM
CHAKA
BOM
ON TOP OF THAT, THROW IN ALL THE INCENTIVES TO BUY MORE – DISCOUNTS, THREE FOR TWO SALES – AND IN A FLASH WE'VE FILLED OUR CARTS WITH TOTALLY POINTLESS STUFF.
CHAKA
BOM
BOOM
CHAKA
CHAKA
BOOM

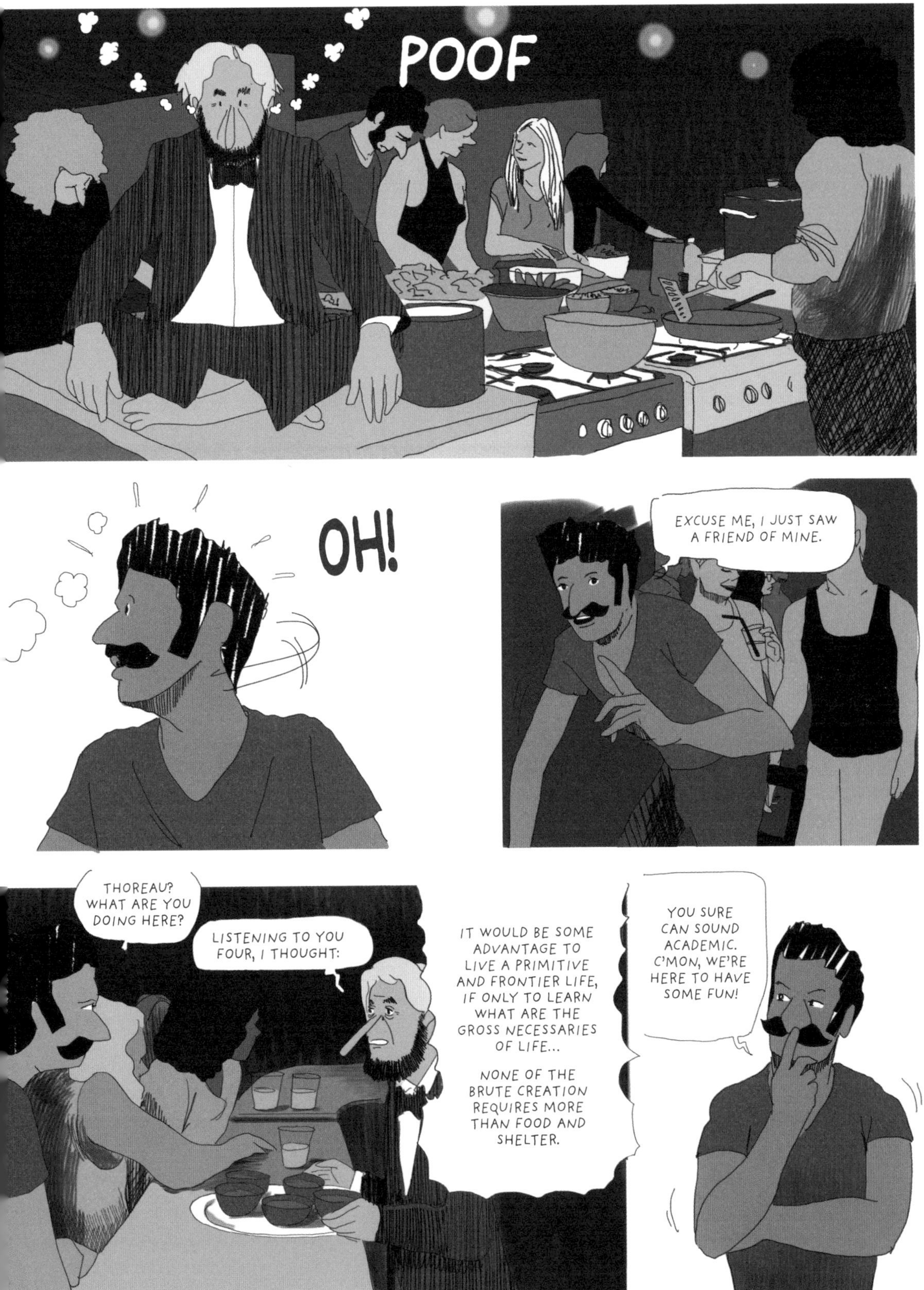
POOF
OH!
EXCUSE ME, I JUST SAW A FRIEND OF MINE.
THOREAU? WHAT ARE YOU DOING HERE?
LISTENING TO YOU FOUR, I THOUGHT:
IT WOULD BE SOME ADVANTAGE TO LIVE A PRIMITIVE AND FRONTIER LIFE, IF ONLY TO LEARN WHAT ARE THE GROSS NECESSARIES OF LIFE...
NONE OF THE BRUTE CREATION REQUIRES MORE THAN FOOD AND SHELTER.
YOU SURE CAN SOUND ACADEMIC. C'MON, WE'RE HERE TO HAVE SOME FUN!

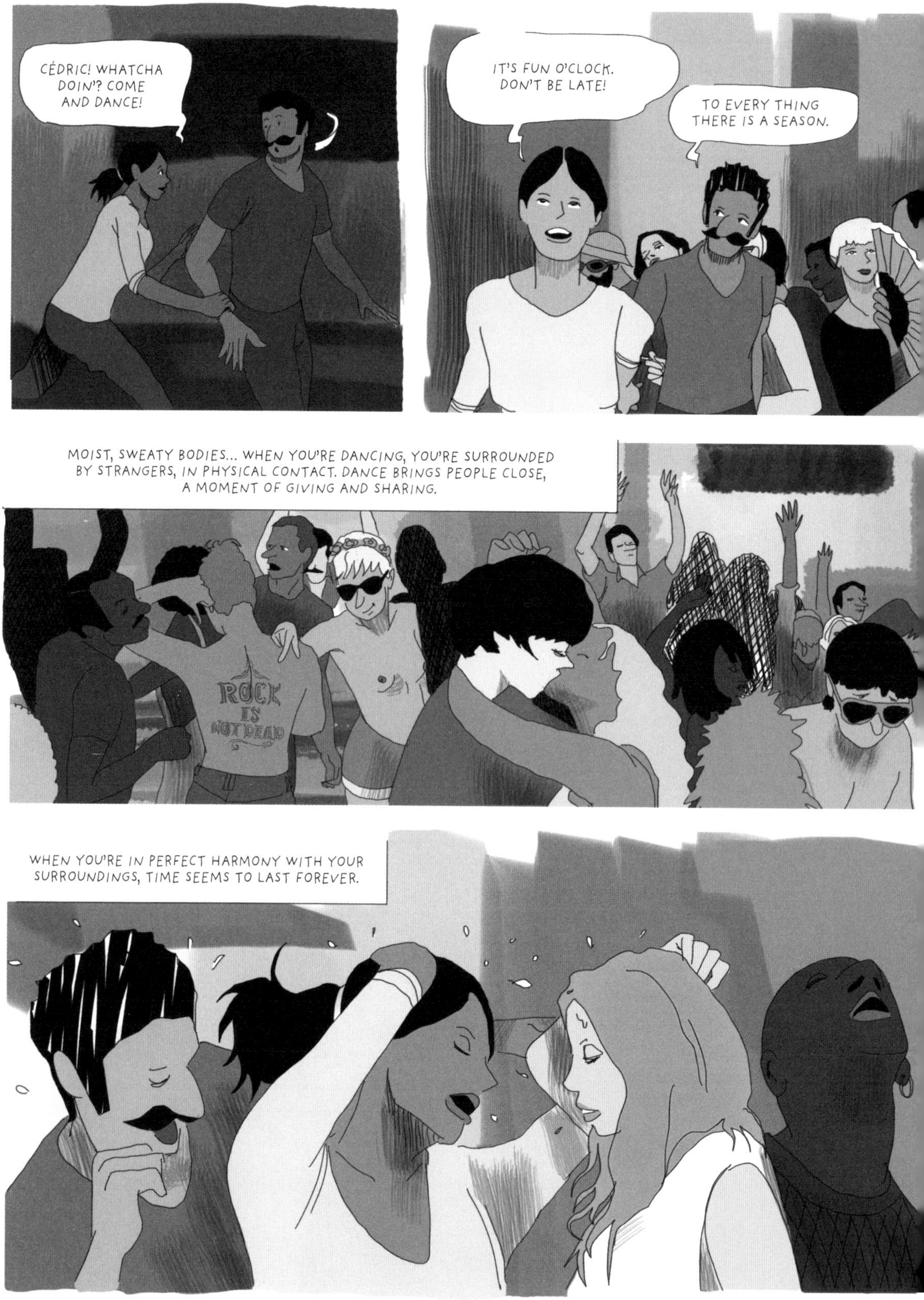
CÉDRIC! WHATCHA DOIN'? COME AND DANCE!
IT'S FUN O'CLOCK. DON'T BE LATE!
TO EVERY THING THERE IS A SEASON.
MOIST, SWEATY BODIES... WHEN YOU'RE DANCING, YOU'RE SURROUNDED BY STRANGERS, IN PHYSICAL CONTACT. DANCE BRINGS PEOPLE CLOSE, A MOMENT OF GIVING AND SHARING.
ROCK IS NOT DEAD
WHEN YOU'RE IN PERFECT HARMONY WITH YOUR SURROUNDINGS, TIME SEEMS TO LAST FOREVER.

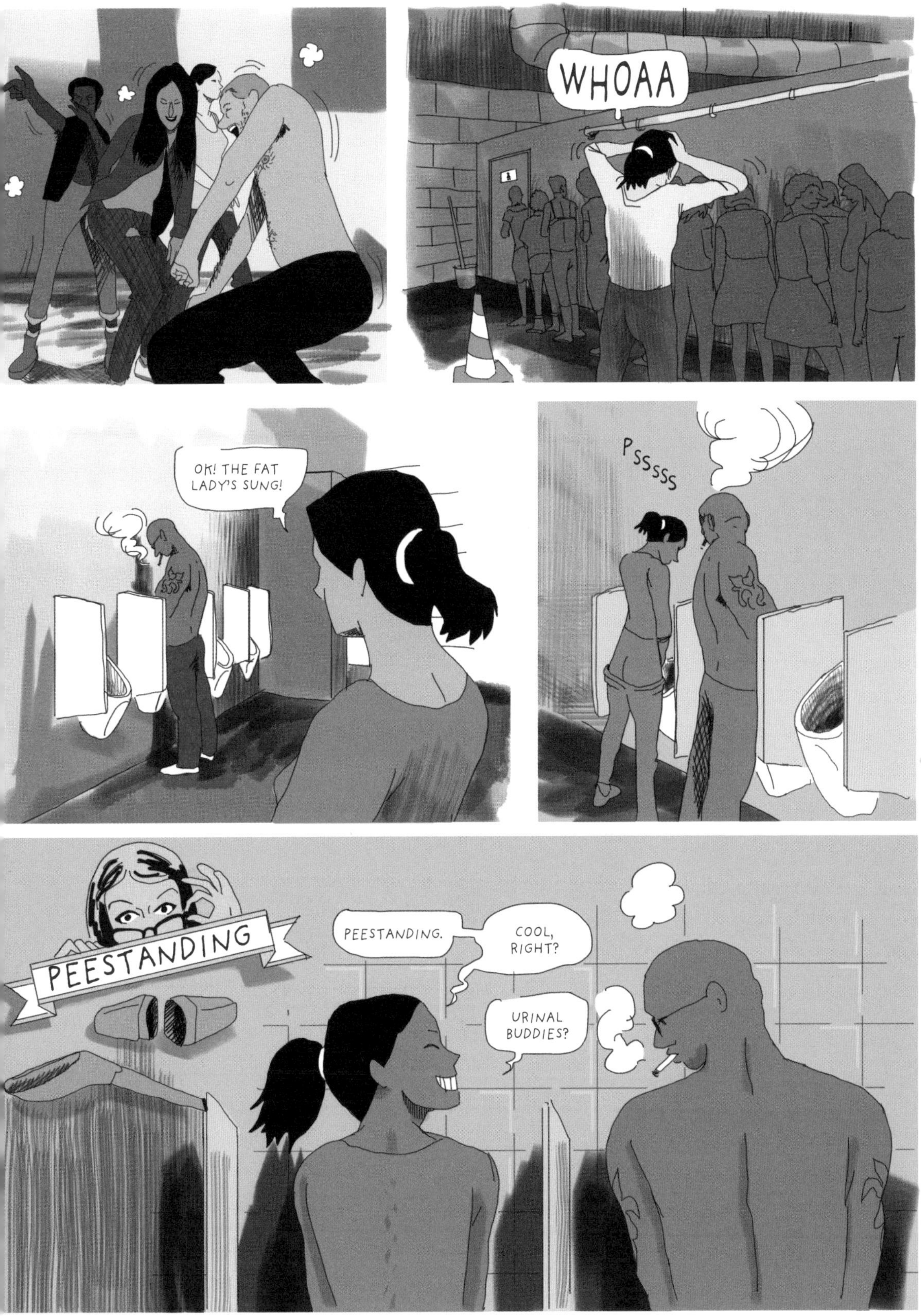
WHOAA
OK! THE FAT LADY'S SUNG!
PSSSSS
PEESTANDING
PEESTANDING.
COOL, RIGHT?
URINAL BUDDIES?

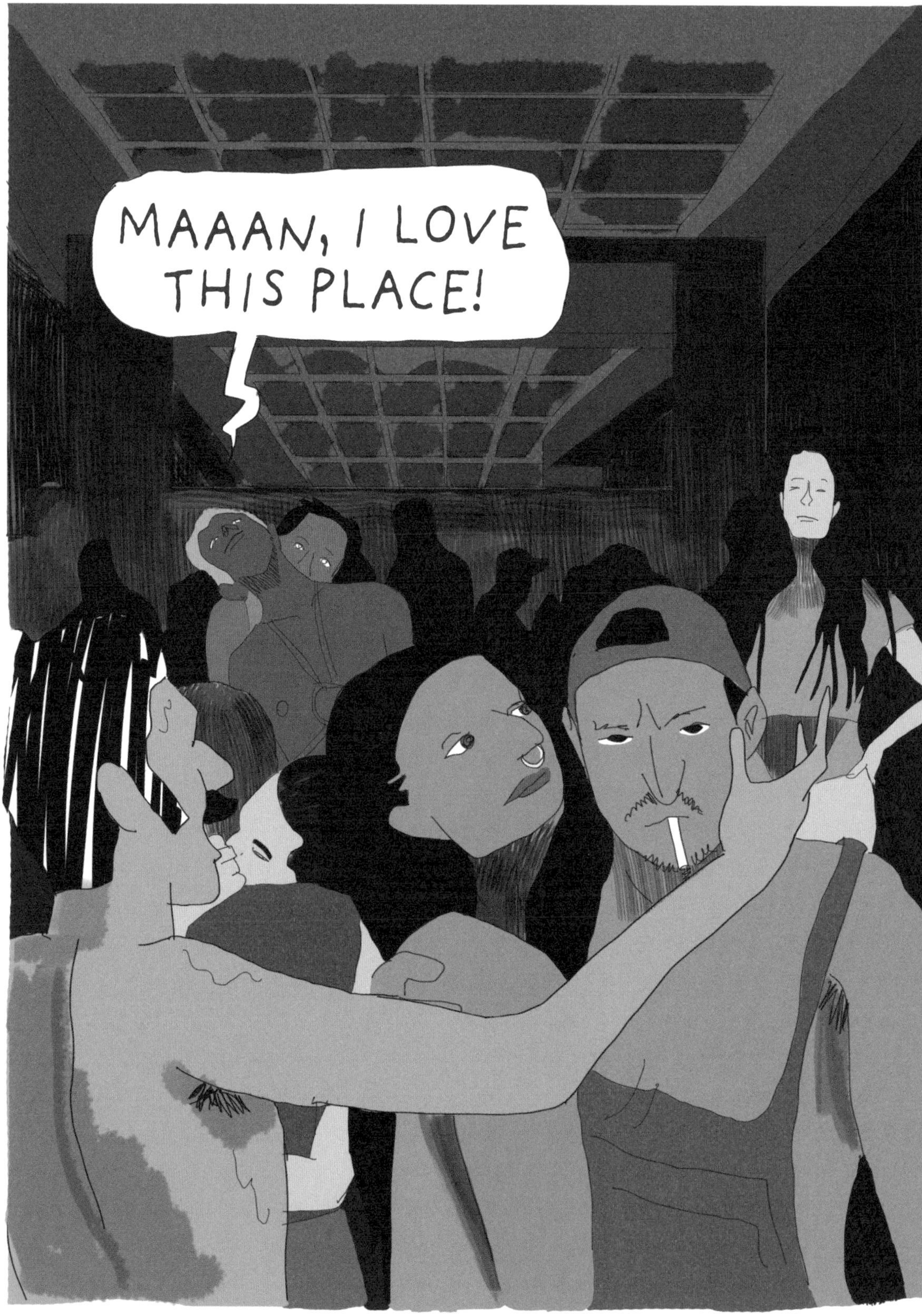
MAAAN, I LOVE THIS PLACE!

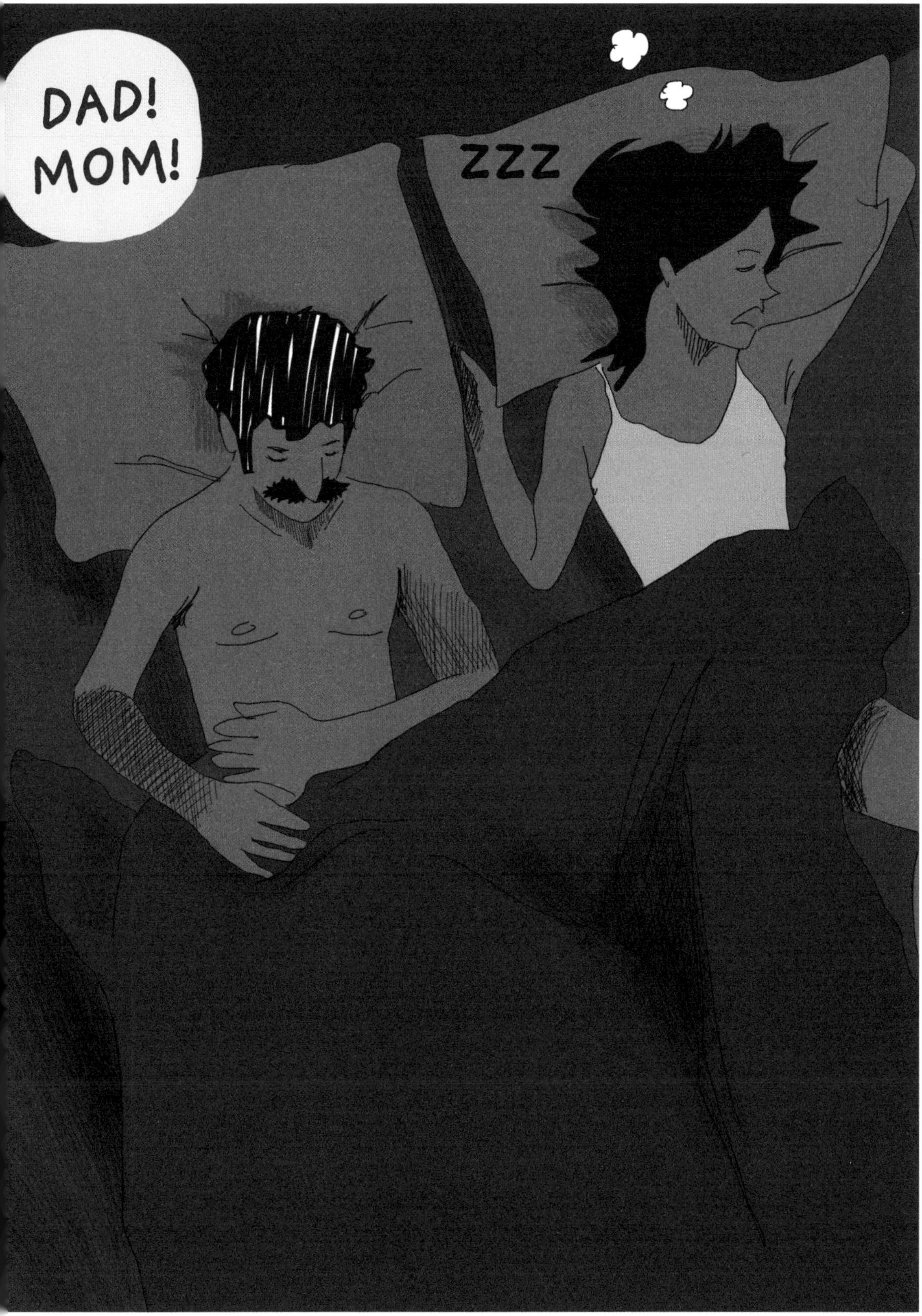
DAD!
MOM!
ZZZ

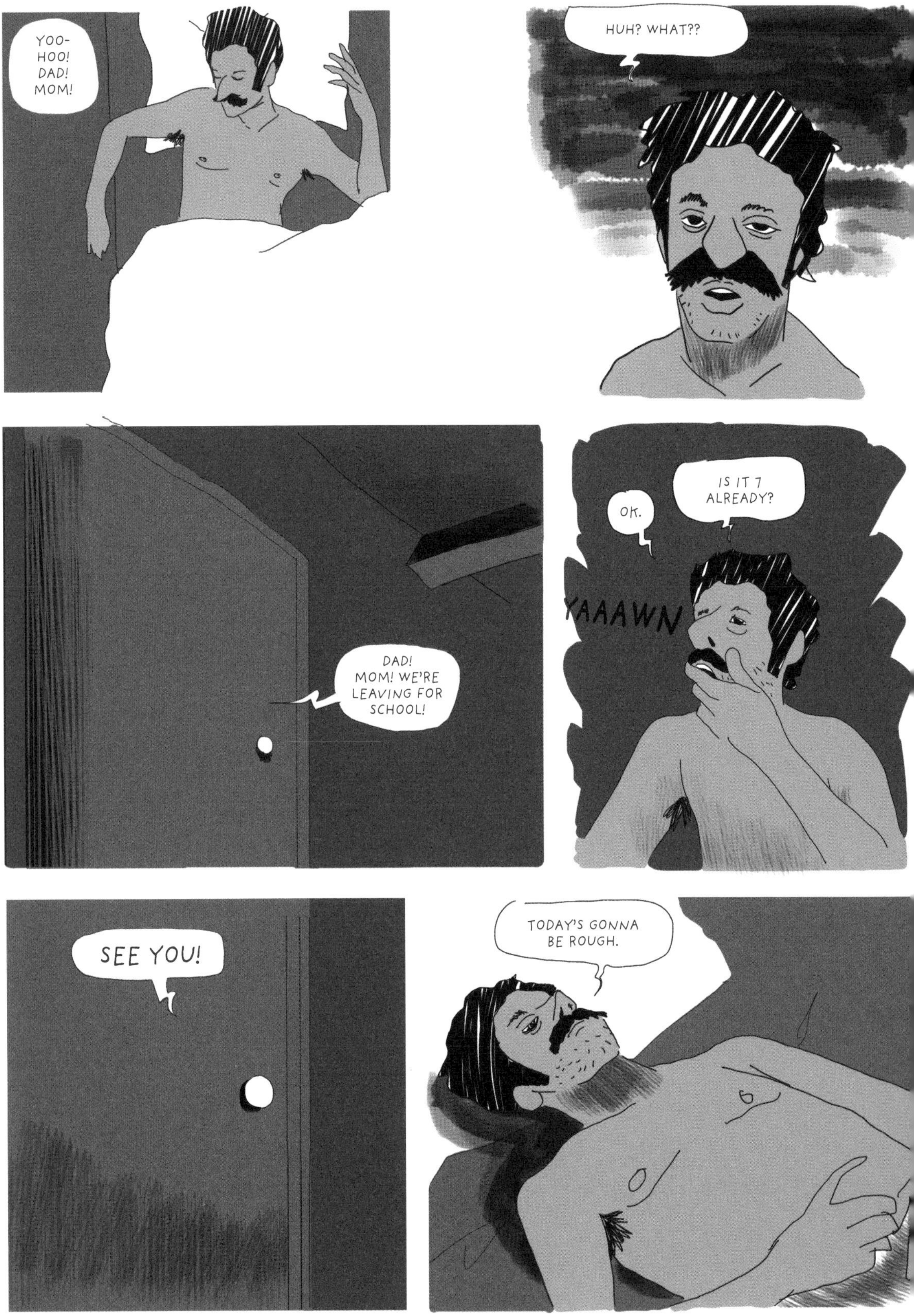
YOO-HOO! DAD! MOM!
HUH? WHAT??
DAD! MOM! WE'RE LEAVING FOR SCHOOL!
IS IT 7 ALREADY?
OK.
YAAAWN
SEE YOU!
TODAY'S GONNA BE ROUGH.

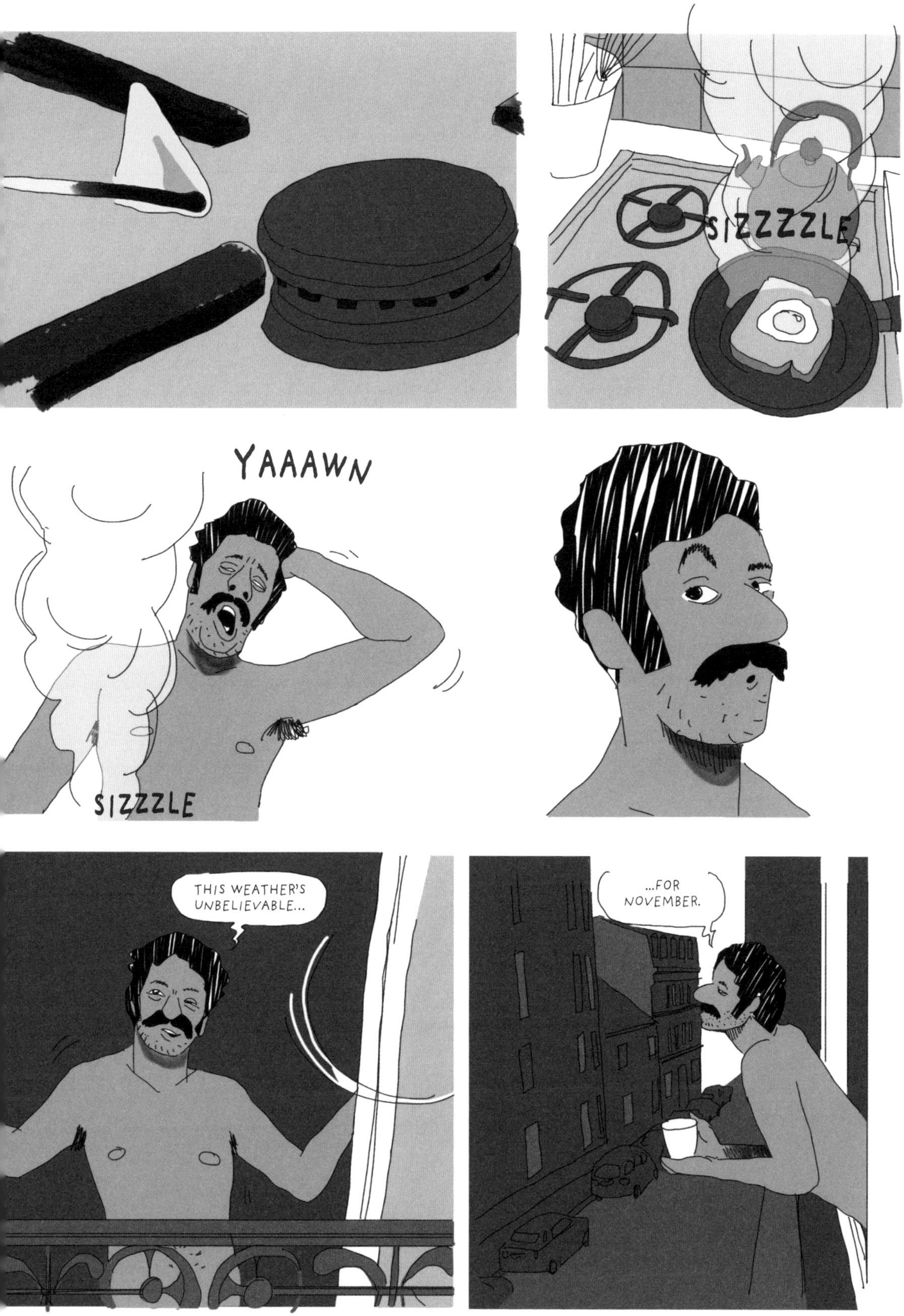
SIZZZZZLE
YAAAWN
SIZZZLE
THIS WEATHER'S UNBELIEVABLE...
...FOR NOVEMBER.

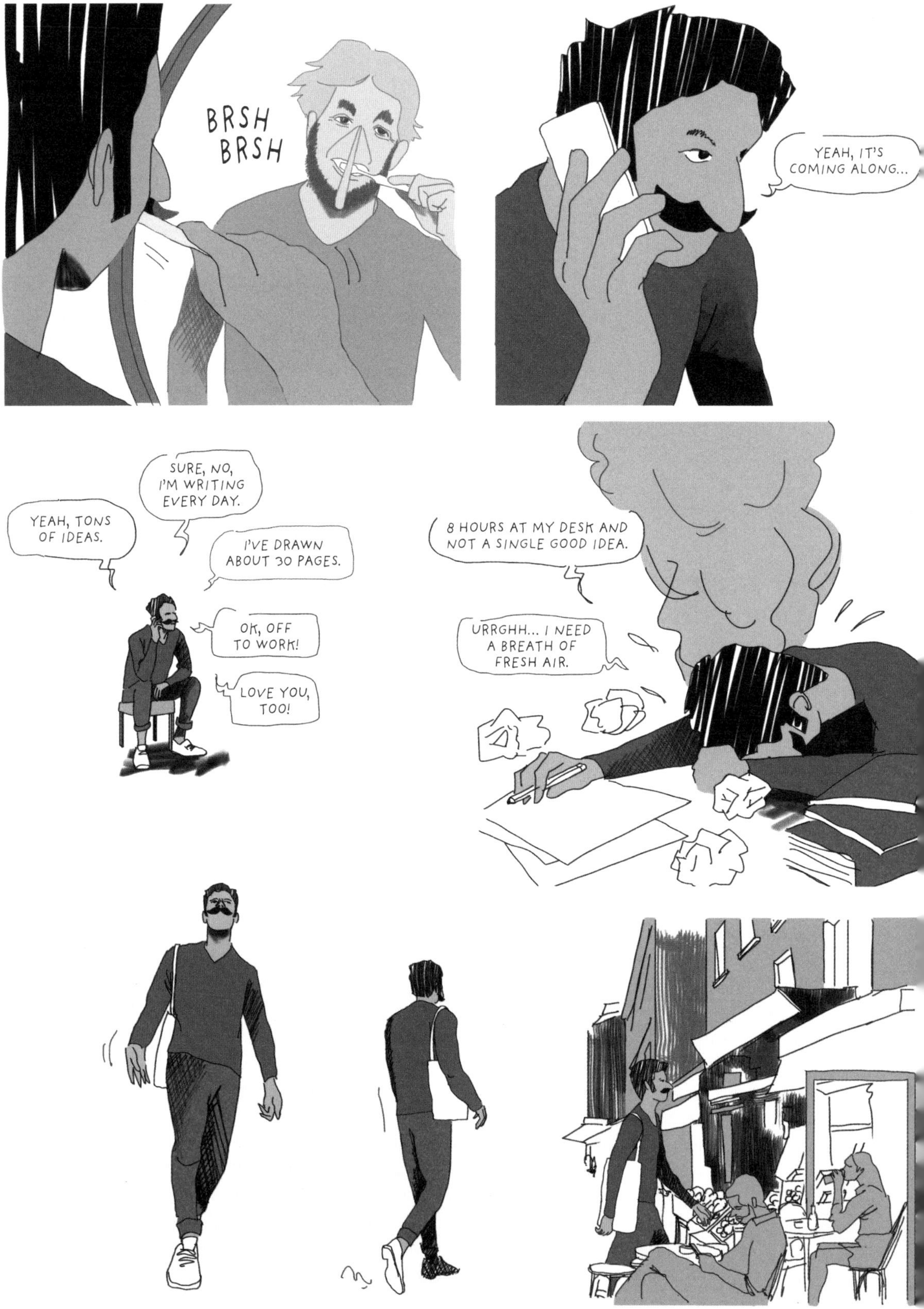

BRSH BRSH
YEAH, IT'S COMING ALONG...
YEAH, TONS OF IDEAS.
SURE, NO, I'M WRITING EVERY DAY.
I'VE DRAWN ABOUT 30 PAGES.
OK, OFF TO WORK!
LOVE YOU, TOO!
8 HOURS AT MY DESK AND NOT A SINGLE GOOD IDEA.
URRGHH... I NEED A BREATH OF FRESH AIR.

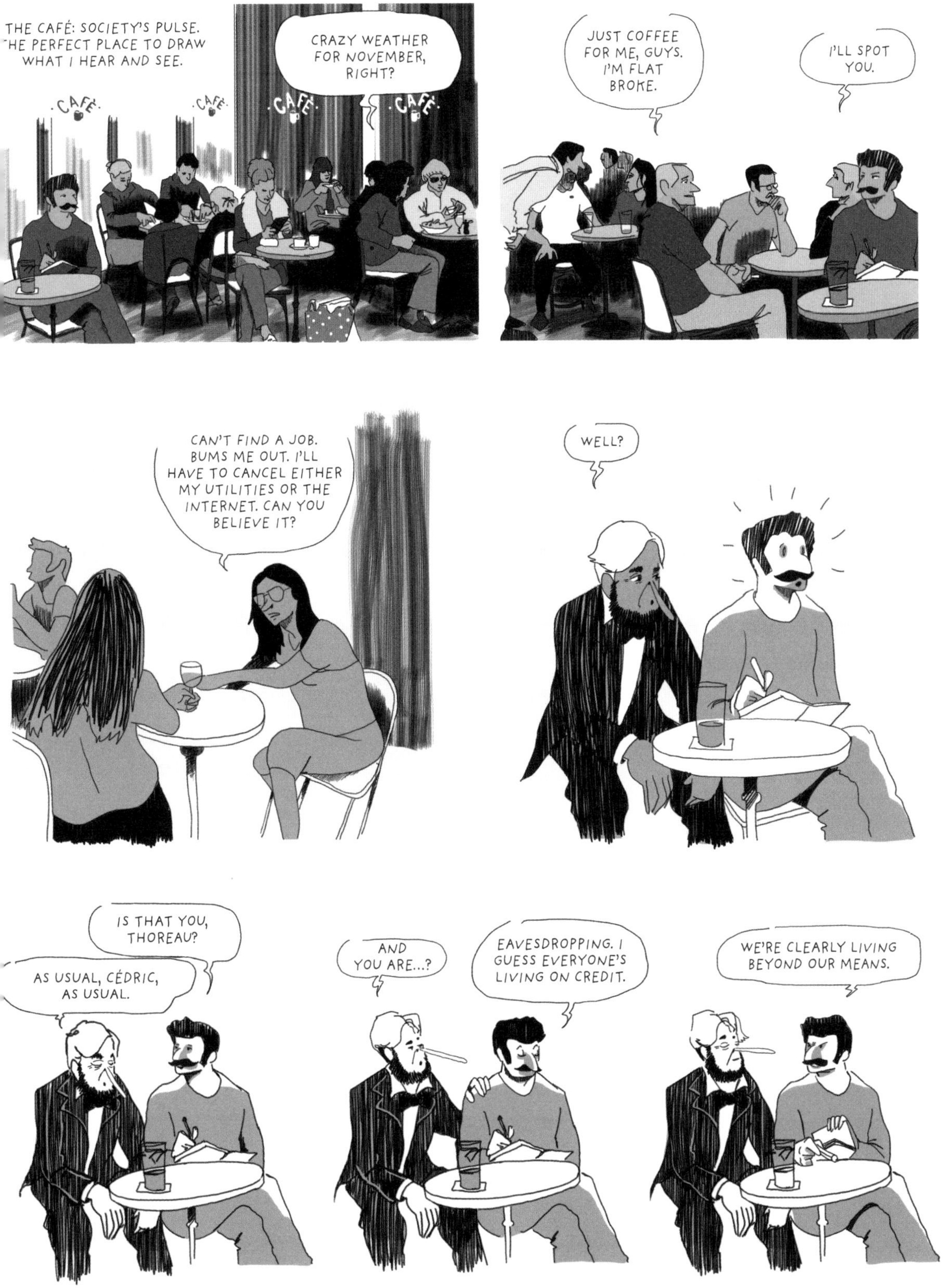
THE CAFÉ: SOCIETY'S PULSE. THE PERFECT PLACE TO DRAW WHAT I HEAR AND SEE.
CAFÉ
CAFÉ
CAFÉ
CAFÉ
CRAZY WEATHER FOR NOVEMBER, RIGHT?
JUST COFFEE FOR ME, GUYS. I'M FLAT BROKE.
I'LL SPOT YOU.
CAN'T FIND A JOB. BUMS ME OUT. I'LL HAVE TO CANCEL EITHER MY UTILITIES OR THE INTERNET. CAN YOU BELIEVE IT?
WELL?
IS THAT YOU, THOREAU?
AS USUAL, CÉDRIC, AS USUAL.
AND YOU ARE...?
EAVESDROPPING. I GUESS EVERYONE'S LIVING ON CREDIT.
WE'RE CLEARLY LIVING BEYOND OUR MEANS.

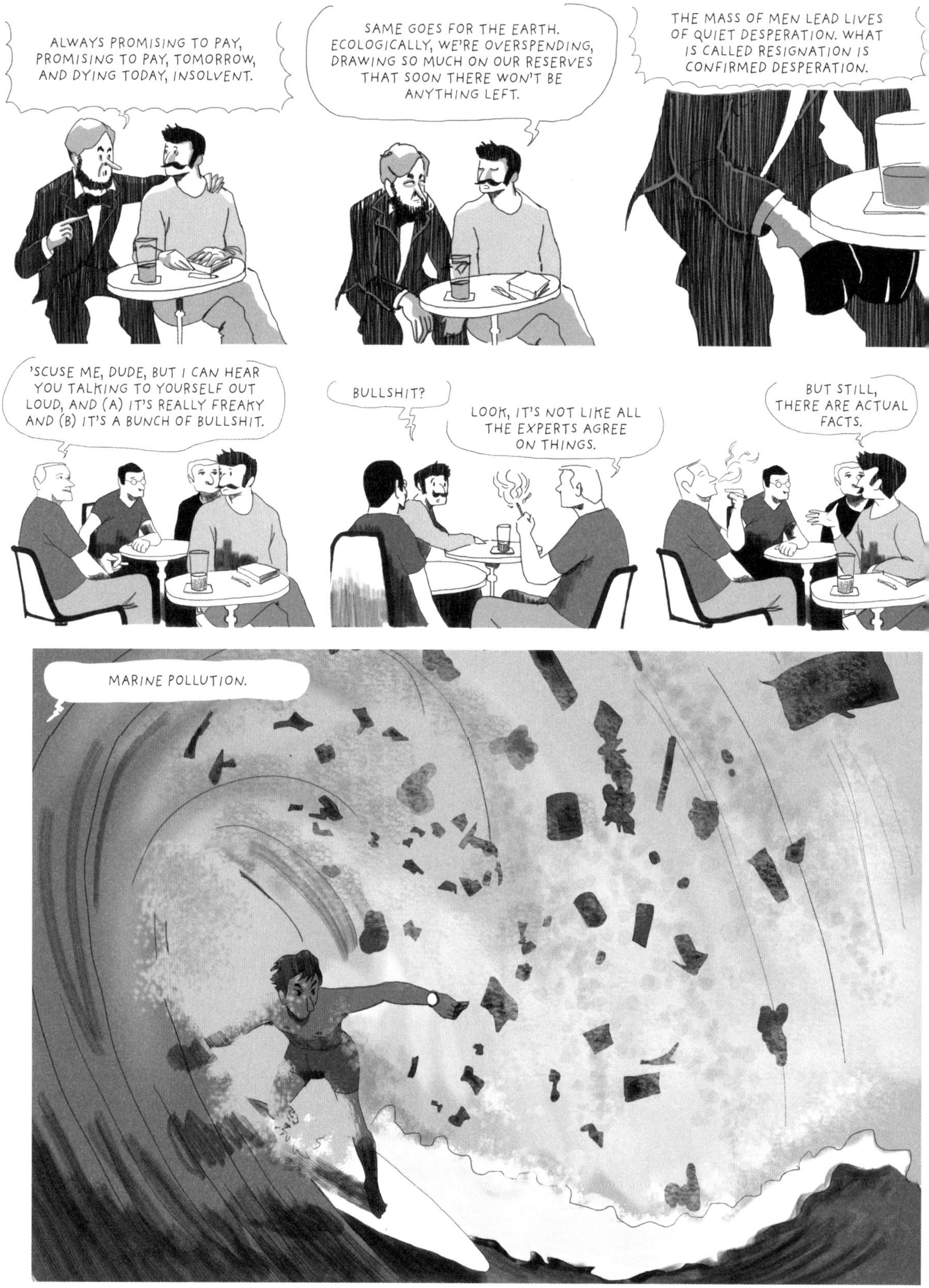
ALWAYS PROMISING TO PAY, PROMISING TO PAY, TOMORROW, AND DYING TODAY, INSOLVENT.
SAME GOES FOR THE EARTH. ECOLOGICALLY, WE'RE OVERSPENDING, DRAWING SO MUCH ON OUR RESERVES THAT SOON THERE WON'T BE ANYTHING LEFT.
THE MASS OF MEN LEAD LIVES OF QUIET DESPERATION. WHAT IS CALLED RESIGNATION IS CONFIRMED DESPERATION.
'SCUSE ME, DUDE, BUT I CAN HEAR YOU TALKING TO YOURSELF OUT LOUD, AND (A) IT'S REALLY FREAKY AND (B) IT'S A BUNCH OF BULLSHIT.
BULLSHIT?
LOOK, IT'S NOT LIKE ALL THE EXPERTS AGREE ON THINGS.
BUT STILL, THERE ARE ACTUAL FACTS.
MARINE POLLUTION.

MASSIVE DEFORESTATION.

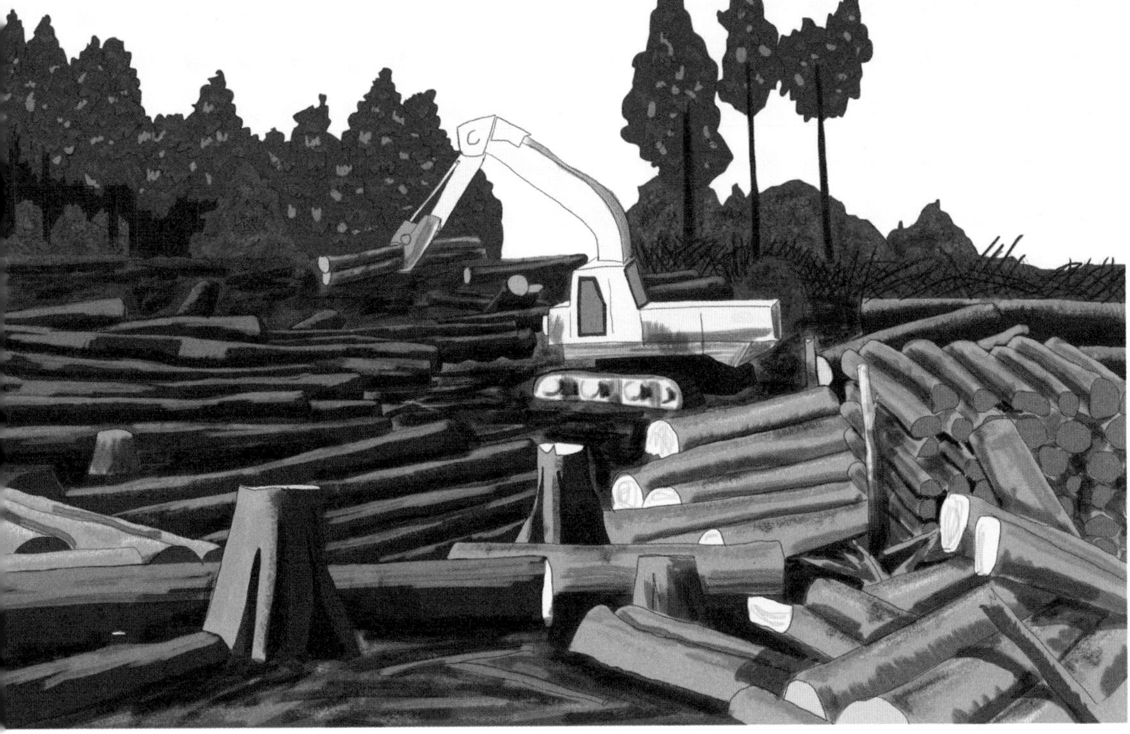

FRESHWATER POLLUTION.

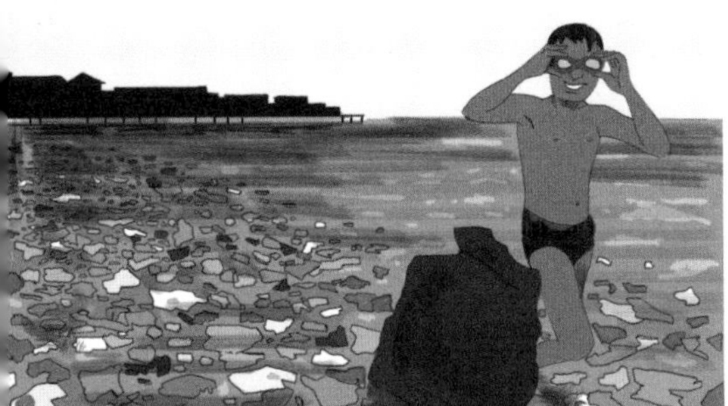

CHEMICAL POLLUTION.

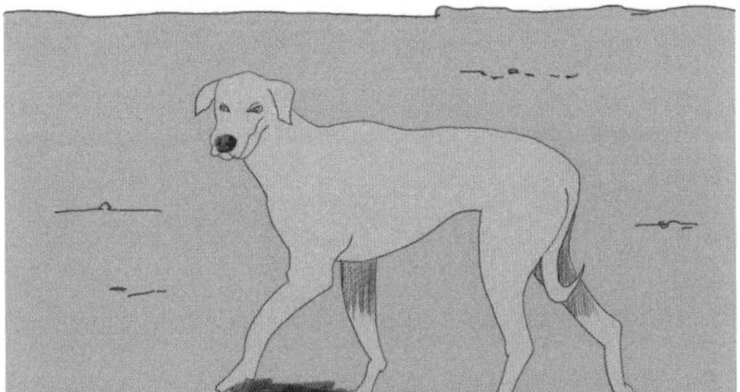

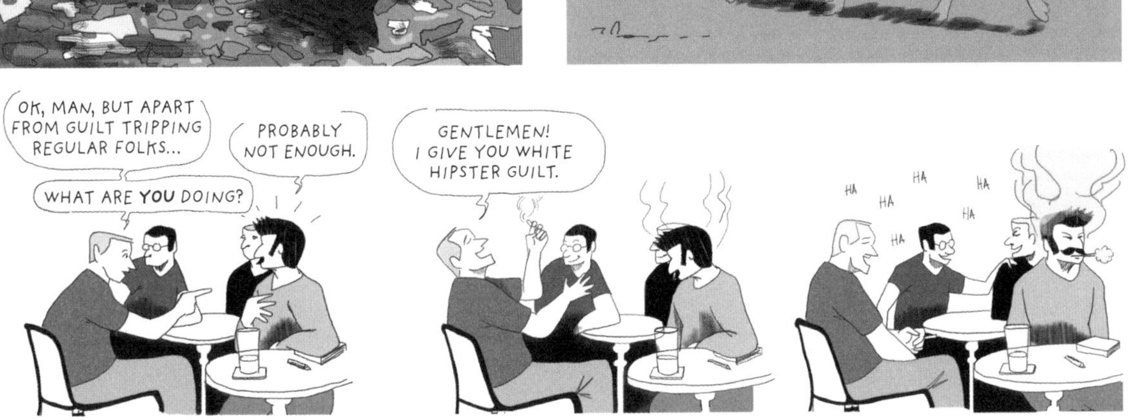
OK, MAN, BUT APART FROM GUILT TRIPPING REGULAR FOLKS...
WHAT ARE YOU DOING?
PROBABLY NOT ENOUGH.
GENTLEMEN! I GIVE YOU WHITE HIPSTER GUILT.
HA HA HA HA HA HA

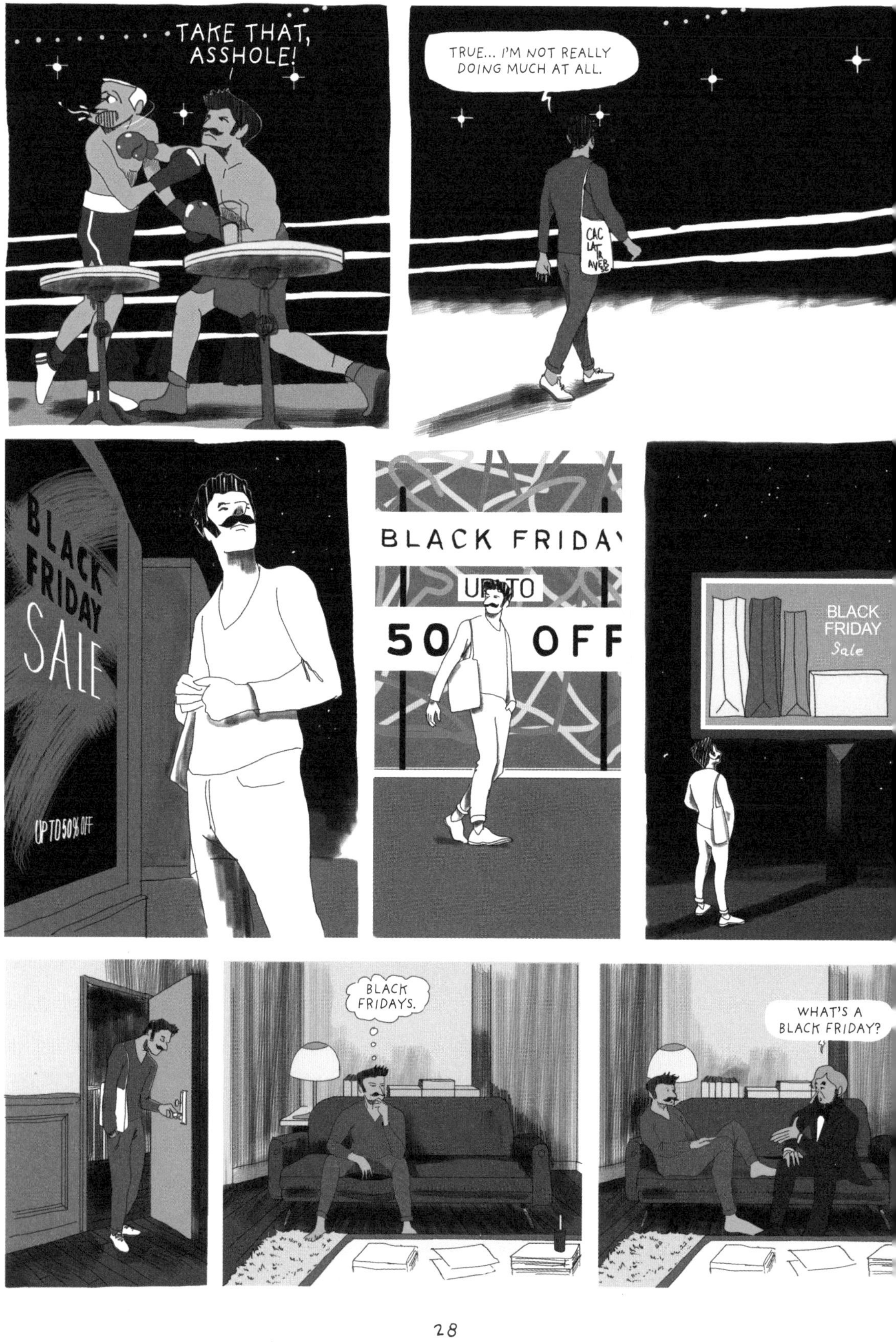

TAKE THAT, ASSHOLE!
TRUE... I'M NOT REALLY DOING MUCH AT ALL.
BLACK FRIDAY SALE
UP TO 50% OFF
BLACK FRIDA
50 OFF
BLACK FRIDAY Sale
BLACK FRIDAYS.
WHAT'S A BLACK FRIDAY?

BLACK FRIDAY

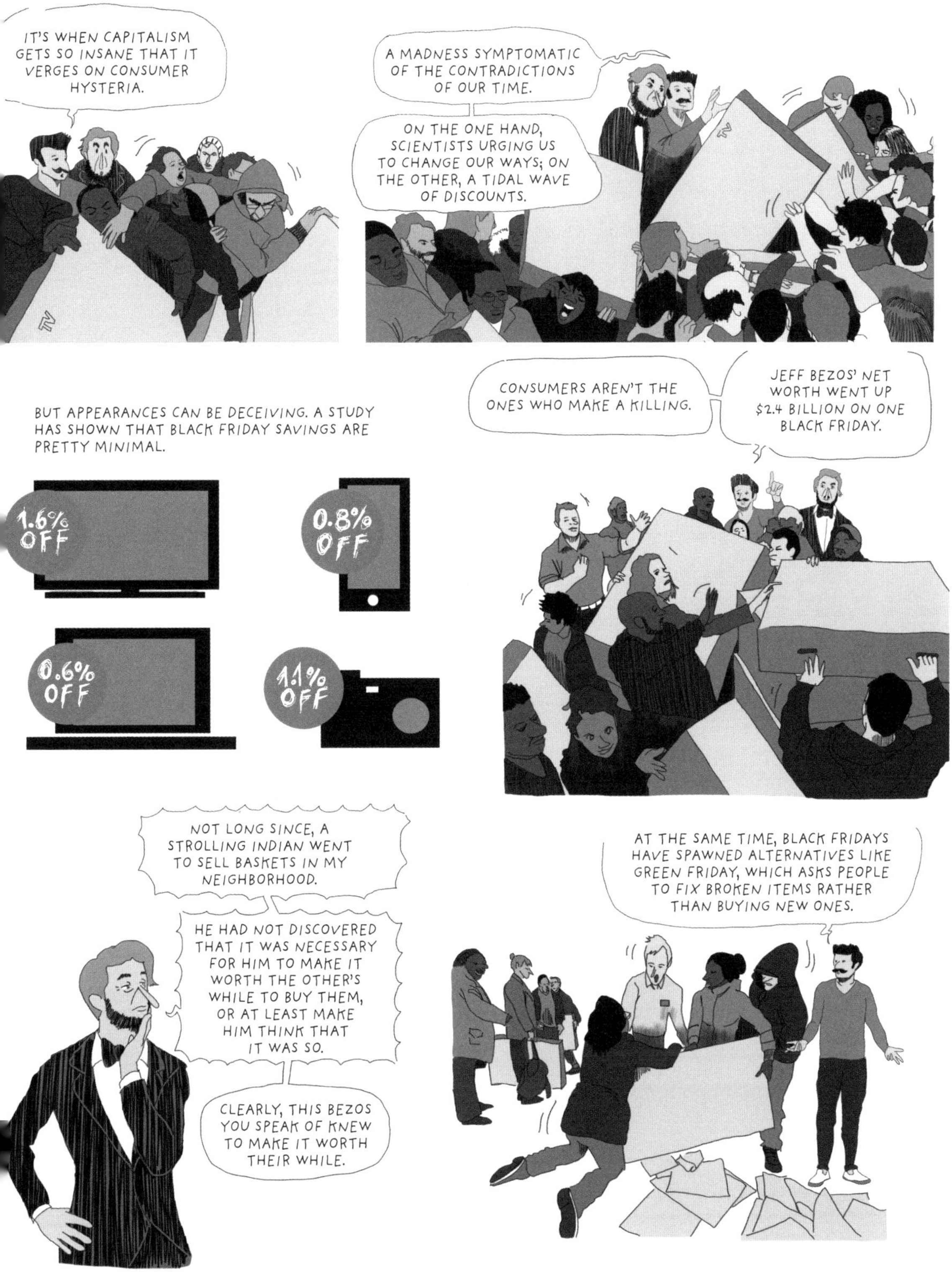

IT'S WHEN CAPITALISM GETS SO INSANE THAT IT VERGES ON CONSUMER HYSTERIA.
A MADNESS SYMPTOMATIC OF THE CONTRADICTIONS OF OUR TIME.
ON THE ONE HAND, SCIENTISTS URGING US TO CHANGE OUR WAYS; ON THE OTHER, A TIDAL WAVE OF DISCOUNTS.
BUT APPEARANCES CAN BE DECEIVING. A STUDY HAS SHOWN THAT BLACK FRIDAY SAVINGS ARE PRETTY MINIMAL.
1.6% OFF
0.8% OFF
0.6% OFF
1.1% OFF
CONSUMERS AREN'T THE ONES WHO MAKE A KILLING.
JEFF BEZOS' NET WORTH WENT UP $2.4 BILLION ON ONE BLACK FRIDAY.
NOT LONG SINCE, A STROLLING INDIAN WENT TO SELL BASKETS IN MY NEIGHBORHOOD.
HE HAD NOT DISCOVERED THAT IT WAS NECESSARY FOR HIM TO MAKE IT WORTH THE OTHER'S WHILE TO BUY THEM, OR AT LEAST MAKE HIM THINK THAT IT WAS SO.
CLEARLY, THIS BEZOS YOU SPEAK OF KNEW TO MAKE IT WORTH THEIR WHILE.
AT THE SAME TIME, BLACK FRIDAYS HAVE SPAWNED ALTERNATIVES LIKE GREEN FRIDAY, WHICH ASKS PEOPLE TO FIX BROKEN ITEMS RATHER THAN BUYING NEW ONES.

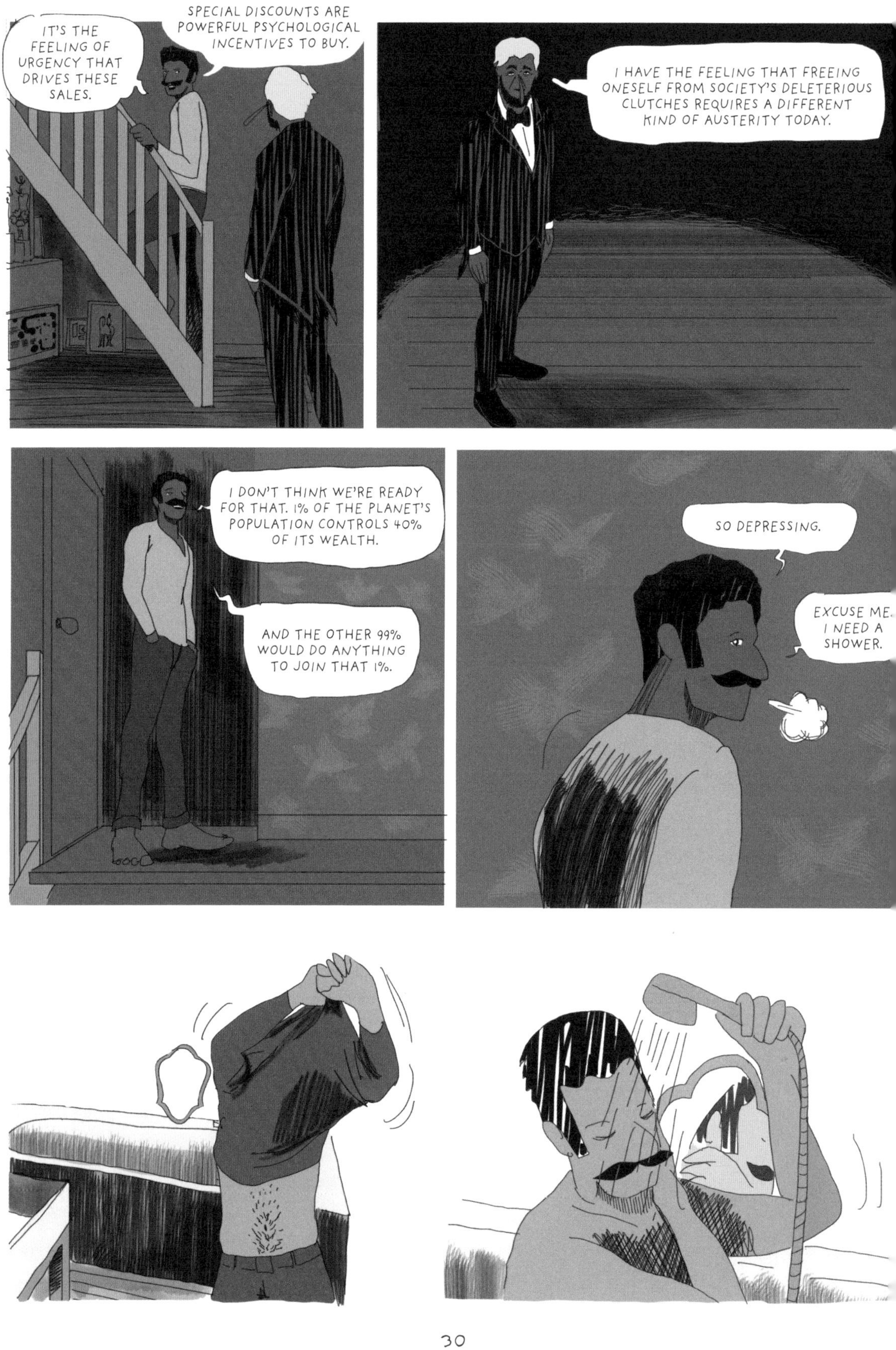
IT'S THE FEELING OF URGENCY THAT DRIVES THESE SALES.
SPECIAL DISCOUNTS ARE POWERFUL PSYCHOLOGICAL INCENTIVES TO BUY.
I HAVE THE FEELING THAT FREEING ONESELF FROM SOCIETY'S DELETERIOUS CLUTCHES REQUIRES A DIFFERENT KIND OF AUSTERITY TODAY.
I DON'T THINK WE'RE READY FOR THAT. 1% OF THE PLANET'S POPULATION CONTROLS 40% OF ITS WEALTH.
AND THE OTHER 99% WOULD DO ANYTHING TO JOIN THAT 1%.
SO DEPRESSING.
EXCUSE ME. I NEED A SHOWER.

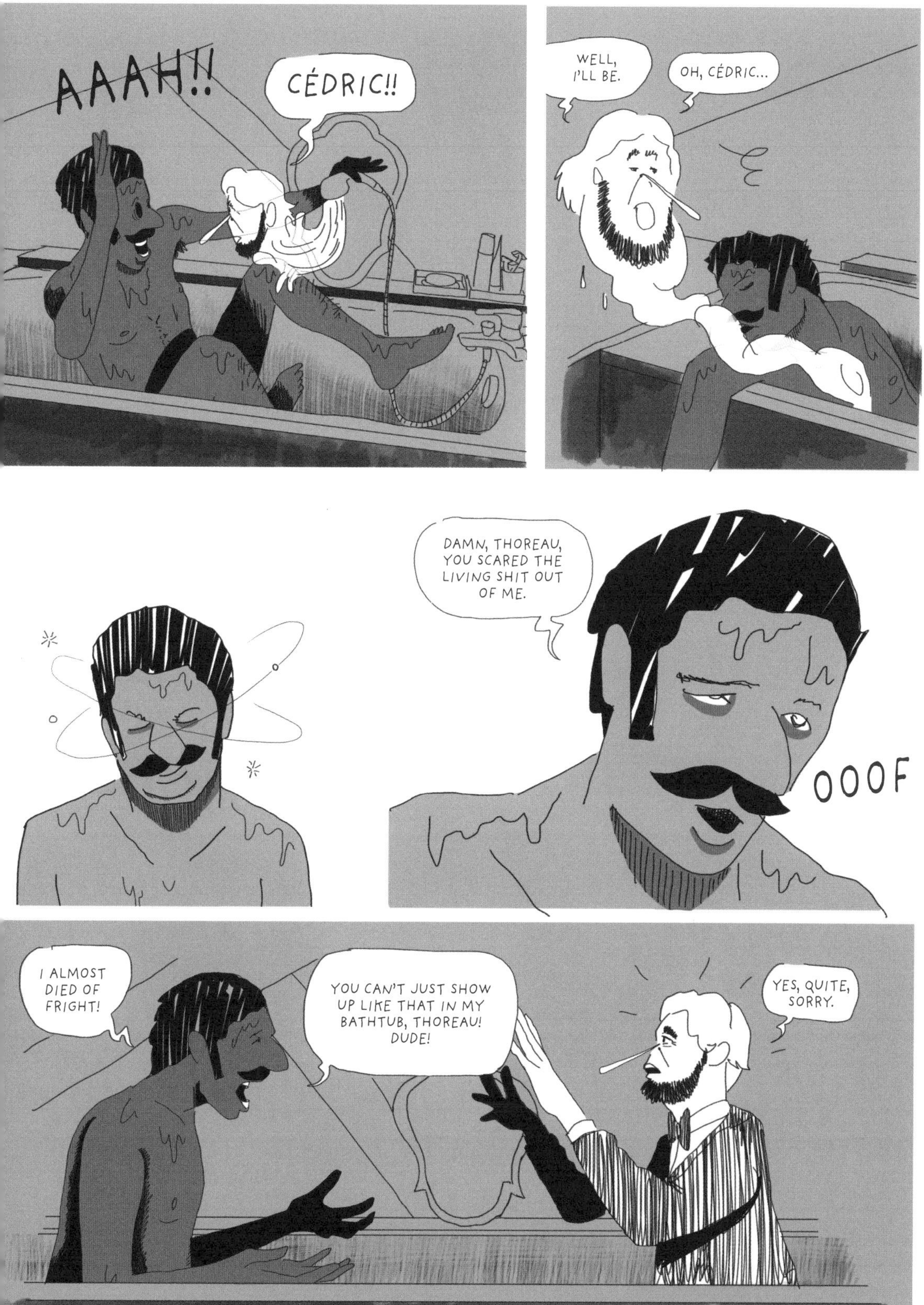
AAAH!!
CÉDRIC!!
WELL, I'LL BE.
OH, CÉDRIC...
DAMN, THOREAU, YOU SCARED THE LIVING SHIT OUT OF ME.
OOOF
I ALMOST DIED OF FRIGHT!
YOU CAN'T JUST SHOW UP LIKE THAT IN MY BATHTUB, THOREAU! DUDE!
YES, QUITE, SORRY.

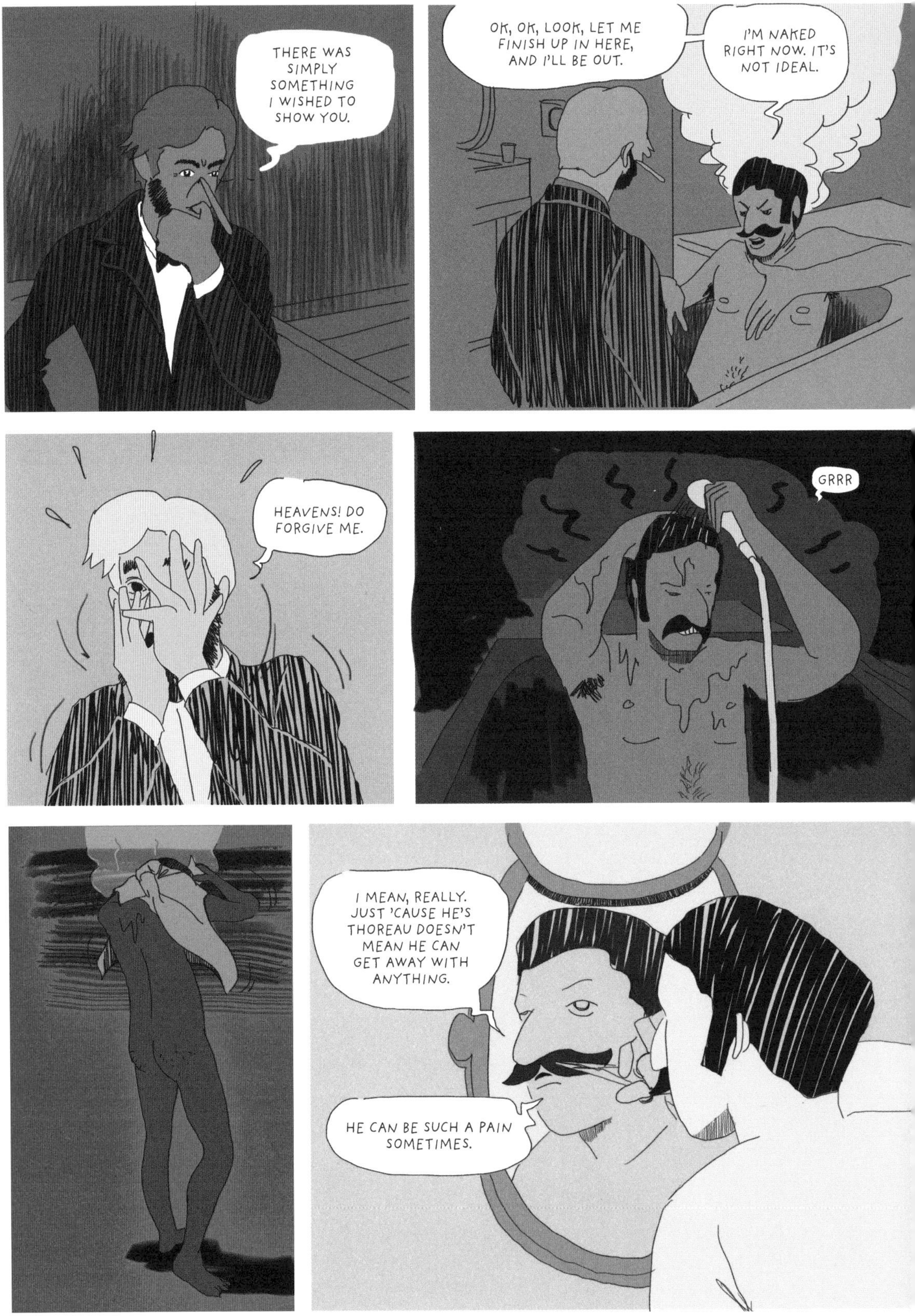
THERE WAS SIMPLY SOMETHING I WISHED TO SHOW YOU.
OK, OK, LOOK, LET ME FINISH UP IN HERE, AND I'LL BE OUT.
I'M NAKED RIGHT NOW. IT'S NOT IDEAL.
HEAVENS! DO FORGIVE ME.
GRRR
I MEAN, REALLY. JUST 'CAUSE HE'S THOREAU DOESN'T MEAN HE CAN GET AWAY WITH ANYTHING.
HE CAN BE SUCH A PAIN SOMETIMES.

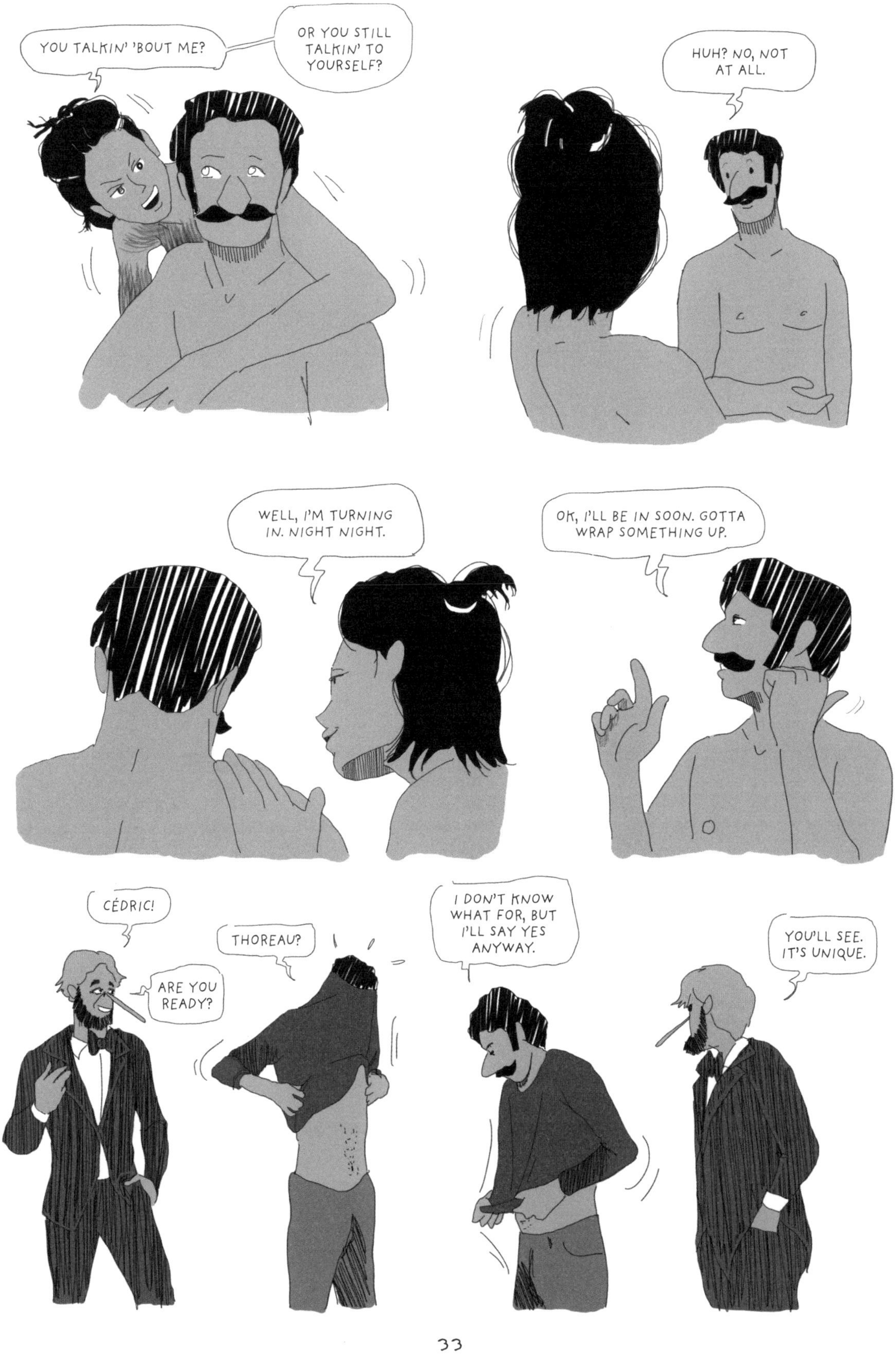
YOU TALKIN' 'BOUT ME?
OR YOU STILL TALKIN' TO YOURSELF?
HUH? NO, NOT AT ALL.
WELL, I'M TURNING IN. NIGHT NIGHT.
OK, I'LL BE IN SOON. GOTTA WRAP SOMETHING UP.
CÉDRIC!
ARE YOU READY?
THOREAU?
I DON'T KNOW WHAT FOR, BUT I'LL SAY YES ANYWAY.
YOU'LL SEE. IT'S UNIQUE.

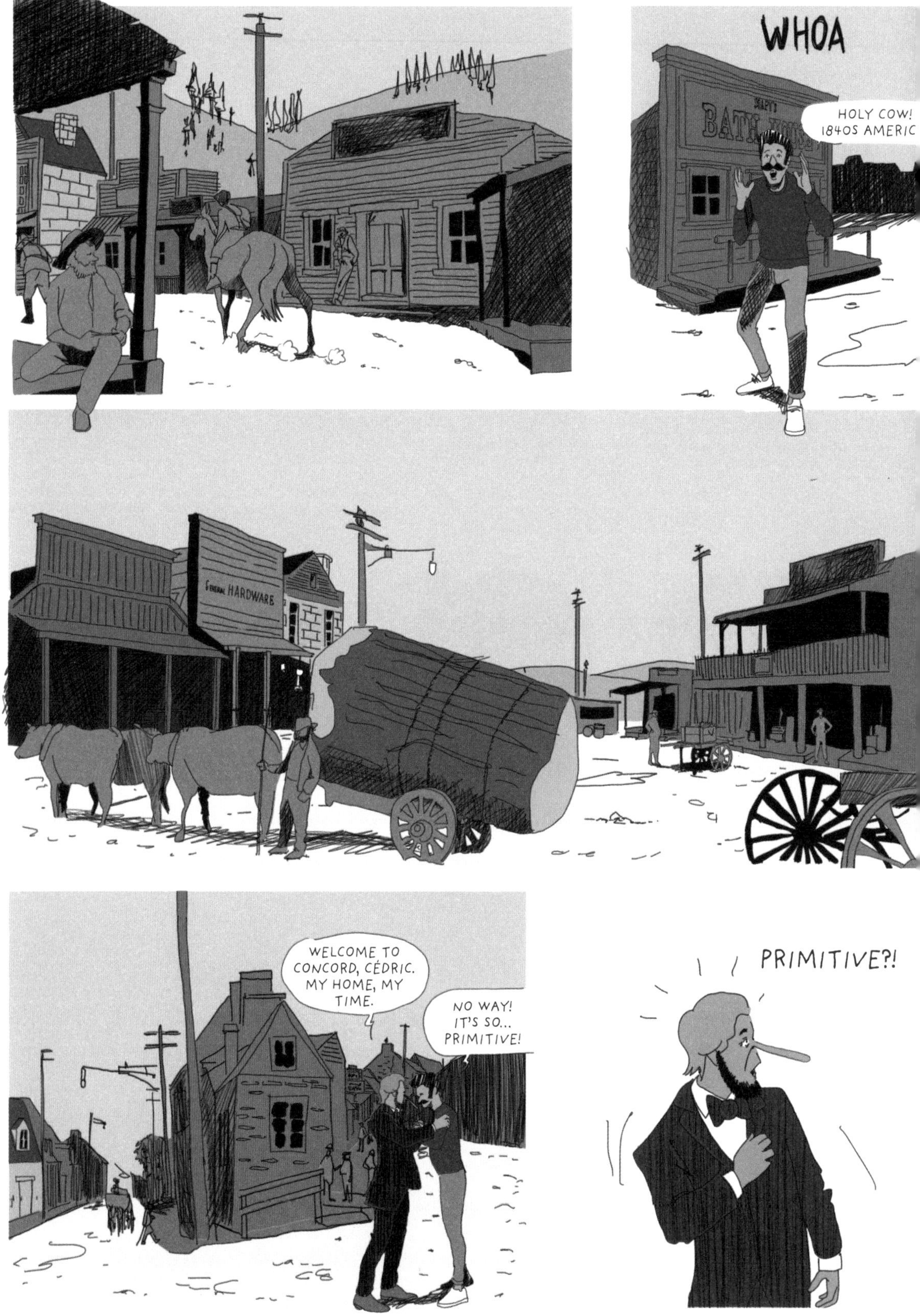
WHOA
HOLY COW!
1840S AMERIC
HARDWARE
WELCOME TO CONCORD, CÉDRIC. MY HOME, MY TIME.
NO WAY! IT'S SO... PRIMITIVE!
PRIMITIVE?!

IT IS THE YEAR 1839. THIS IS AS MODERN AS IT GETS. THIS IS MY ERA.

EVEN YOURS, HOWEVER MODERN AND ADVANCED, WILL LOOK PRIMITIVE TO THE FUTURE.

EVERY ERA LOOKS DOWN UPON THE PAST, CONVINCED THAT THEY THEMSELVES WERE THE PINNACLE.

MY CENTURY FORMS THE BEDROCK OF YOUR OWN. THE FOUNDATIONS OF YOUR TIME WERE LAID IN MINE.

YOUR ERA'S SYSTEMS OF PRODUCTION ARE SYMBOLIC OF THE MIDDLE CLASS' TRIUMPH IN THE 19TH CENTURY.

YOU MERELY INCREASED CONSUMERISM, THE PROFIT MARGIN AND ESTRANGEMENT FROM NATURE...

...PROBLEMS ALREADY PRESENT IN MY DAY.

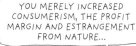

FOLLOW ME.

STEP INSIDE.

35

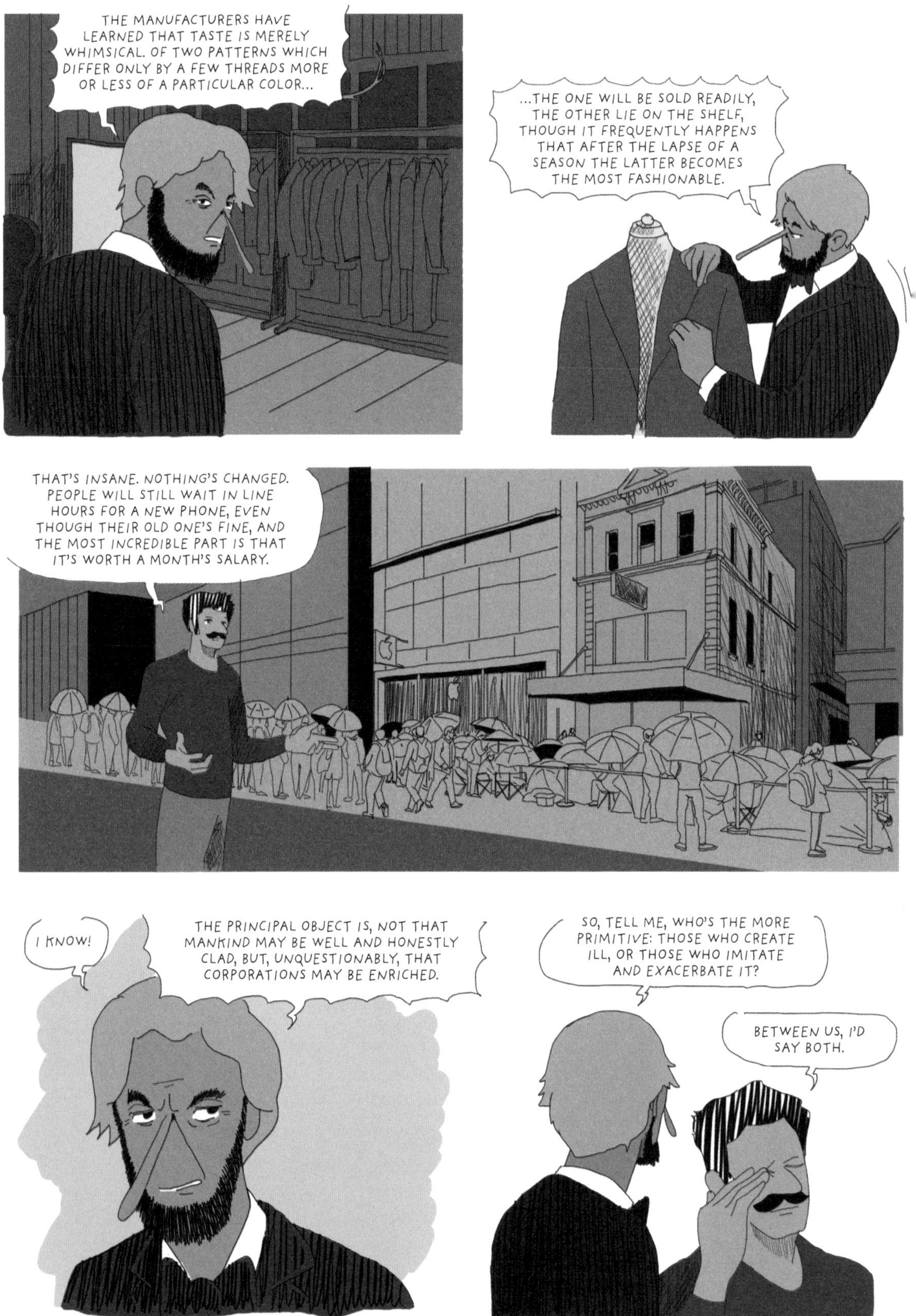
THE MANUFACTURERS HAVE LEARNED THAT TASTE IS MERELY WHIMSICAL. OF TWO PATTERNS WHICH DIFFER ONLY BY A FEW THREADS MORE OR LESS OF A PARTICULAR COLOR...
...THE ONE WILL BE SOLD READILY, THE OTHER LIE ON THE SHELF, THOUGH IT FREQUENTLY HAPPENS THAT AFTER THE LAPSE OF A SEASON THE LATTER BECOMES THE MOST FASHIONABLE.
THAT'S *INSANE*. NOTHING'S CHANGED. PEOPLE WILL STILL WAIT IN LINE HOURS FOR A NEW PHONE, EVEN THOUGH THEIR OLD ONE'S *FINE*, AND THE MOST *INCREDIBLE* PART IS THAT IT'S WORTH A MONTH'S SALARY.
I KNOW!
THE PRINCIPAL OBJECT IS, NOT THAT MANKIND MAY BE WELL AND HONESTLY CLAD, BUT, UNQUESTIONABLY, THAT CORPORATIONS MAY BE ENRICHED.
SO, TELL ME, WHO'S THE MORE *PRIMITIVE*: THOSE WHO CREATE ILL, OR THOSE WHO IMITATE AND EXACERBATE IT?
BETWEEN US, I'D SAY BOTH.

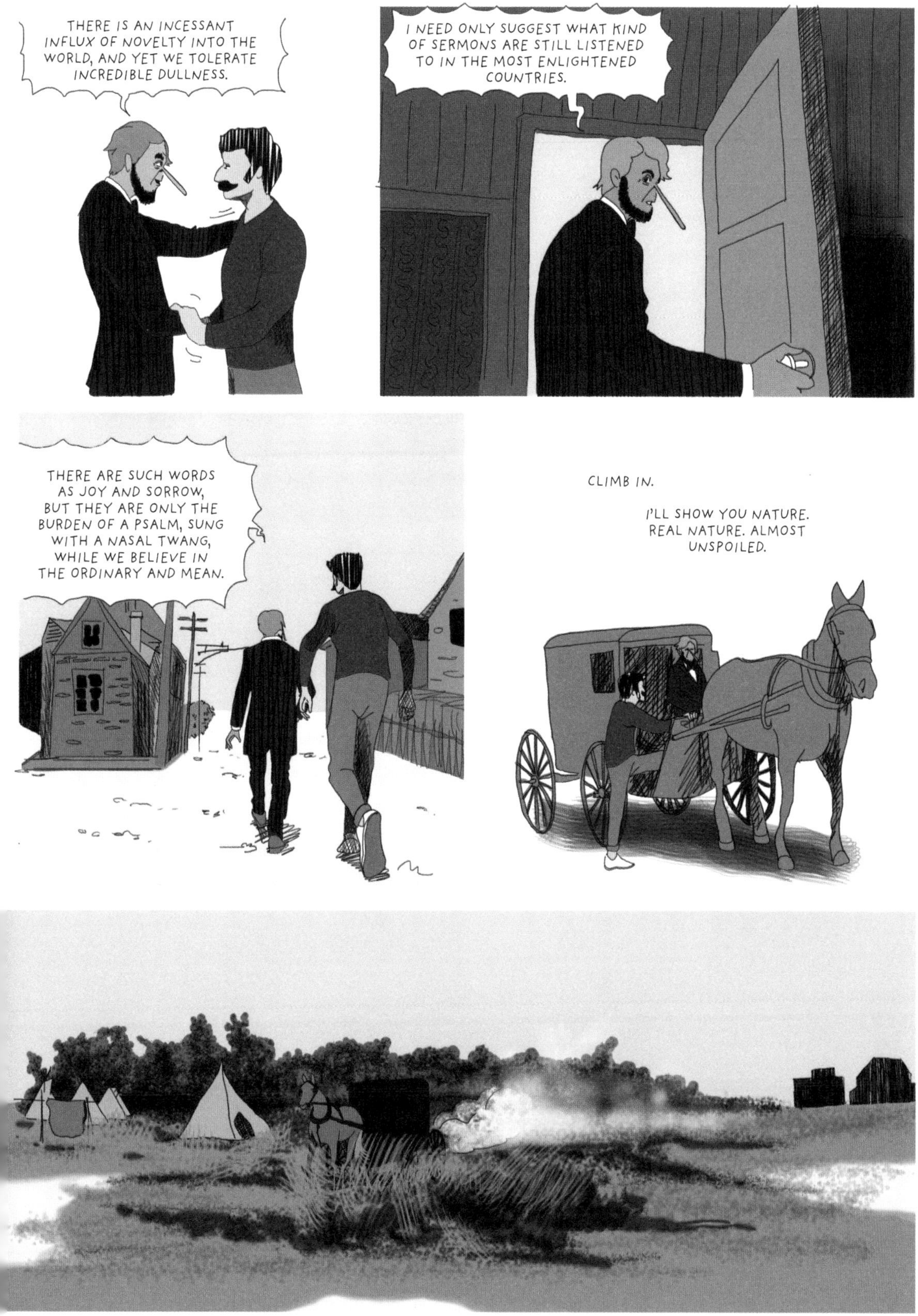
THERE IS AN INCESSANT INFLUX OF NOVELTY INTO THE WORLD, AND YET WE TOLERATE INCREDIBLE DULLNESS.
I NEED ONLY SUGGEST WHAT KIND OF SERMONS ARE STILL LISTENED TO IN THE MOST ENLIGHTENED COUNTRIES.
THERE ARE SUCH WORDS AS JOY AND SORROW, BUT THEY ARE ONLY THE BURDEN OF A PSALM, SUNG WITH A NASAL TWANG, WHILE WE BELIEVE IN THE ORDINARY AND MEAN.
CLIMB IN.
I'LL SHOW YOU NATURE. REAL NATURE. ALMOST UNSPOILED.

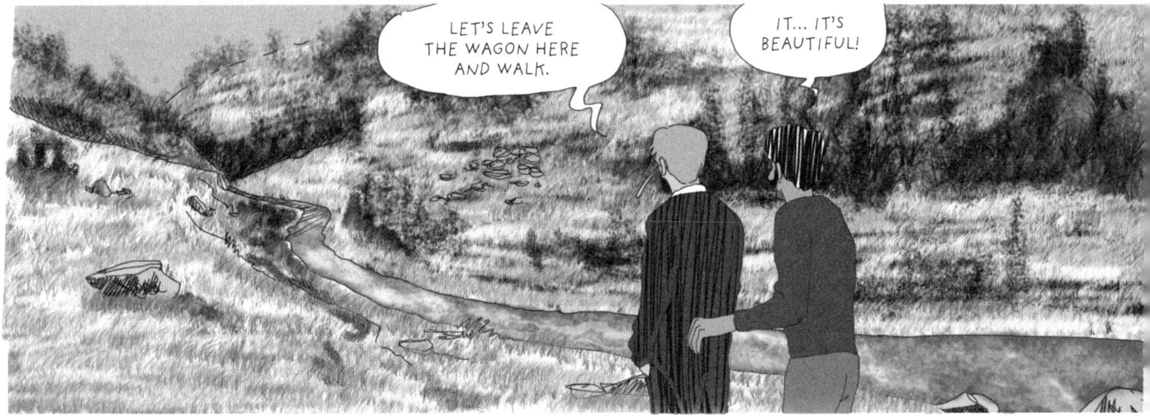
LET'S LEAVE THE WAGON HERE AND WALK.
IT... IT'S BEAUTIFUL!

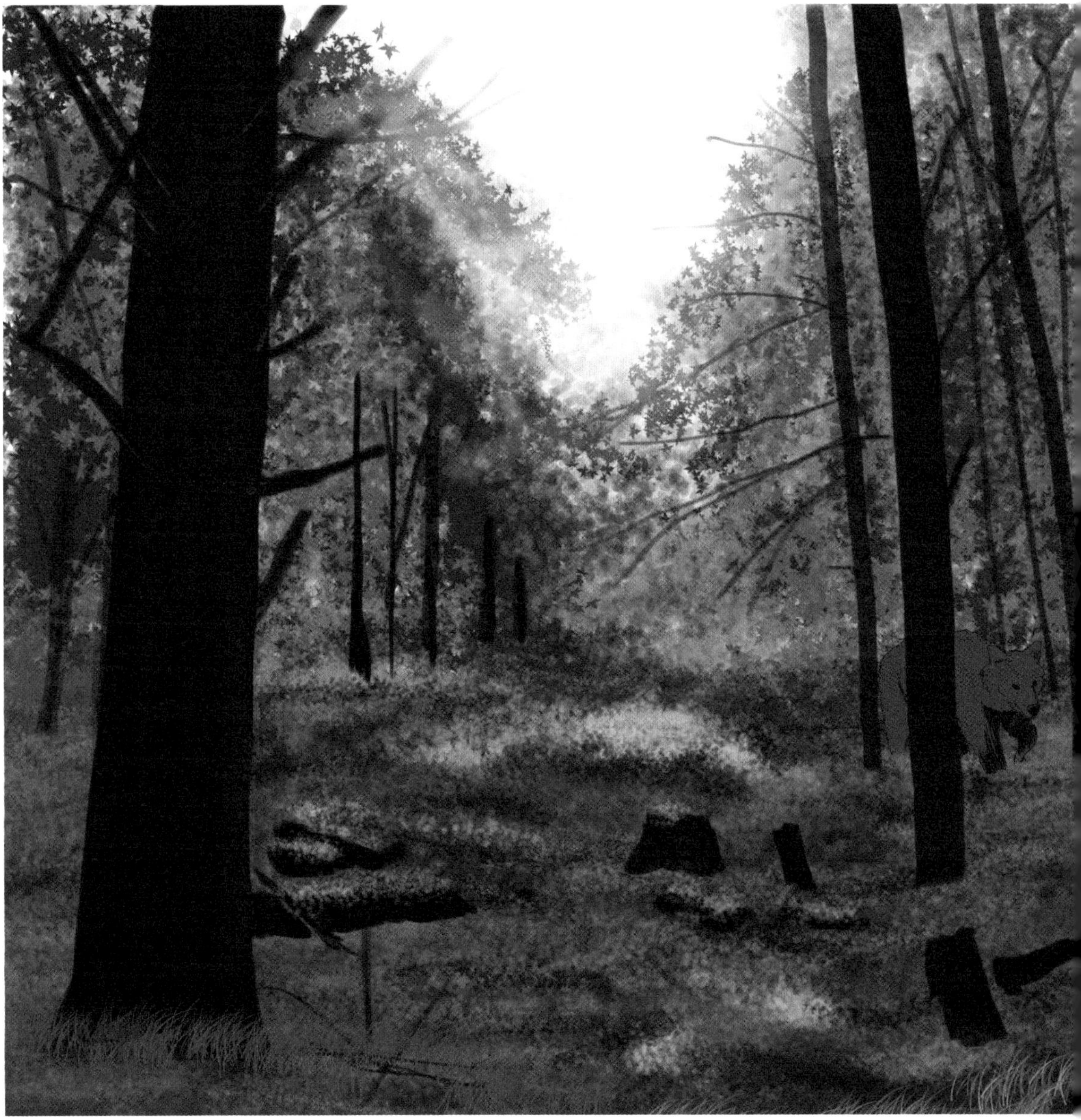

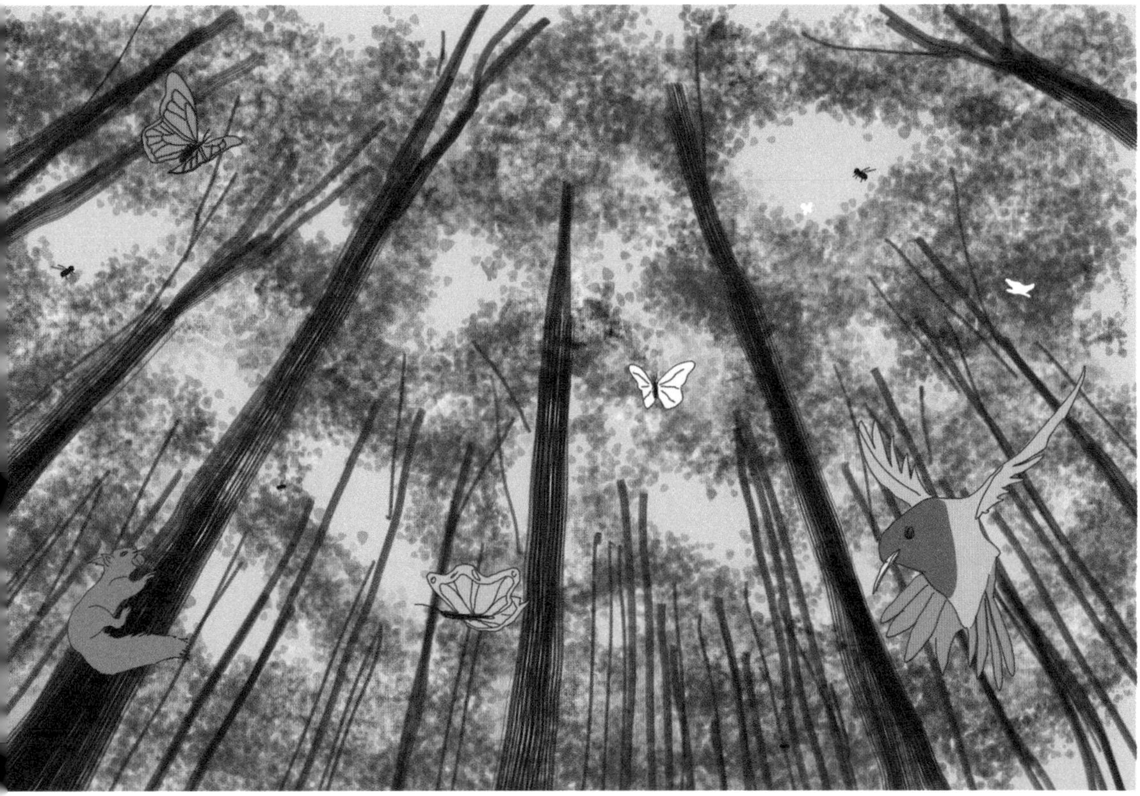

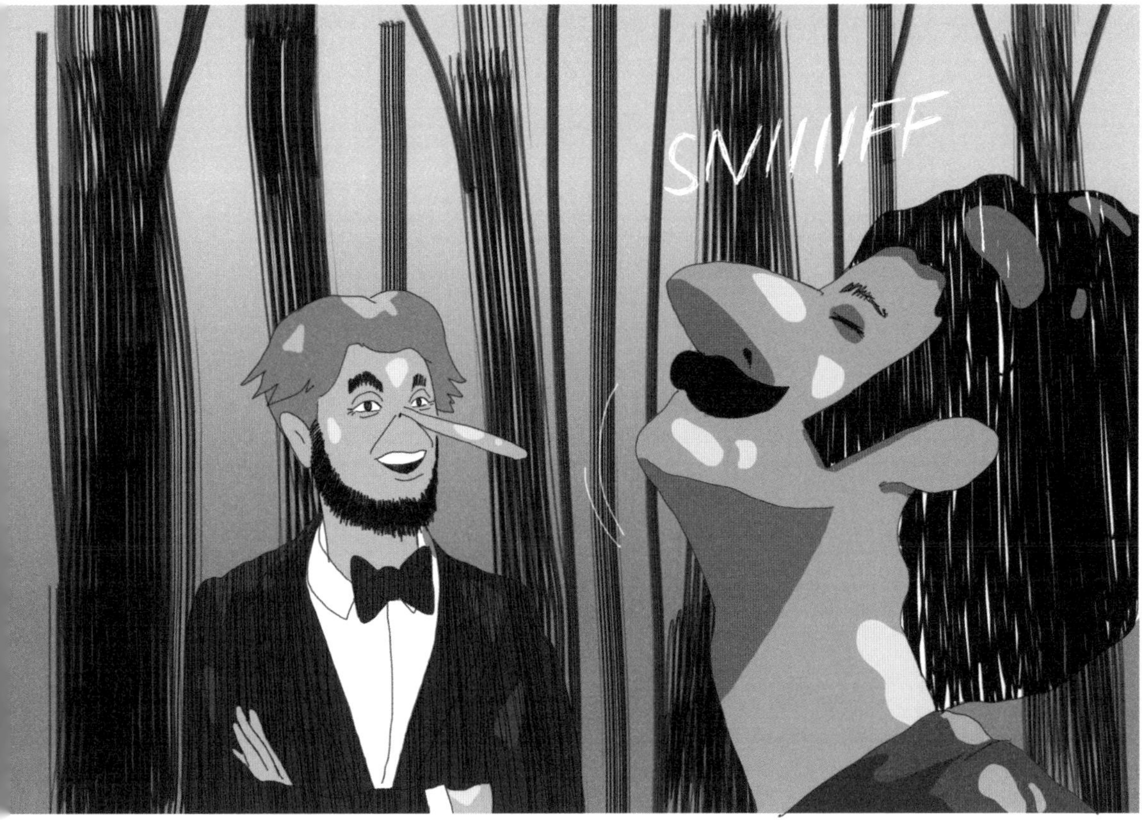
SNIIIIFF

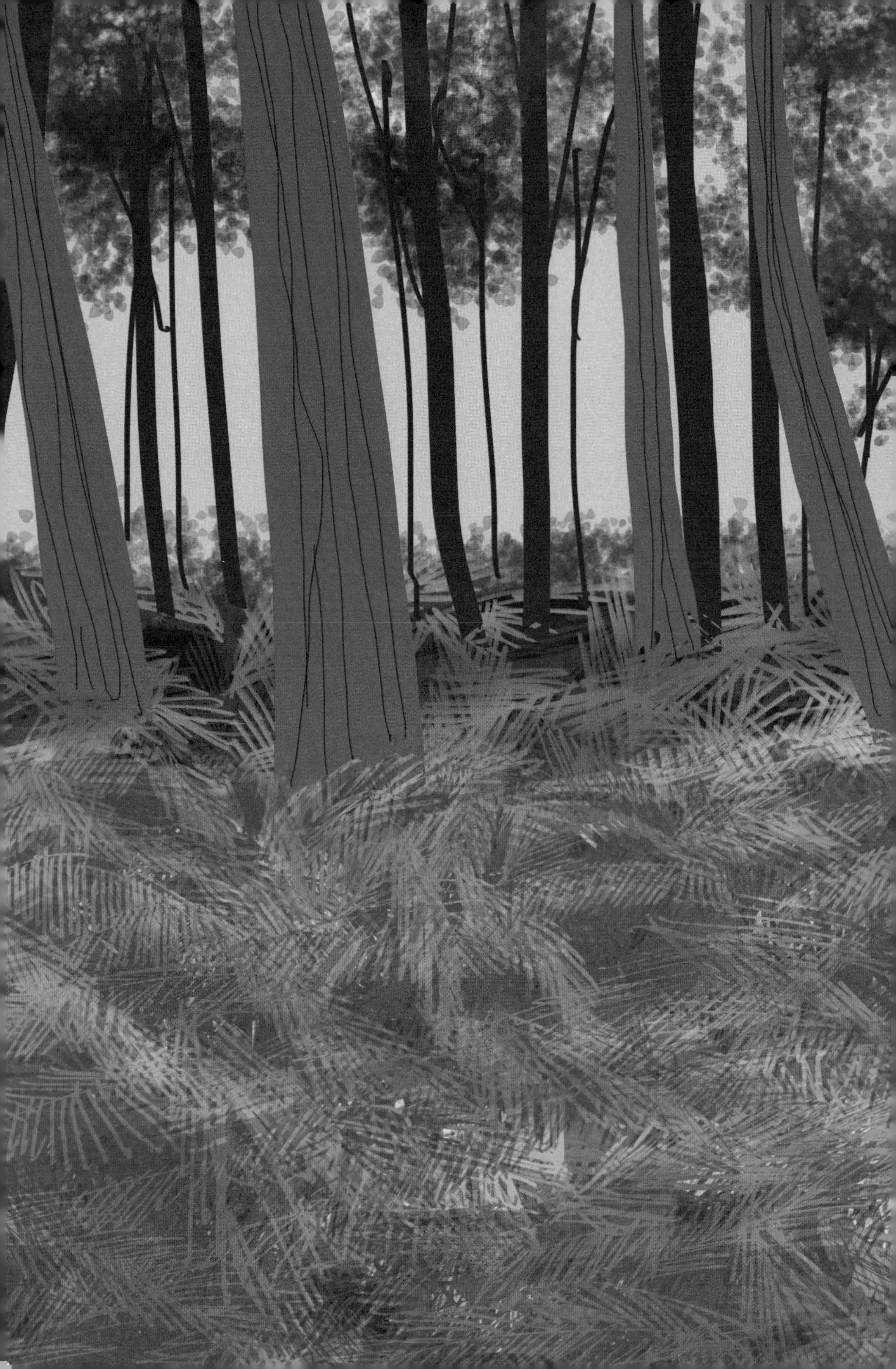

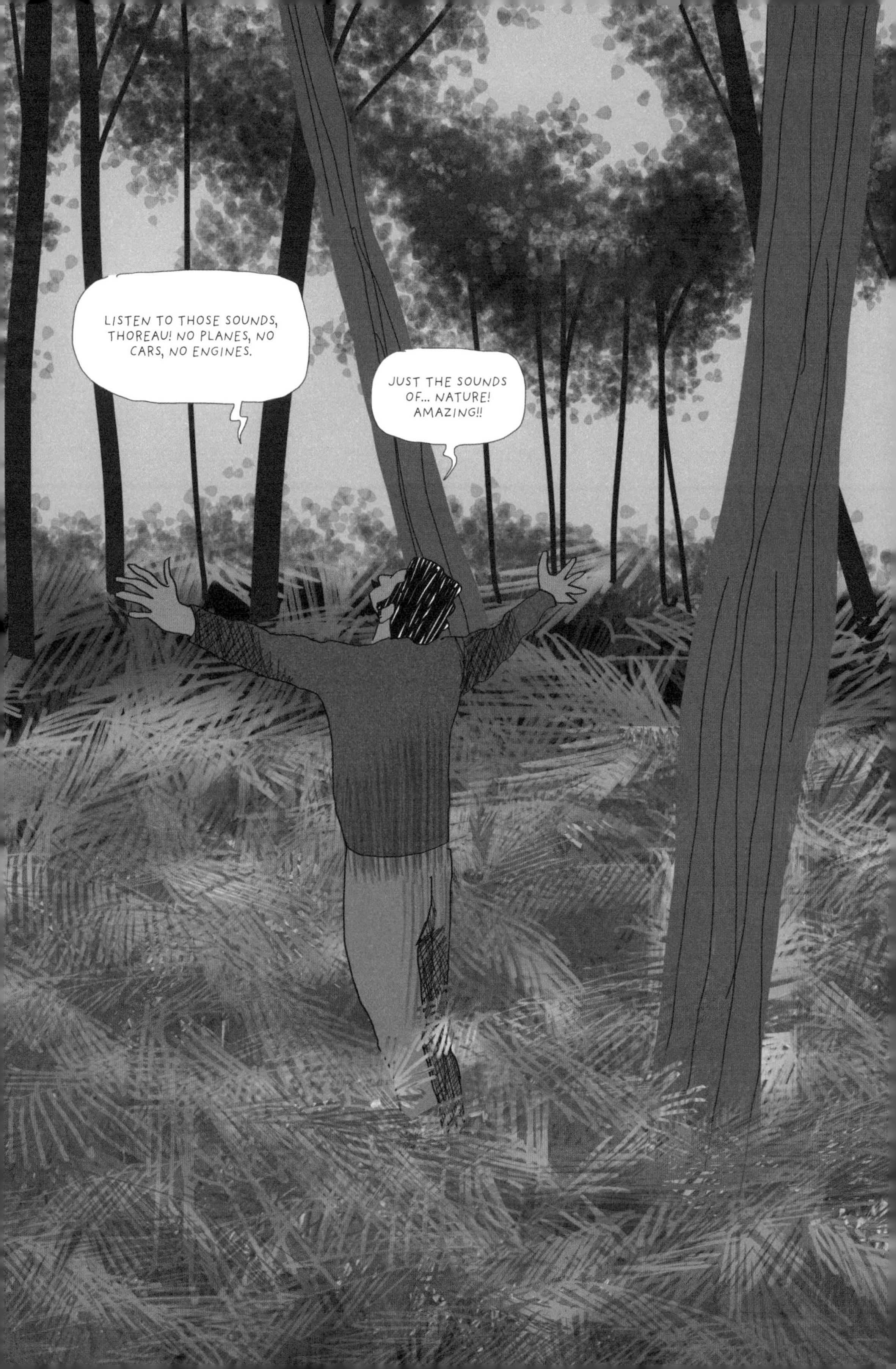
LISTEN TO THOSE SOUNDS, THOREAU! NO PLANES, NO CARS, NO ENGINES.
JUST THE SOUNDS OF... NATURE! AMAZING!!

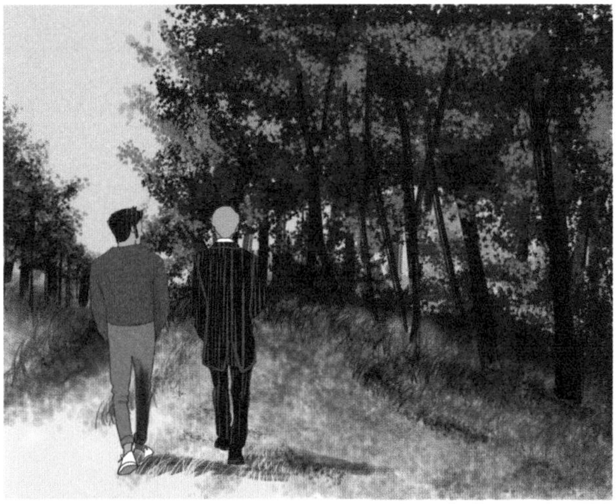

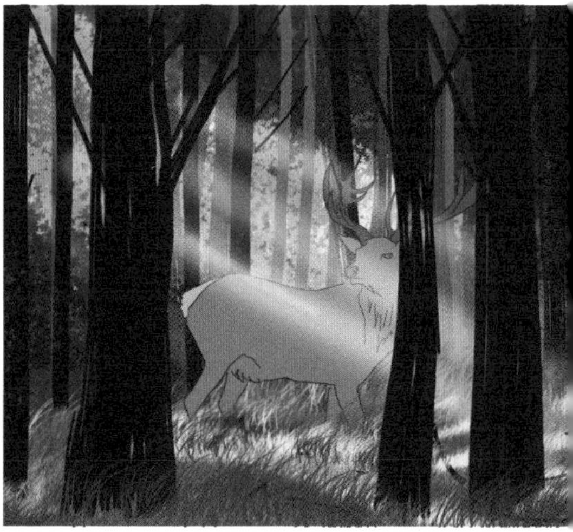

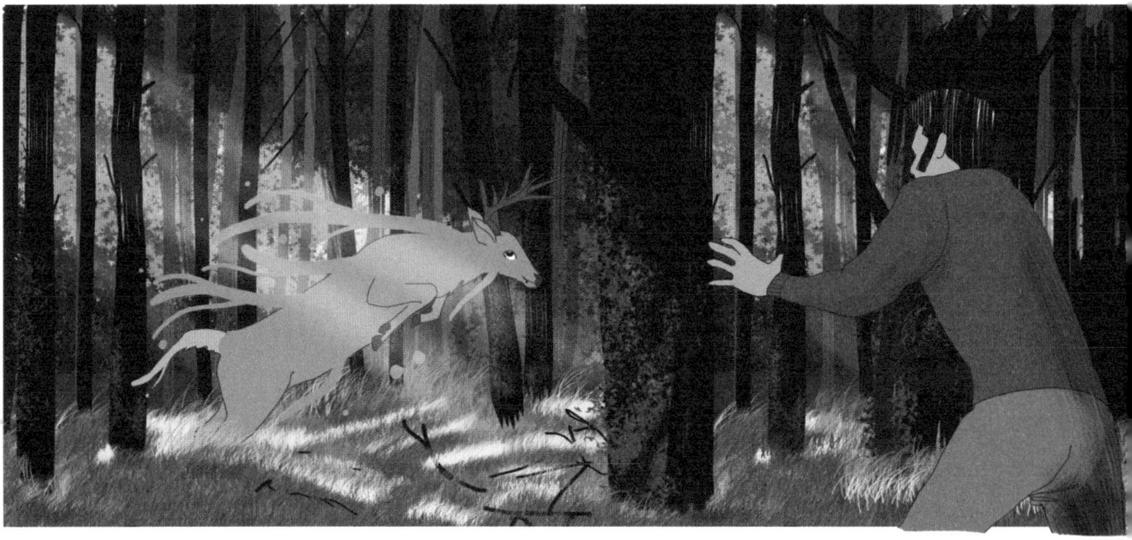

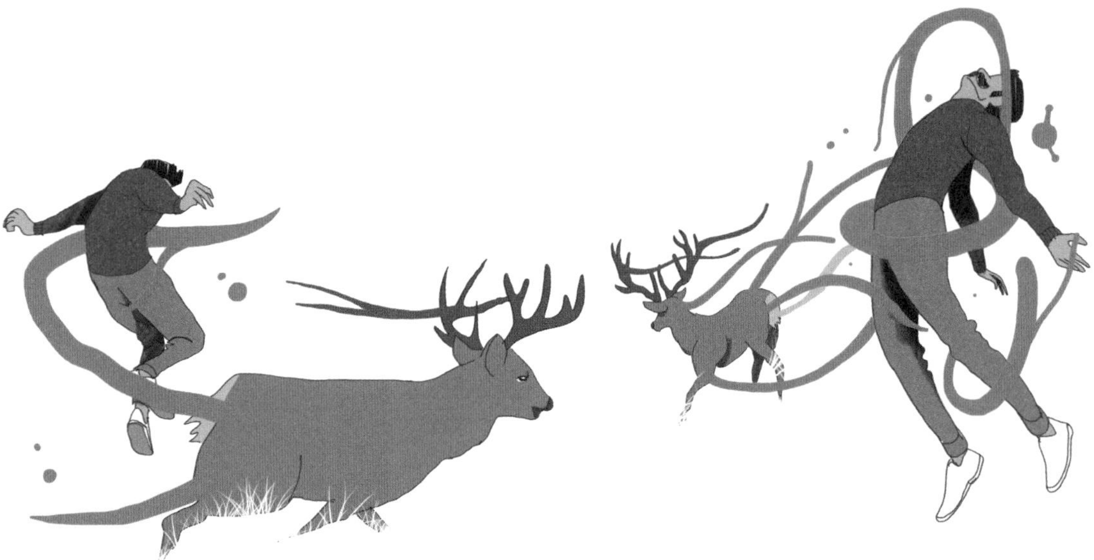

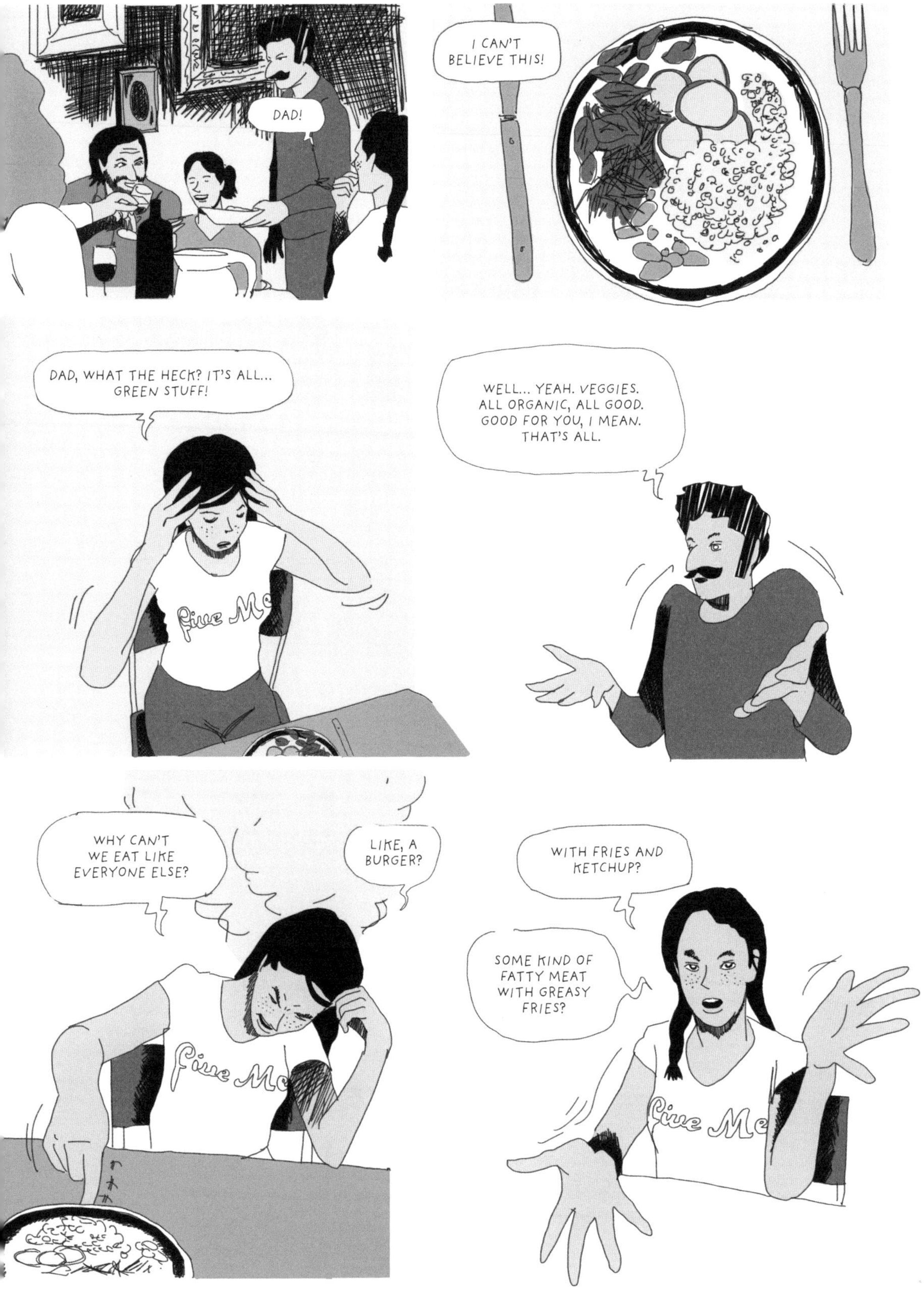
DAD!
I CAN'T BELIEVE THIS!
DAD, WHAT THE HECK? IT'S ALL... GREEN STUFF!
WELL... YEAH. VEGGIES. ALL ORGANIC, ALL GOOD. GOOD FOR YOU, I MEAN. THAT'S ALL.
WHY CAN'T WE EAT LIKE EVERYONE ELSE?
LIKE, A BURGER?
WITH FRIES AND KETCHUP?
SOME KIND OF FATTY MEAT WITH GREASY FRIES?

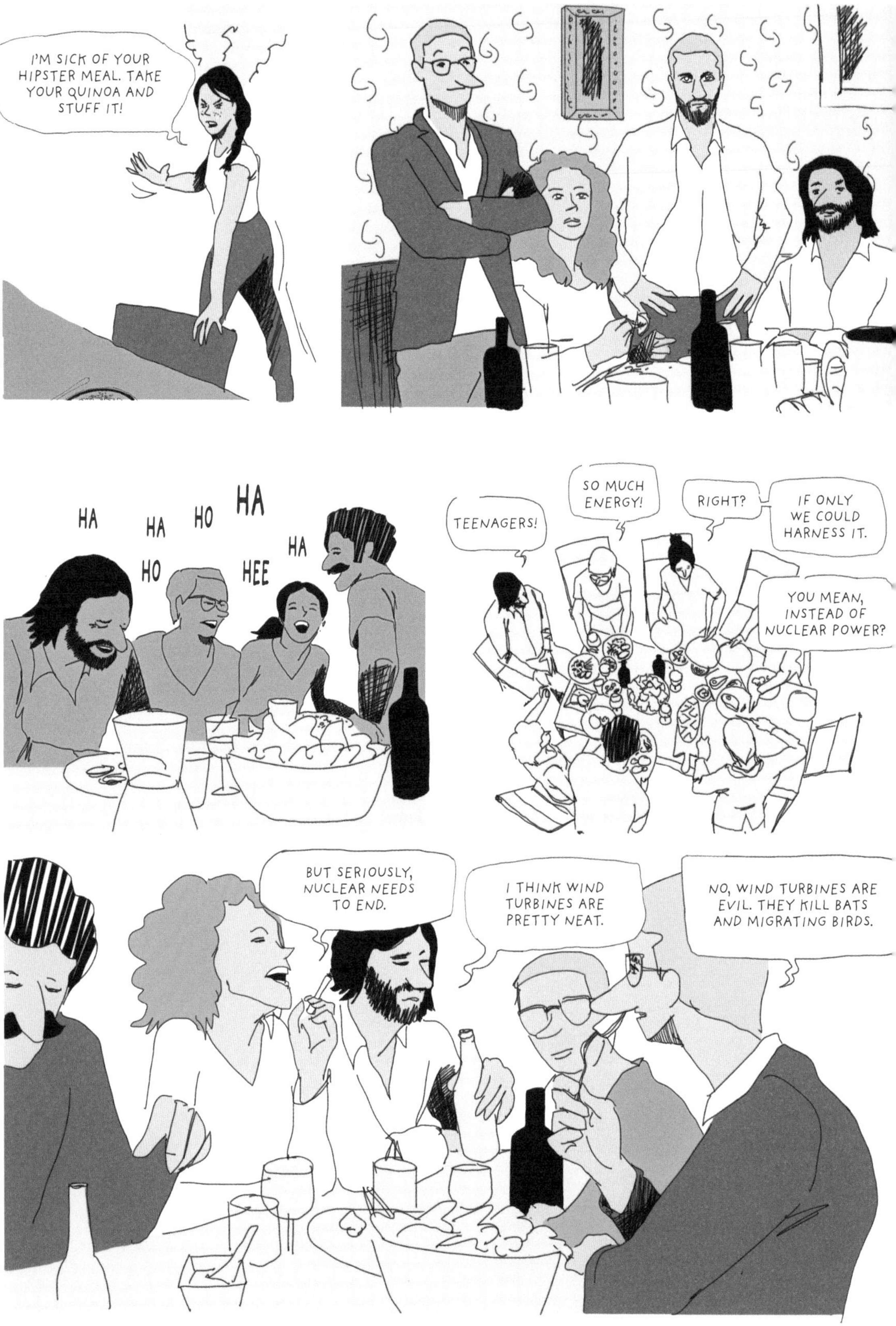

I'M SICK OF YOUR HIPSTER MEAL. TAKE YOUR QUINOA AND STUFF IT!
HA
HA
HO
HA
HO
HEE
HA
TEENAGERS!
SO MUCH ENERGY!
RIGHT?
IF ONLY WE COULD HARNESS IT.
YOU MEAN, INSTEAD OF NUCLEAR POWER?
BUT SERIOUSLY, NUCLEAR NEEDS TO END.
I THINK WIND TURBINES ARE PRETTY NEAT.
NO, WIND TURBINES ARE EVIL. THEY KILL BATS AND MIGRATING BIRDS.

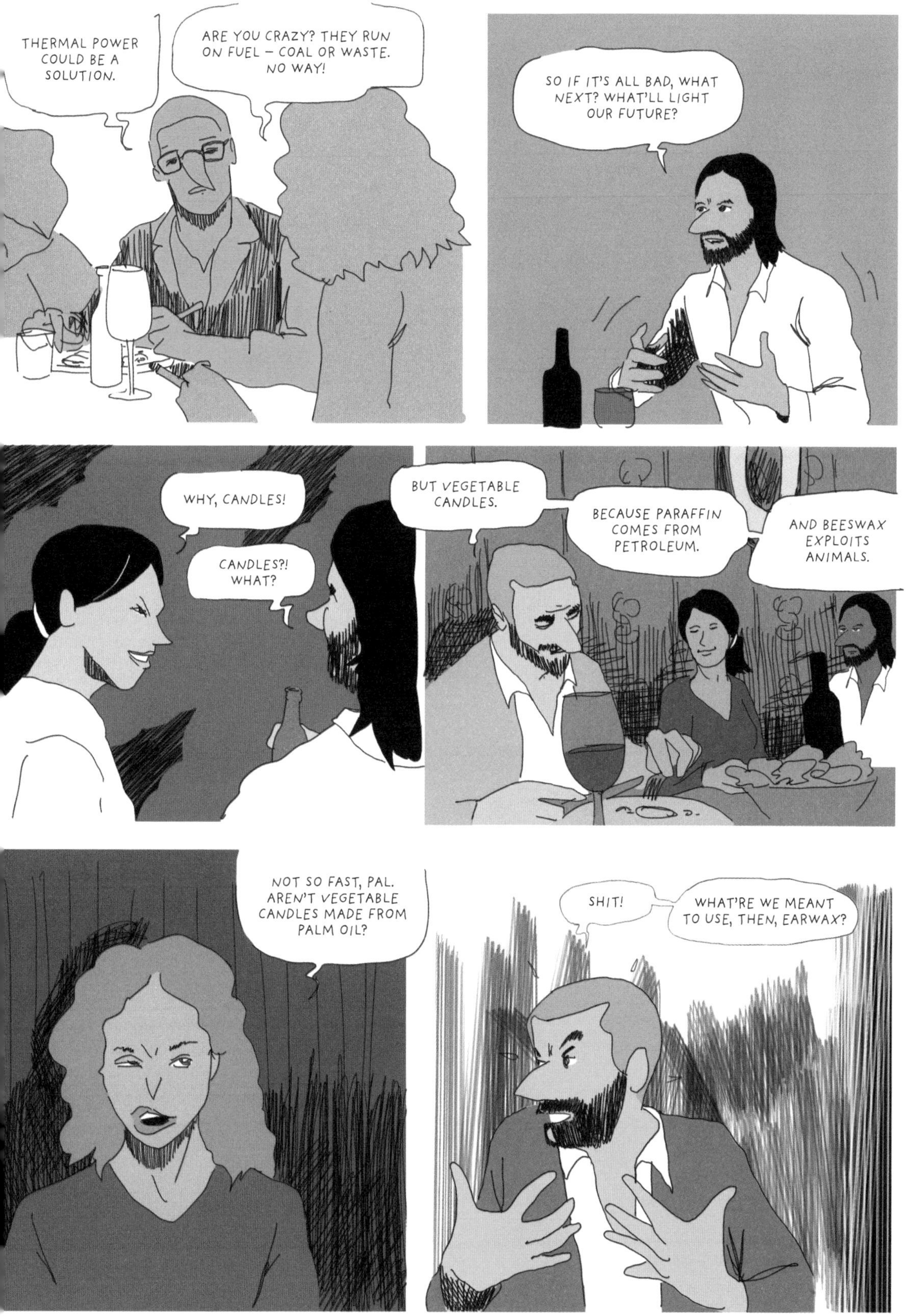
THERMAL POWER COULD BE A SOLUTION.
ARE YOU CRAZY? THEY RUN ON FUEL – COAL OR WASTE. NO WAY!
SO IF IT'S ALL BAD, WHAT NEXT? WHAT'LL LIGHT OUR FUTURE?
WHY, CANDLES!
CANDLES?! WHAT?
BUT VEGETABLE CANDLES.
BECAUSE PARAFFIN COMES FROM PETROLEUM.
AND BEESWAX EXPLOITS ANIMALS.
NOT SO FAST, PAL. AREN'T VEGETABLE CANDLES MADE FROM PALM OIL?
SHIT!
WHAT'RE WE MEANT TO USE, THEN, EARWAX?

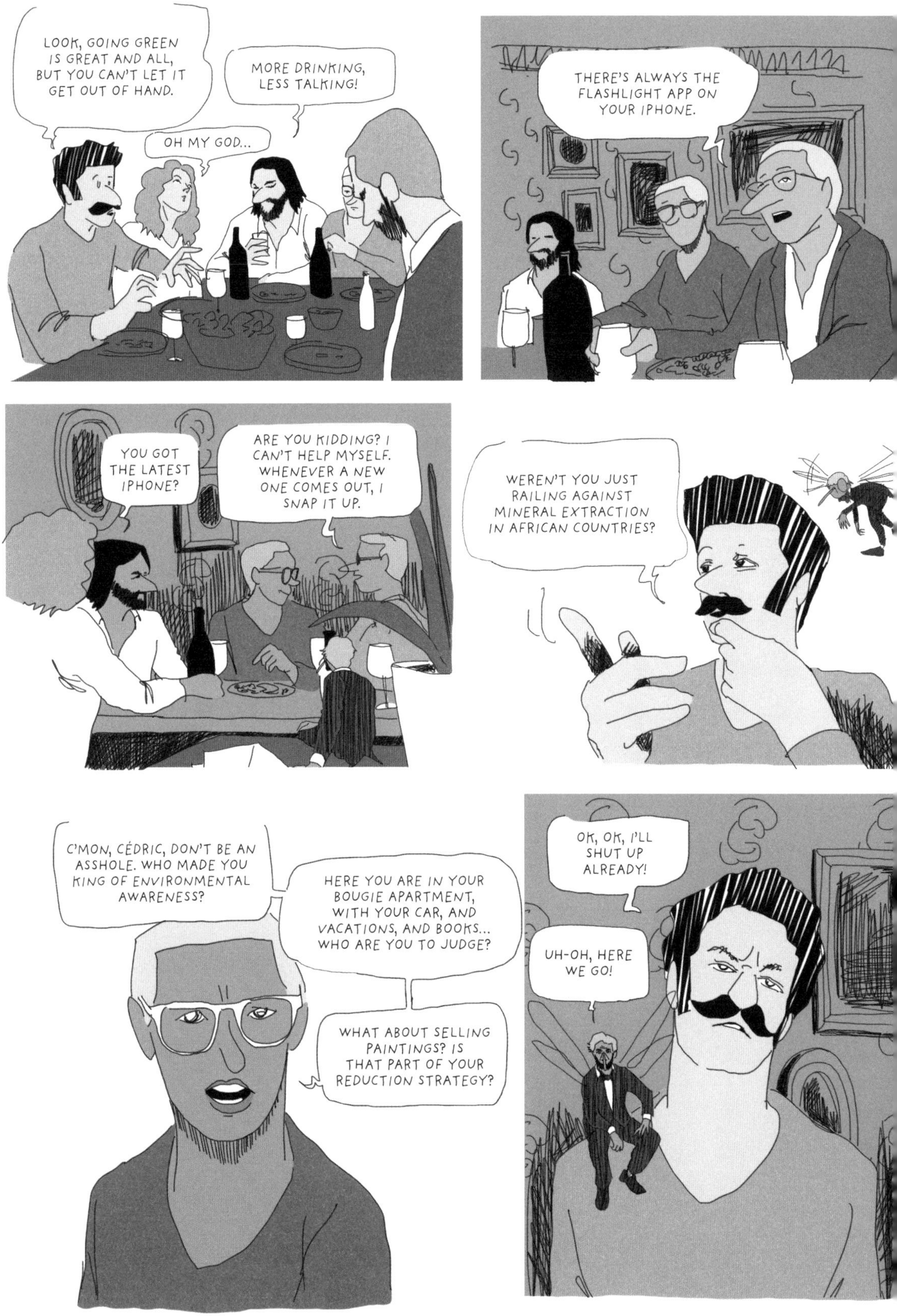
LOOK, GOING GREEN IS GREAT AND ALL, BUT YOU CAN'T LET IT GET OUT OF HAND.
MORE DRINKING, LESS TALKING!
OH MY GOD...
THERE'S ALWAYS THE FLASHLIGHT APP ON YOUR IPHONE.
YOU GOT THE LATEST IPHONE?
ARE YOU KIDDING? I CAN'T HELP MYSELF. WHENEVER A NEW ONE COMES OUT, I SNAP IT UP.
WEREN'T YOU JUST RAILING AGAINST MINERAL EXTRACTION IN AFRICAN COUNTRIES?
C'MON, CÉDRIC, DON'T BE AN ASSHOLE. WHO MADE YOU KING OF ENVIRONMENTAL AWARENESS?
HERE YOU ARE IN YOUR BOUGIE APARTMENT, WITH YOUR CAR, AND VACATIONS, AND BOOKS... WHO ARE YOU TO JUDGE?
WHAT ABOUT SELLING PAINTINGS? IS THAT PART OF YOUR REDUCTION STRATEGY?
OK, OK, I'LL SHUT UP ALREADY!
UH-OH, HERE WE GO!

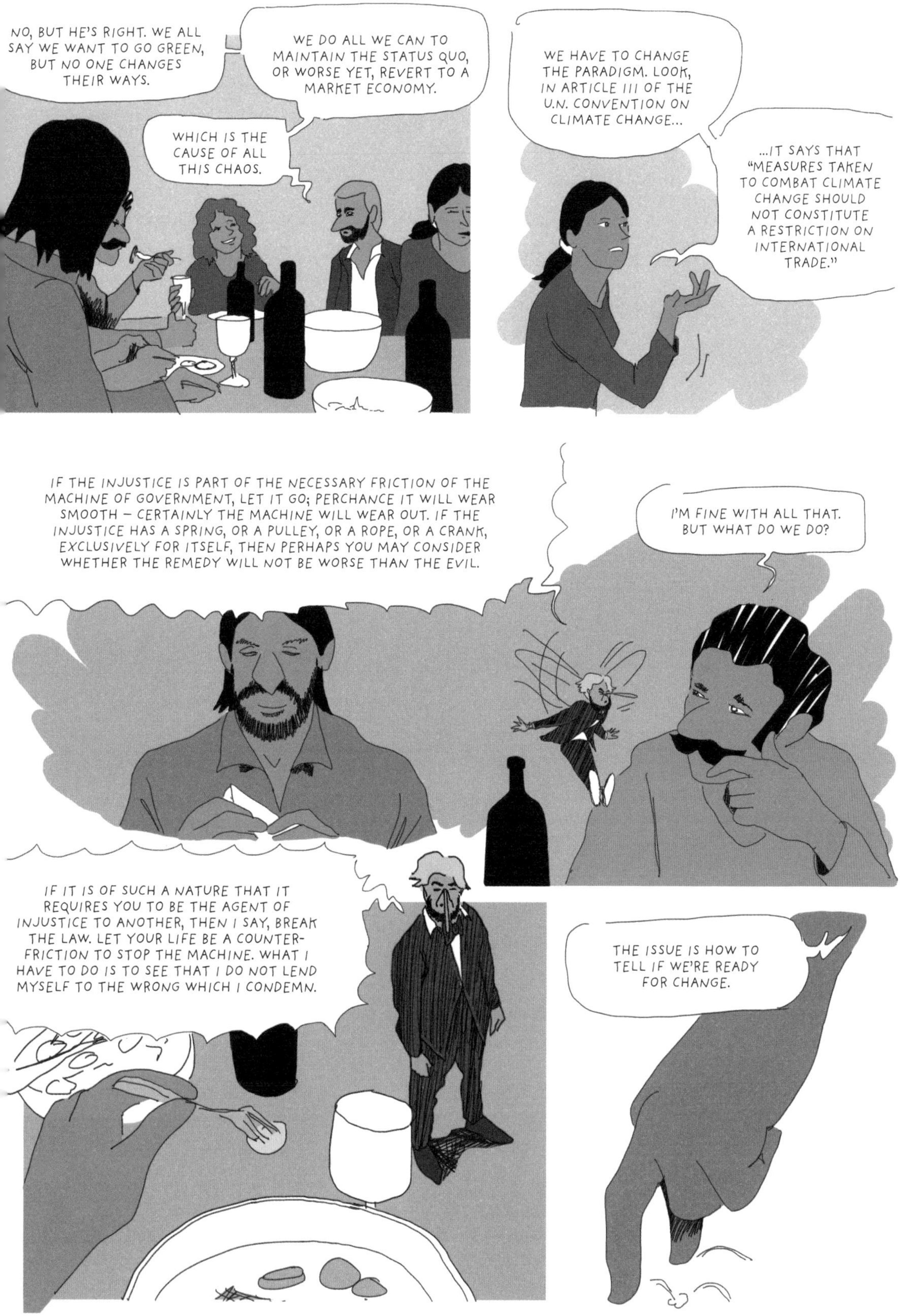
NO, BUT HE'S RIGHT. WE ALL SAY WE WANT TO GO GREEN, BUT NO ONE CHANGES THEIR WAYS.
WE DO ALL WE CAN TO MAINTAIN THE STATUS QUO, OR WORSE YET, REVERT TO A MARKET ECONOMY.
WHICH IS THE CAUSE OF ALL THIS CHAOS.
WE HAVE TO CHANGE THE PARADIGM. LOOK, IN ARTICLE III OF THE U.N. CONVENTION ON CLIMATE CHANGE...
...IT SAYS THAT "MEASURES TAKEN TO COMBAT CLIMATE CHANGE SHOULD NOT CONSTITUTE A RESTRICTION ON INTERNATIONAL TRADE."
IF THE INJUSTICE IS PART OF THE NECESSARY FRICTION OF THE MACHINE OF GOVERNMENT, LET IT GO; PERCHANCE IT WILL WEAR SMOOTH — CERTAINLY THE MACHINE WILL WEAR OUT. IF THE INJUSTICE HAS A SPRING, OR A PULLEY, OR A ROPE, OR A CRANK, EXCLUSIVELY FOR ITSELF, THEN PERHAPS YOU MAY CONSIDER WHETHER THE REMEDY WILL NOT BE WORSE THAN THE EVIL.
I'M FINE WITH ALL THAT. BUT WHAT DO WE DO?
IF IT IS OF SUCH A NATURE THAT IT REQUIRES YOU TO BE THE AGENT OF INJUSTICE TO ANOTHER, THEN I SAY, BREAK THE LAW. LET YOUR LIFE BE A COUNTER-FRICTION TO STOP THE MACHINE. WHAT I HAVE TO DO IS TO SEE THAT I DO NOT LEND MYSELF TO THE WRONG WHICH I CONDEMN.
THE ISSUE IS HOW TO TELL IF WE'RE READY FOR CHANGE.

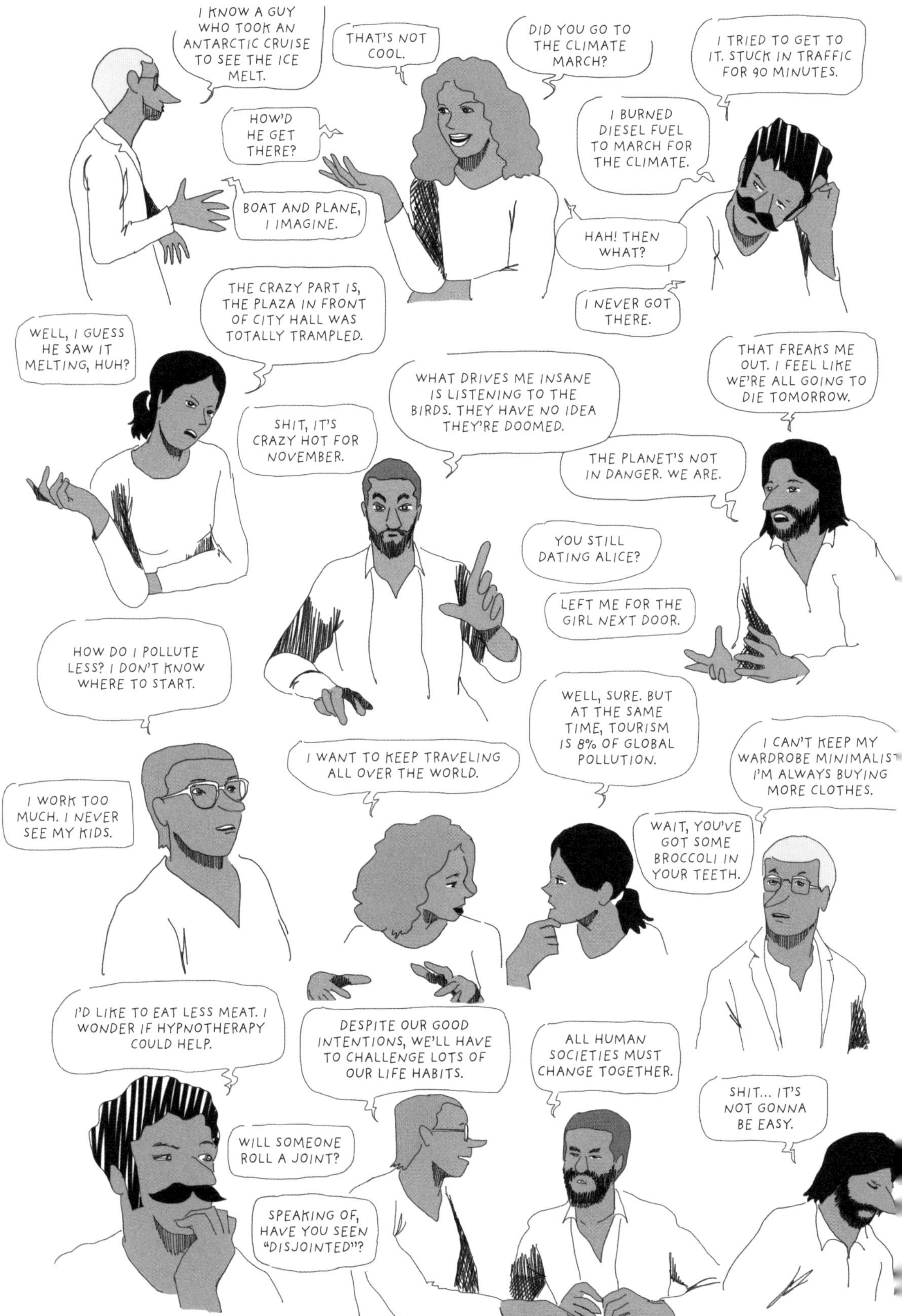
I KNOW A GUY WHO TOOK AN ANTARCTIC CRUISE TO SEE THE ICE MELT.
THAT'S NOT COOL.
HOW'D HE GET THERE?
BOAT AND PLANE, I IMAGINE.
DID YOU GO TO THE CLIMATE MARCH?
I TRIED TO GET TO IT. STUCK IN TRAFFIC FOR 90 MINUTES.
I BURNED DIESEL FUEL TO MARCH FOR THE CLIMATE.
HAH! THEN WHAT?
I NEVER GOT THERE.
WELL, I GUESS HE SAW IT MELTING, HUH?
THE CRAZY PART IS, THE PLAZA IN FRONT OF CITY HALL WAS TOTALLY TRAMPLED.
WHAT DRIVES ME INSANE IS LISTENING TO THE BIRDS. THEY HAVE NO IDEA THEY'RE DOOMED.
SHIT, IT'S CRAZY HOT FOR NOVEMBER.
THAT FREAKS ME OUT. I FEEL LIKE WE'RE ALL GOING TO DIE TOMORROW.
THE PLANET'S NOT IN DANGER. WE ARE.
YOU STILL DATING ALICE?
LEFT ME FOR THE GIRL NEXT DOOR.
HOW DO I POLLUTE LESS? I DON'T KNOW WHERE TO START.
WELL, SURE. BUT AT THE SAME TIME, TOURISM IS 8% OF GLOBAL POLLUTION.
I WANT TO KEEP TRAVELING ALL OVER THE WORLD.
I CAN'T KEEP MY WARDROBE MINIMALIST. I'M ALWAYS BUYING MORE CLOTHES.
I WORK TOO MUCH. I NEVER SEE MY KIDS.
WAIT, YOU'VE GOT SOME BROCCOLI IN YOUR TEETH.
I'D LIKE TO EAT LESS MEAT. I WONDER IF HYPNOTHERAPY COULD HELP.
DESPITE OUR GOOD INTENTIONS, WE'LL HAVE TO CHALLENGE LOTS OF OUR LIFE HABITS.
ALL HUMAN SOCIETIES MUST CHANGE TOGETHER.
SHIT... IT'S NOT GONNA BE EASY.
WILL SOMEONE ROLL A JOINT?
SPEAKING OF, HAVE YOU SEEN "DISJOINTED"?

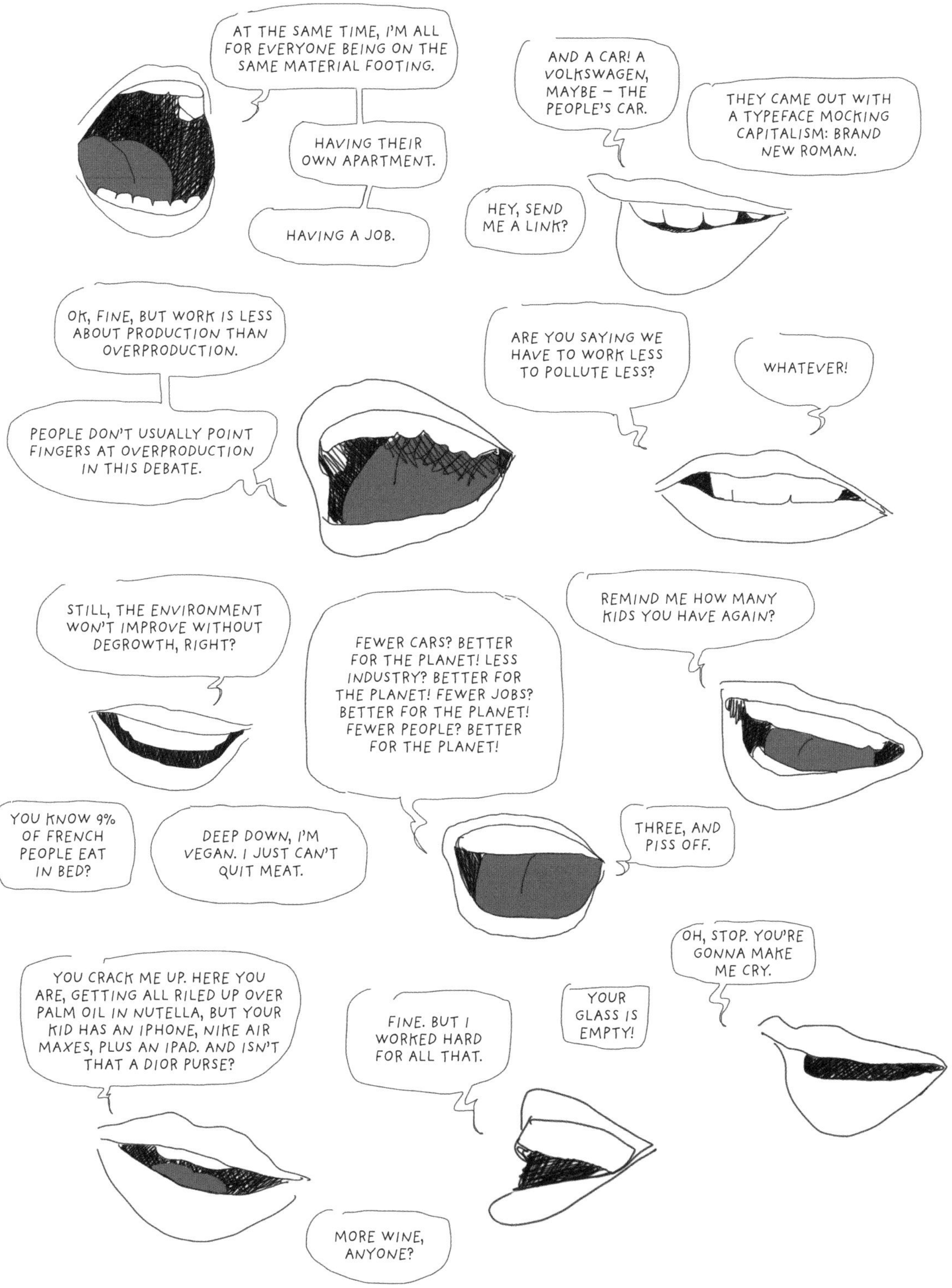
AT THE SAME TIME, I'M ALL FOR EVERYONE BEING ON THE SAME MATERIAL FOOTING.
HAVING THEIR OWN APARTMENT.
HAVING A JOB.
AND A CAR! A VOLKSWAGEN, MAYBE — THE PEOPLE'S CAR.
THEY CAME OUT WITH A TYPEFACE MOCKING CAPITALISM: BRAND NEW ROMAN.
HEY, SEND ME A LINK?
OK, FINE, BUT WORK IS LESS ABOUT PRODUCTION THAN OVERPRODUCTION.
PEOPLE DON'T USUALLY POINT FINGERS AT OVERPRODUCTION IN THIS DEBATE.
ARE YOU SAYING WE HAVE TO WORK LESS TO POLLUTE LESS?
WHATEVER!
STILL, THE ENVIRONMENT WON'T IMPROVE WITHOUT DEGROWTH, RIGHT?
FEWER CARS? BETTER FOR THE PLANET! LESS INDUSTRY? BETTER FOR THE PLANET! FEWER JOBS? BETTER FOR THE PLANET! FEWER PEOPLE? BETTER FOR THE PLANET!
REMIND ME HOW MANY KIDS YOU HAVE AGAIN?
YOU KNOW 9% OF FRENCH PEOPLE EAT IN BED?
DEEP DOWN, I'M VEGAN. I JUST CAN'T QUIT MEAT.
THREE, AND PISS OFF.
YOU CRACK ME UP. HERE YOU ARE, GETTING ALL RILED UP OVER PALM OIL IN NUTELLA, BUT YOUR KID HAS AN IPHONE, NIKE AIR MAXES, PLUS AN IPAD. AND ISN'T THAT A DIOR PURSE?
FINE. BUT I WORKED HARD FOR ALL THAT.
YOUR GLASS IS EMPTY!
OH, STOP. YOU'RE GONNA MAKE ME CRY.
MORE WINE, ANYONE?

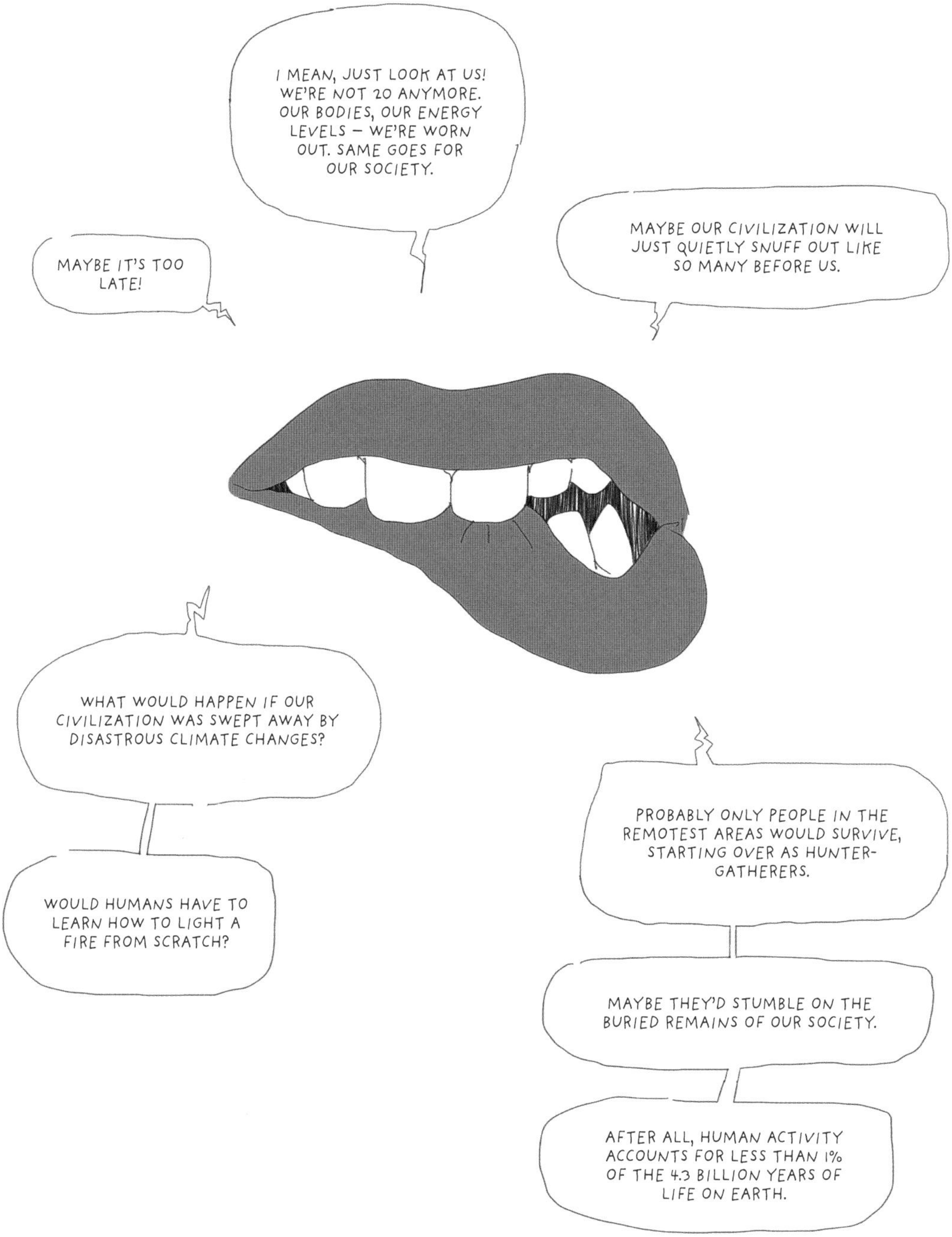
I MEAN, JUST LOOK AT US! WE'RE NOT 20 ANYMORE. OUR BODIES, OUR ENERGY LEVELS – WE'RE WORN OUT. SAME GOES FOR OUR SOCIETY.
MAYBE IT'S TOO LATE!
MAYBE OUR CIVILIZATION WILL JUST QUIETLY SNUFF OUT LIKE SO MANY BEFORE US.
WHAT WOULD HAPPEN IF OUR CIVILIZATION WAS SWEPT AWAY BY DISASTROUS CLIMATE CHANGES?
WOULD HUMANS HAVE TO LEARN HOW TO LIGHT A FIRE FROM SCRATCH?
PROBABLY ONLY PEOPLE IN THE REMOTEST AREAS WOULD SURVIVE, STARTING OVER AS HUNTER-GATHERERS.
MAYBE THEY'D STUMBLE ON THE BURIED REMAINS OF OUR SOCIETY.
AFTER ALL, HUMAN ACTIVITY ACCOUNTS FOR LESS THAN 1% OF THE 4.3 BILLION YEARS OF LIFE ON EARTH.

11. Exacerbation

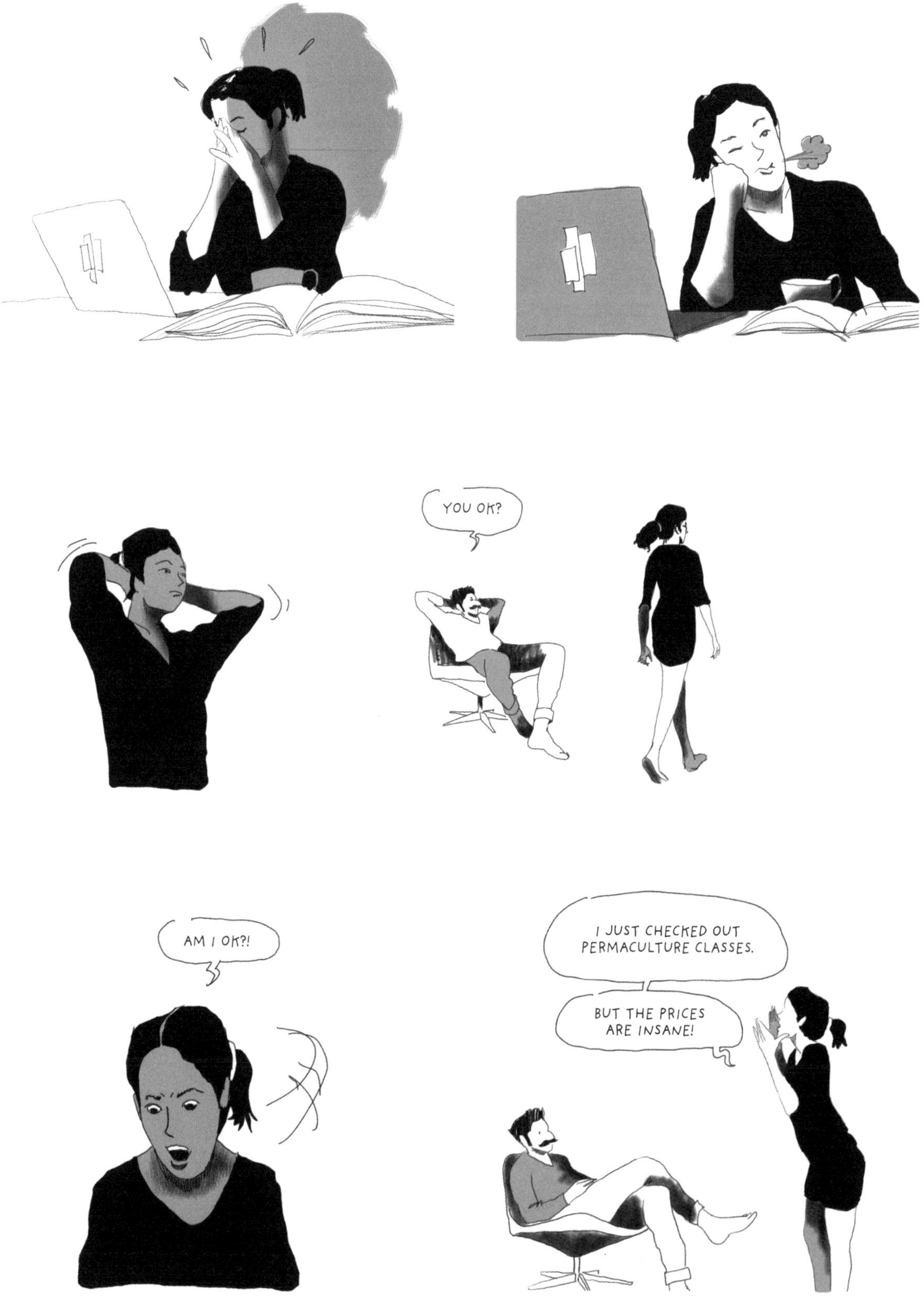
YOU OK?
AM I OK?!
I JUST CHECKED OUT PERMACULTURE CLASSES.
BUT THE PRICES ARE INSANE!

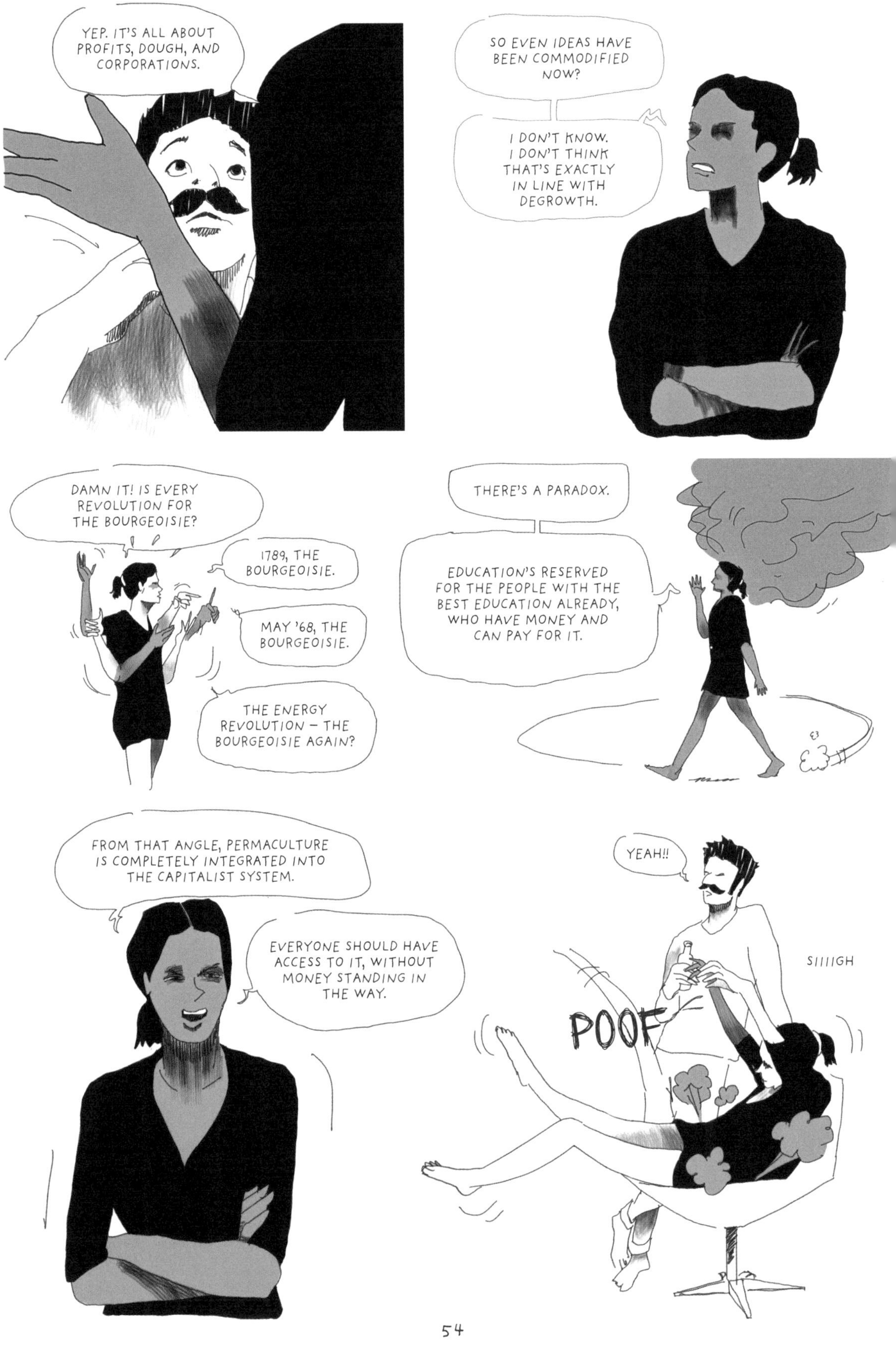
YEP. IT'S ALL ABOUT PROFITS, DOUGH, AND CORPORATIONS.
SO EVEN IDEAS HAVE BEEN COMMODIFIED NOW?
I DON'T KNOW. I DON'T THINK THAT'S EXACTLY IN LINE WITH DEGROWTH.
DAMN IT! IS EVERY REVOLUTION FOR THE BOURGEOISIE?
1789, THE BOURGEOISIE.
MAY '68, THE BOURGEOISIE.
THE ENERGY REVOLUTION – THE BOURGEOISIE AGAIN?
THERE'S A PARADOX.
EDUCATION'S RESERVED FOR THE PEOPLE WITH THE BEST EDUCATION ALREADY, WHO HAVE MONEY AND CAN PAY FOR IT.
FROM THAT ANGLE, PERMACULTURE IS COMPLETELY INTEGRATED INTO THE CAPITALIST SYSTEM.
EVERYONE SHOULD HAVE ACCESS TO IT, WITHOUT MONEY STANDING IN THE WAY.
YEAH!!
SIIIIGH
POOF

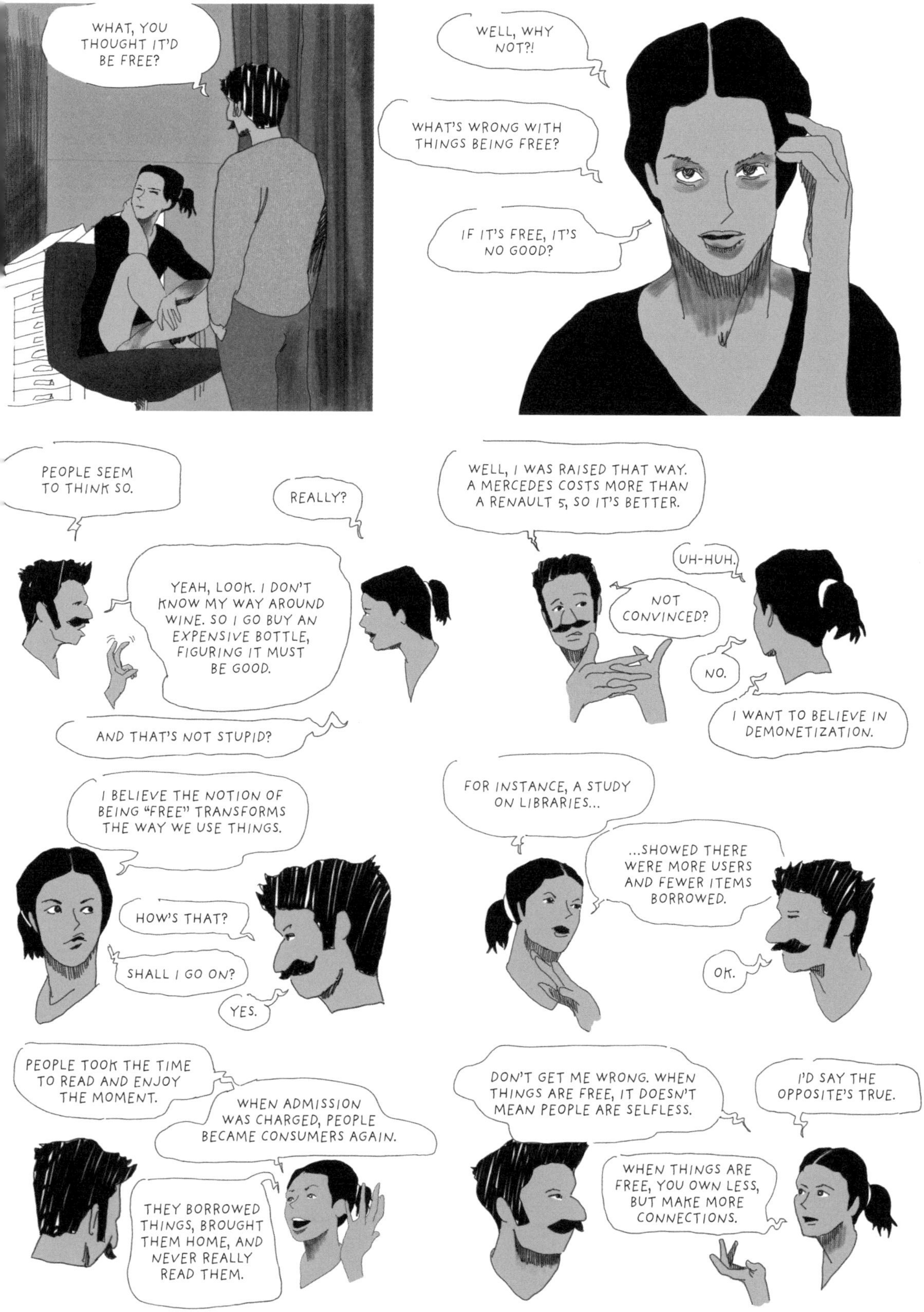
WHAT, YOU THOUGHT IT'D BE FREE?
WELL, WHY NOT?!
WHAT'S WRONG WITH THINGS BEING FREE?
IF IT'S FREE, IT'S NO GOOD?
PEOPLE SEEM TO THINK SO.
REALLY?
YEAH, LOOK. I DON'T KNOW MY WAY AROUND WINE. SO I GO BUY AN EXPENSIVE BOTTLE, FIGURING IT MUST BE GOOD.
AND THAT'S NOT STUPID?
WELL, I WAS RAISED THAT WAY. A MERCEDES COSTS MORE THAN A RENAULT 5, SO IT'S BETTER.
UH-HUH.
NOT CONVINCED?
NO.
I WANT TO BELIEVE IN DEMONETIZATION.
I BELIEVE THE NOTION OF BEING "FREE" TRANSFORMS THE WAY WE USE THINGS.
HOW'S THAT?
SHALL I GO ON?
YES.
FOR INSTANCE, A STUDY ON LIBRARIES...
...SHOWED THERE WERE MORE USERS AND FEWER ITEMS BORROWED.
OK.
PEOPLE TOOK THE TIME TO READ AND ENJOY THE MOMENT.
WHEN ADMISSION WAS CHARGED, PEOPLE BECAME CONSUMERS AGAIN.
THEY BORROWED THINGS, BROUGHT THEM HOME, AND NEVER REALLY READ THEM.
DON'T GET ME WRONG. WHEN THINGS ARE FREE, IT DOESN'T MEAN PEOPLE ARE SELFLESS.
I'D SAY THE OPPOSITE'S TRUE.
WHEN THINGS ARE FREE, YOU OWN LESS, BUT MAKE MORE CONNECTIONS.

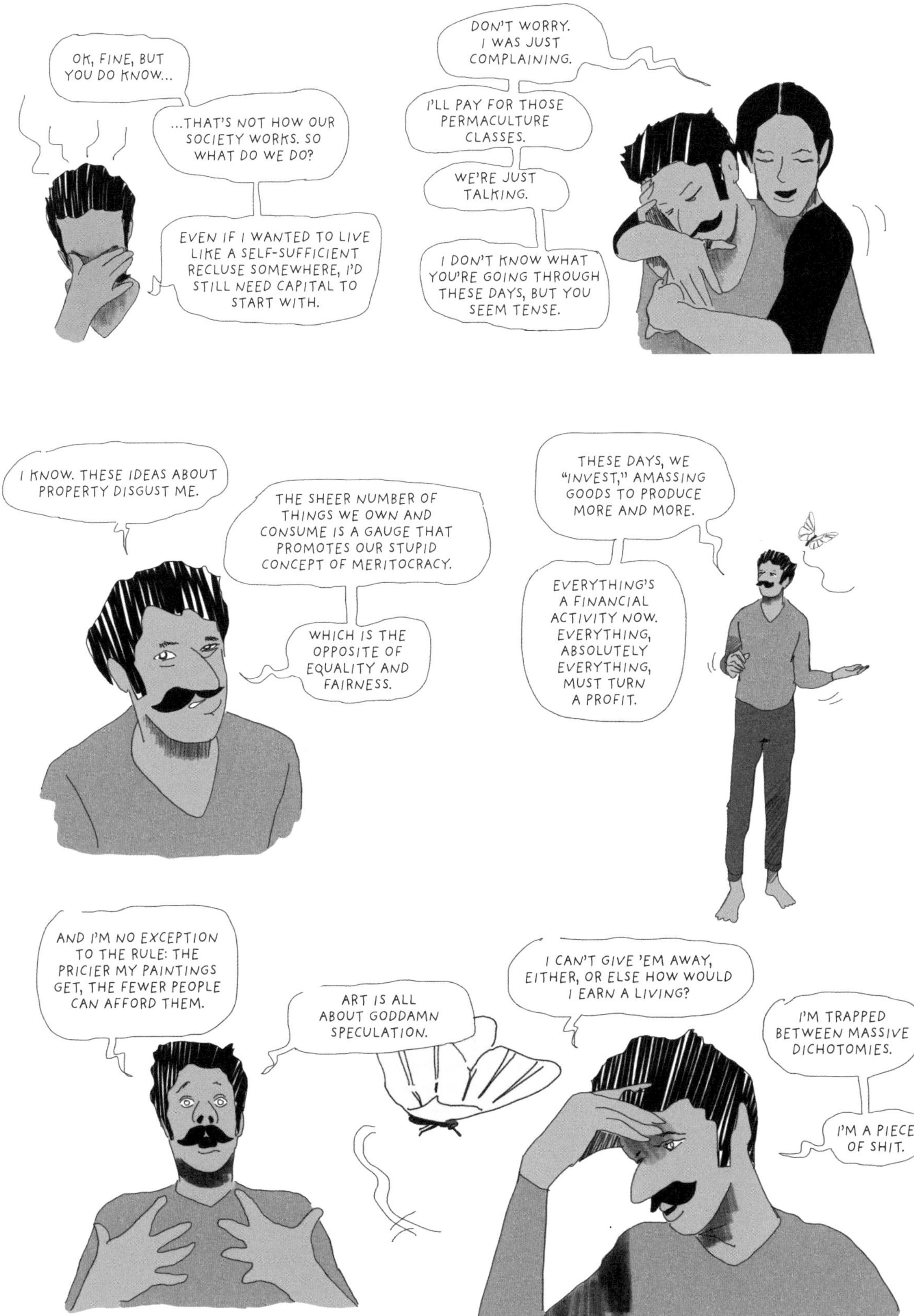
OK, FINE, BUT YOU DO KNOW...
...THAT'S NOT HOW OUR SOCIETY WORKS. SO WHAT DO WE DO?
EVEN IF I WANTED TO LIVE LIKE A SELF-SUFFICIENT RECLUSE SOMEWHERE, I'D STILL NEED CAPITAL TO START WITH.
DON'T WORRY. I WAS JUST COMPLAINING.
I'LL PAY FOR THOSE PERMACULTURE CLASSES.
WE'RE JUST TALKING.
I DON'T KNOW WHAT YOU'RE GOING THROUGH THESE DAYS, BUT YOU SEEM TENSE.
I KNOW. THESE IDEAS ABOUT PROPERTY DISGUST ME.
THE SHEER NUMBER OF THINGS WE OWN AND CONSUME IS A GAUGE THAT PROMOTES OUR STUPID CONCEPT OF MERITOCRACY.
WHICH IS THE OPPOSITE OF EQUALITY AND FAIRNESS.
THESE DAYS, WE "INVEST," AMASSING GOODS TO PRODUCE MORE AND MORE.
EVERYTHING'S A FINANCIAL ACTIVITY NOW. EVERYTHING, ABSOLUTELY EVERYTHING, MUST TURN A PROFIT.
AND I'M NO EXCEPTION TO THE RULE: THE PRICIER MY PAINTINGS GET, THE FEWER PEOPLE CAN AFFORD THEM.
ART IS ALL ABOUT GODDAMN SPECULATION.
I CAN'T GIVE 'EM AWAY, EITHER, OR ELSE HOW WOULD I EARN A LIVING?
I'M TRAPPED BETWEEN MASSIVE DICHOTOMIES.
I'M A PIECE OF SHIT.

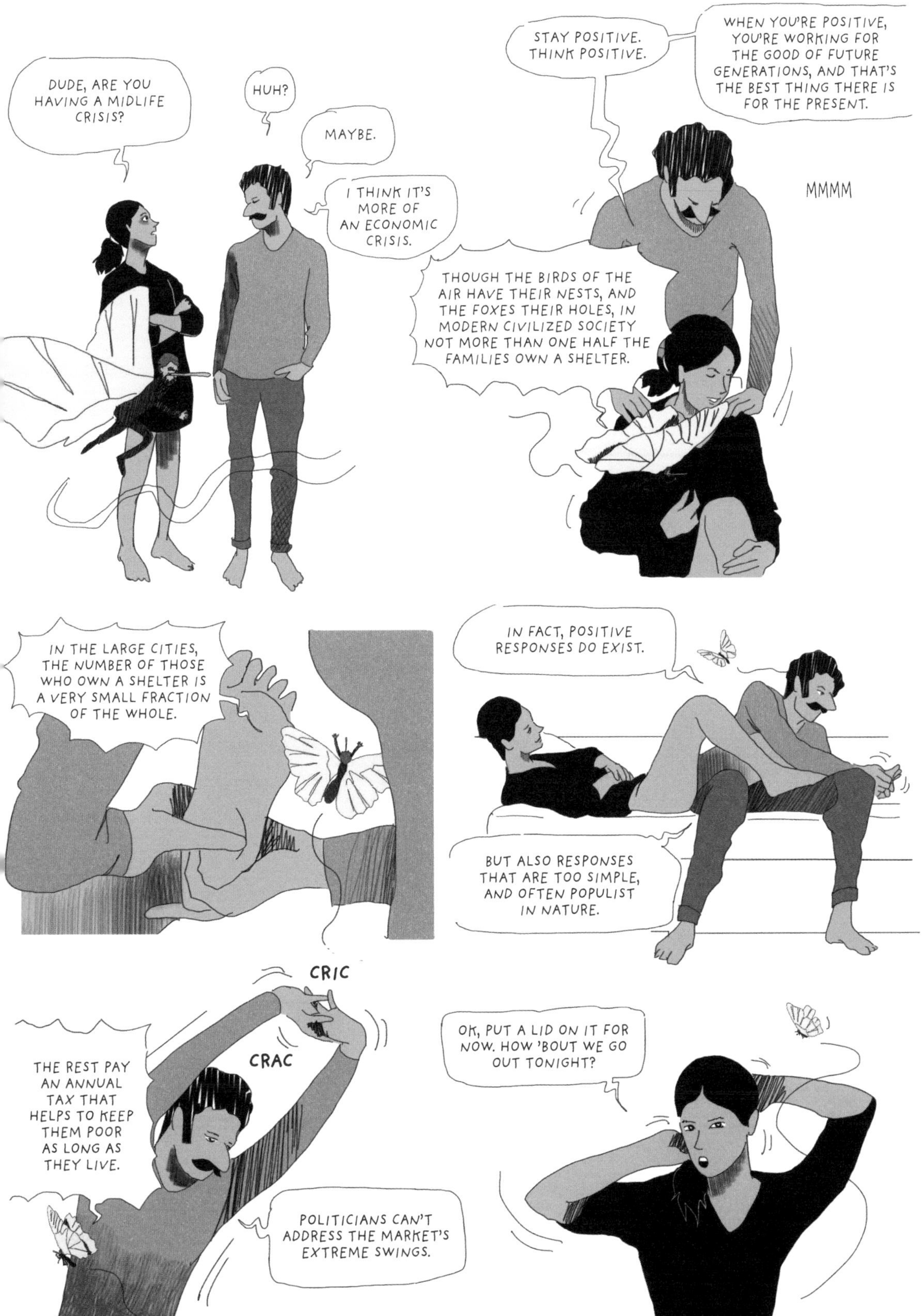
DUDE, ARE YOU HAVING A MIDLIFE CRISIS?
HUH?
MAYBE.
I THINK IT'S MORE OF AN ECONOMIC CRISIS.
STAY POSITIVE. THINK POSITIVE.
WHEN YOU'RE POSITIVE, YOU'RE WORKING FOR THE GOOD OF FUTURE GENERATIONS, AND THAT'S THE BEST THING THERE IS FOR THE PRESENT.
MMMM
THOUGH THE BIRDS OF THE AIR HAVE THEIR NESTS, AND THE FOXES THEIR HOLES, IN MODERN CIVILIZED SOCIETY NOT MORE THAN ONE HALF THE FAMILIES OWN A SHELTER.
IN THE LARGE CITIES, THE NUMBER OF THOSE WHO OWN A SHELTER IS A VERY SMALL FRACTION OF THE WHOLE.
IN FACT, POSITIVE RESPONSES DO EXIST.
BUT ALSO RESPONSES THAT ARE TOO SIMPLE, AND OFTEN POPULIST IN NATURE.
CRIC
CRAC
THE REST PAY AN ANNUAL TAX THAT HELPS TO KEEP THEM POOR AS LONG AS THEY LIVE.
POLITICIANS CAN'T ADDRESS THE MARKET'S EXTREME SWINGS.
OK, PUT A LID ON IT FOR NOW. HOW 'BOUT WE GO OUT TONIGHT?

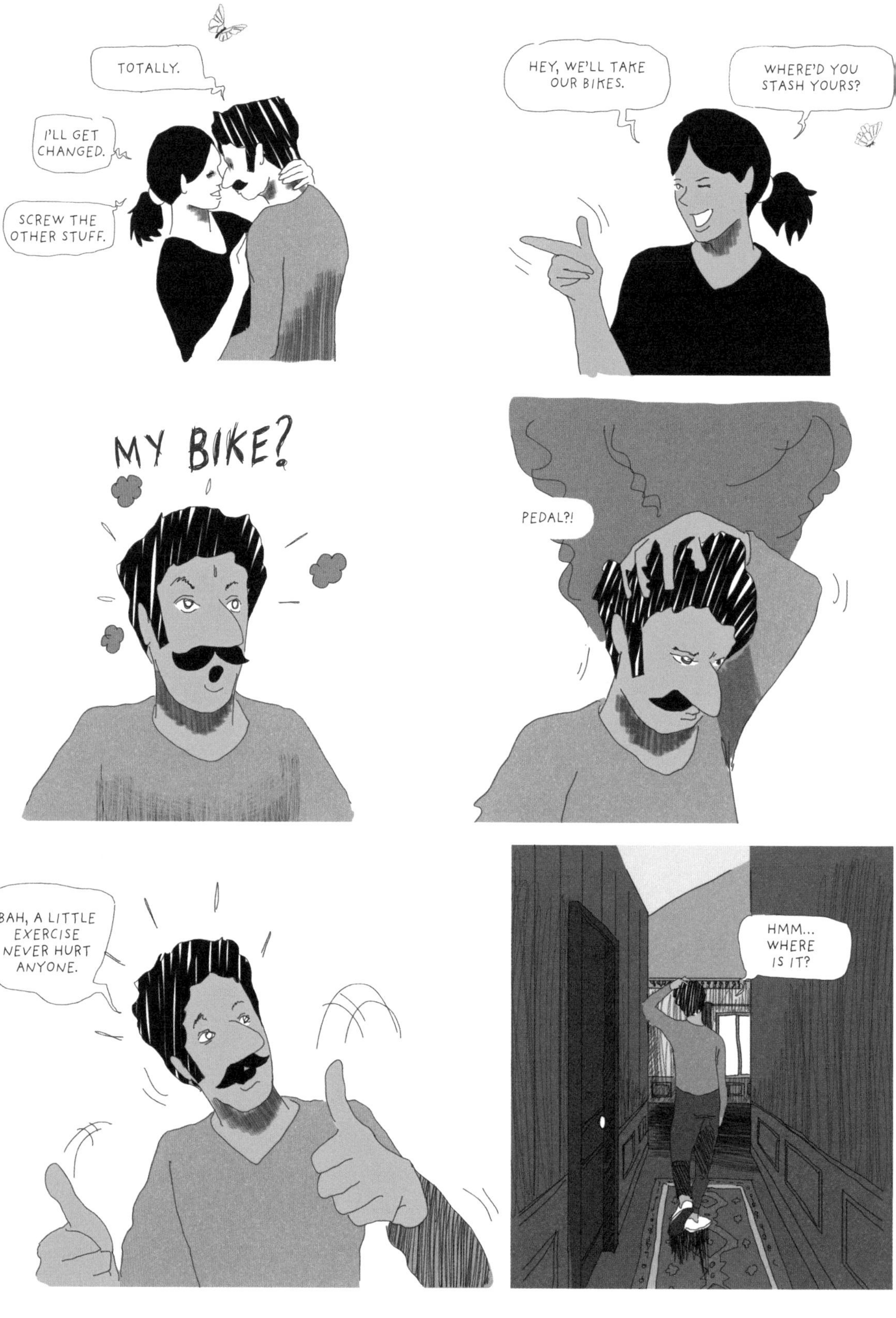
TOTALLY.
I'LL GET CHANGED.
SCREW THE OTHER STUFF.
HEY, WE'LL TAKE OUR BIKES.
WHERE'D YOU STASH YOURS?
MY BIKE?
PEDAL?!
BAH, A LITTLE EXERCISE NEVER HURT ANYONE.
HMM... WHERE IS IT?

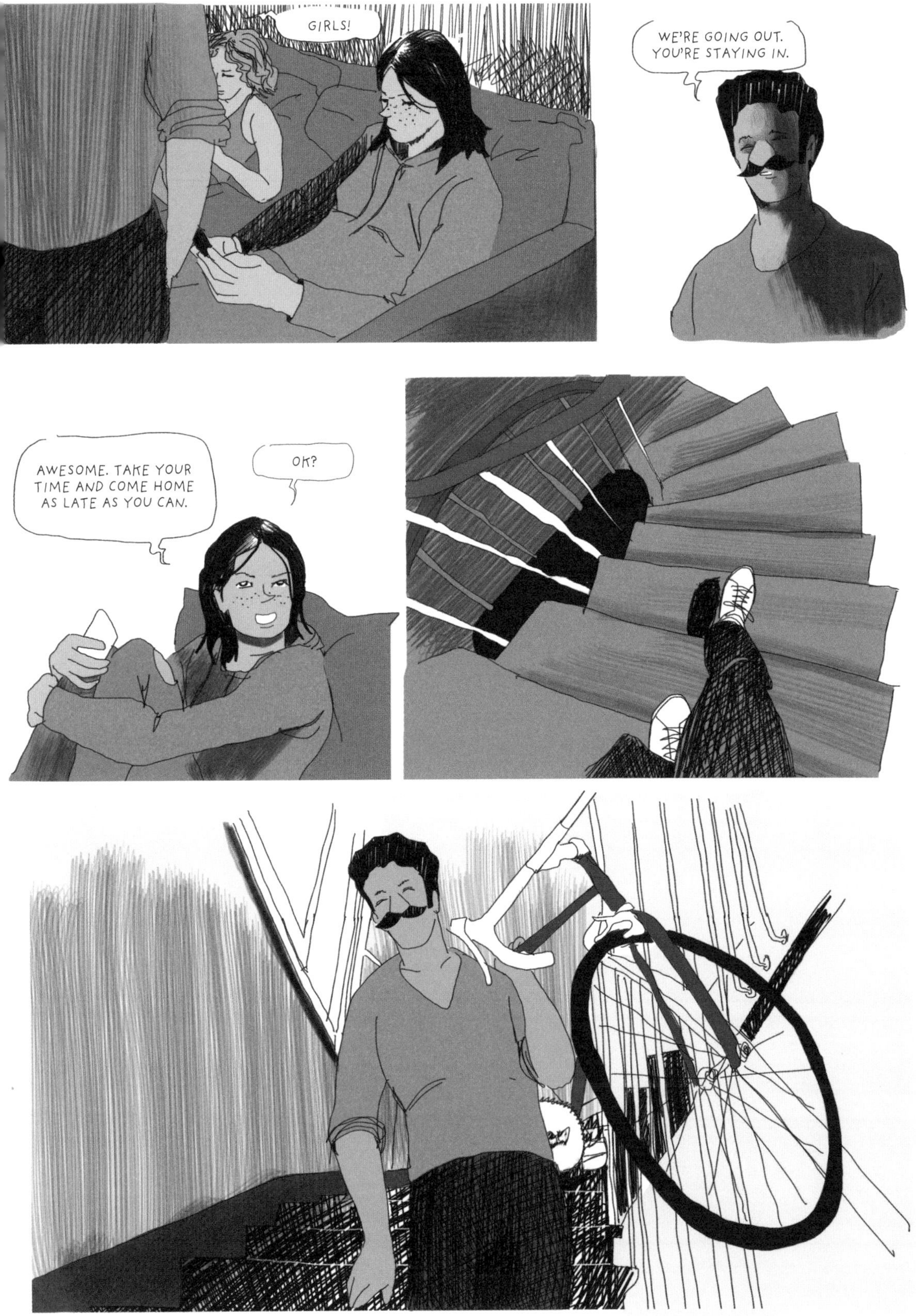
GIRLS!
WE'RE GOING OUT. YOU'RE STAYING IN.
AWESOME. TAKE YOUR TIME AND COME HOME AS LATE AS YOU CAN.
OK?

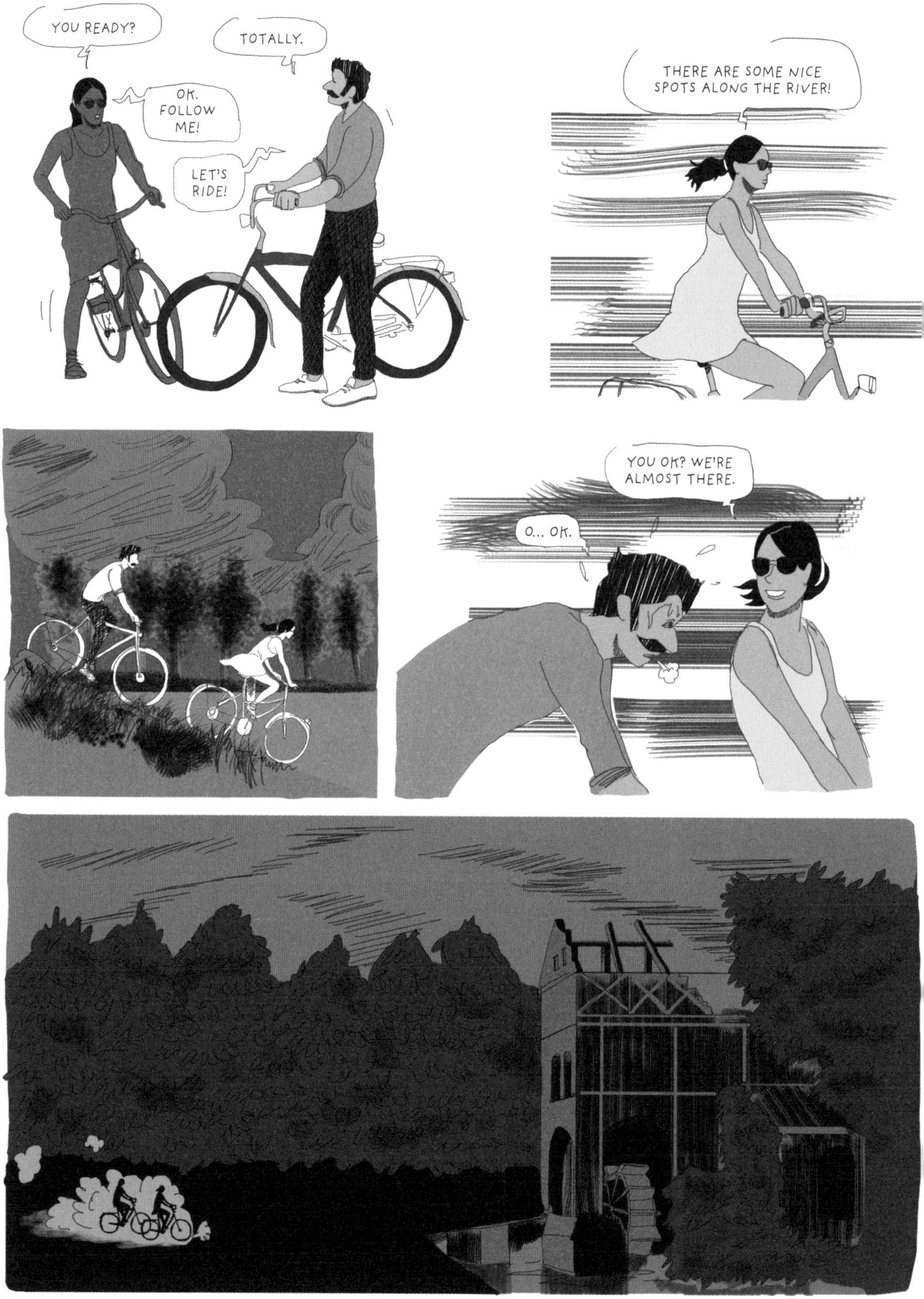
YOU READY?
TOTALLY.
OK. FOLLOW ME!
LET'S RIDE!
THERE ARE SOME NICE SPOTS ALONG THE RIVER!
YOU OK? WE'RE ALMOST THERE.
O... OK.

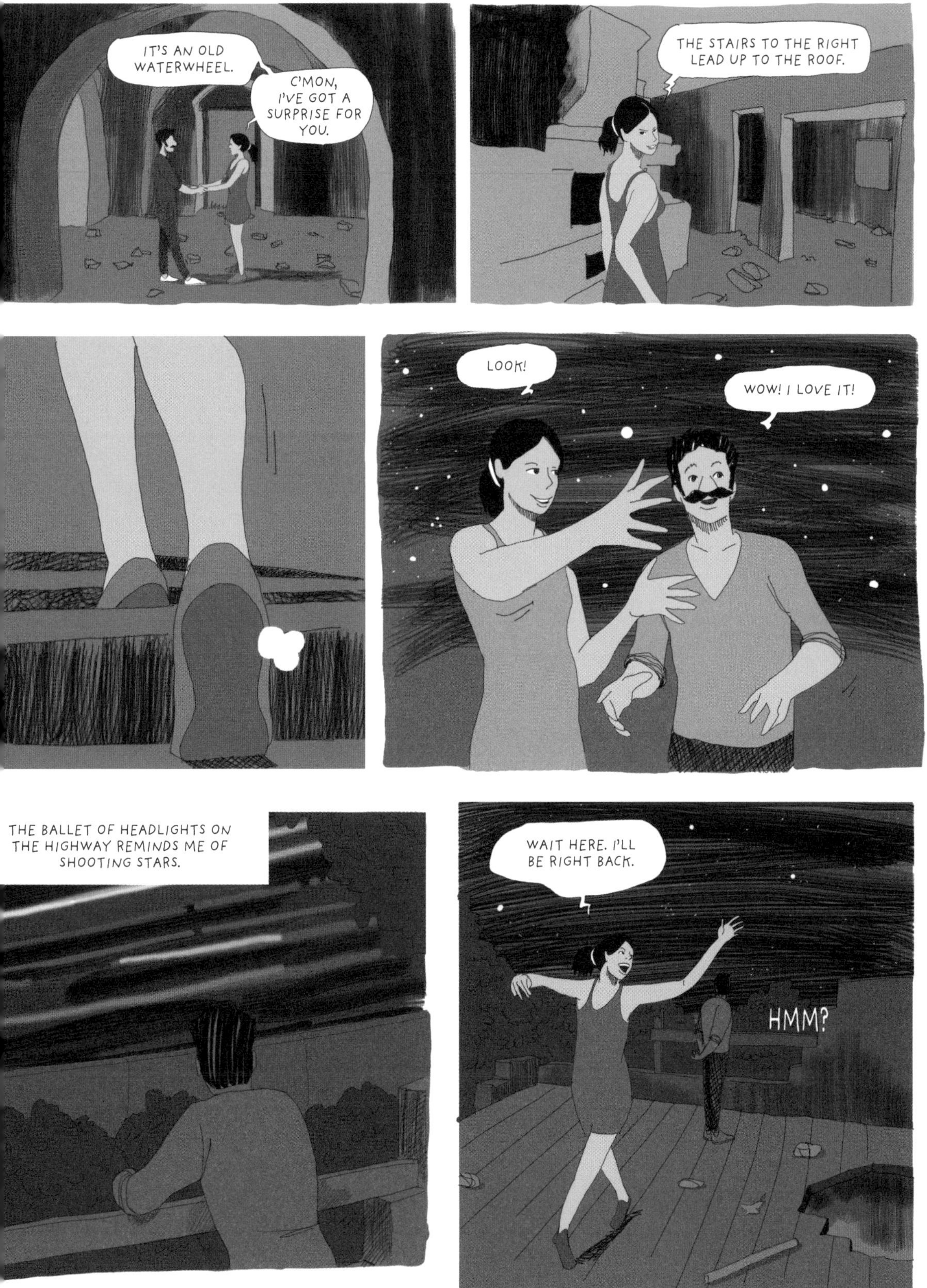
IT'S AN OLD WATERWHEEL.
C'MON, I'VE GOT A SURPRISE FOR YOU.
THE STAIRS TO THE RIGHT LEAD UP TO THE ROOF.
LOOK!
WOW! I LOVE IT!
THE BALLET OF HEADLIGHTS ON THE HIGHWAY REMINDS ME OF SHOOTING STARS.
WAIT HERE. I'LL BE RIGHT BACK.
HMM?

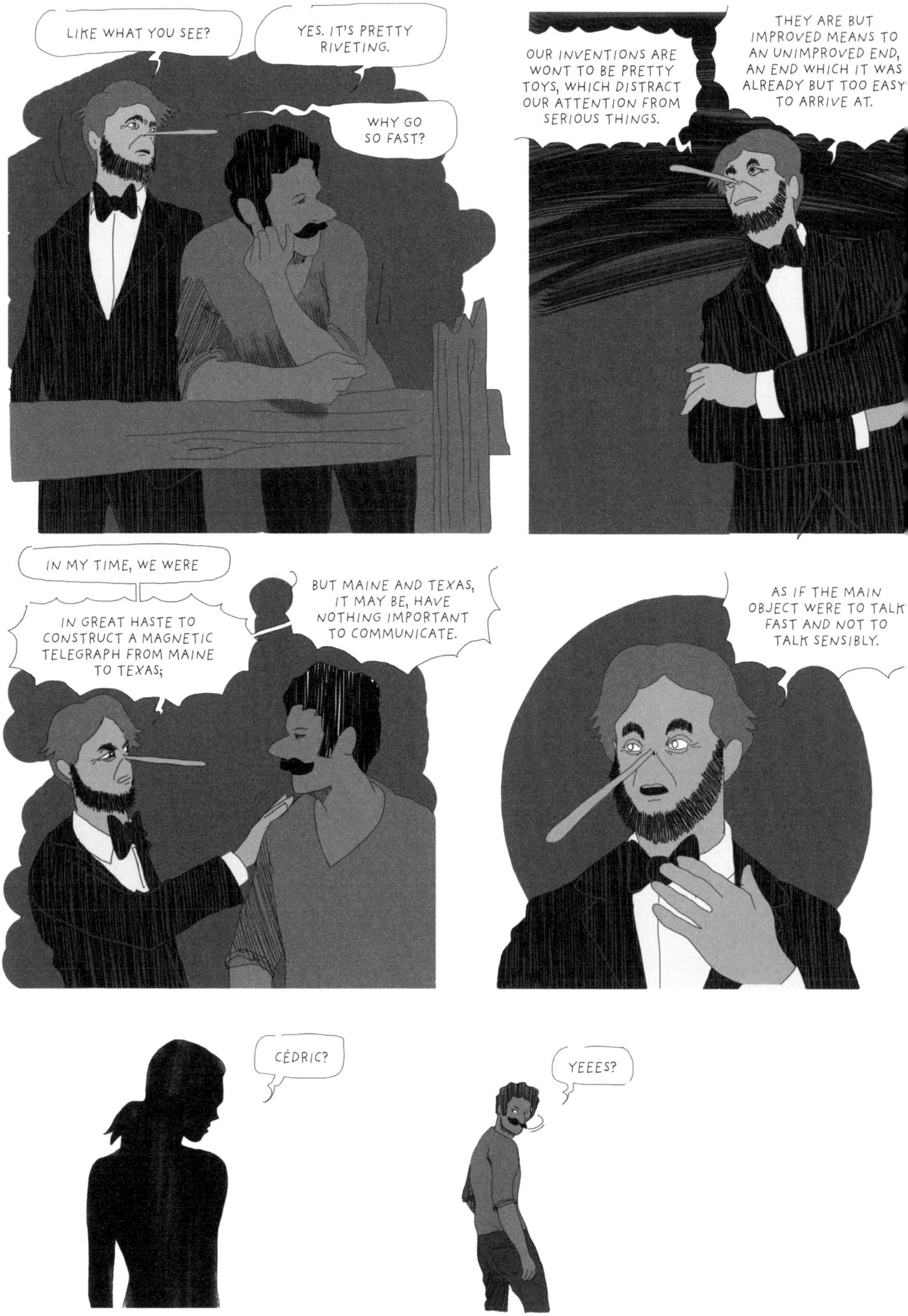

LIKE WHAT YOU SEE?
YES. IT'S PRETTY RIVETING.
WHY GO SO FAST?
OUR INVENTIONS ARE WONT TO BE PRETTY TOYS, WHICH DISTRACT OUR ATTENTION FROM SERIOUS THINGS.
THEY ARE BUT IMPROVED MEANS TO AN UNIMPROVED END, AN END WHICH IT WAS ALREADY BUT TOO EASY TO ARRIVE AT.
IN MY TIME, WE WERE
IN GREAT HASTE TO CONSTRUCT A MAGNETIC TELEGRAPH FROM MAINE TO TEXAS;
BUT MAINE AND TEXAS, IT MAY BE, HAVE NOTHING IMPORTANT TO COMMUNICATE.
AS IF THE MAIN OBJECT WERE TO TALK FAST AND NOT TO TALK SENSIBLY.
CÉDRIC?
YEEES?

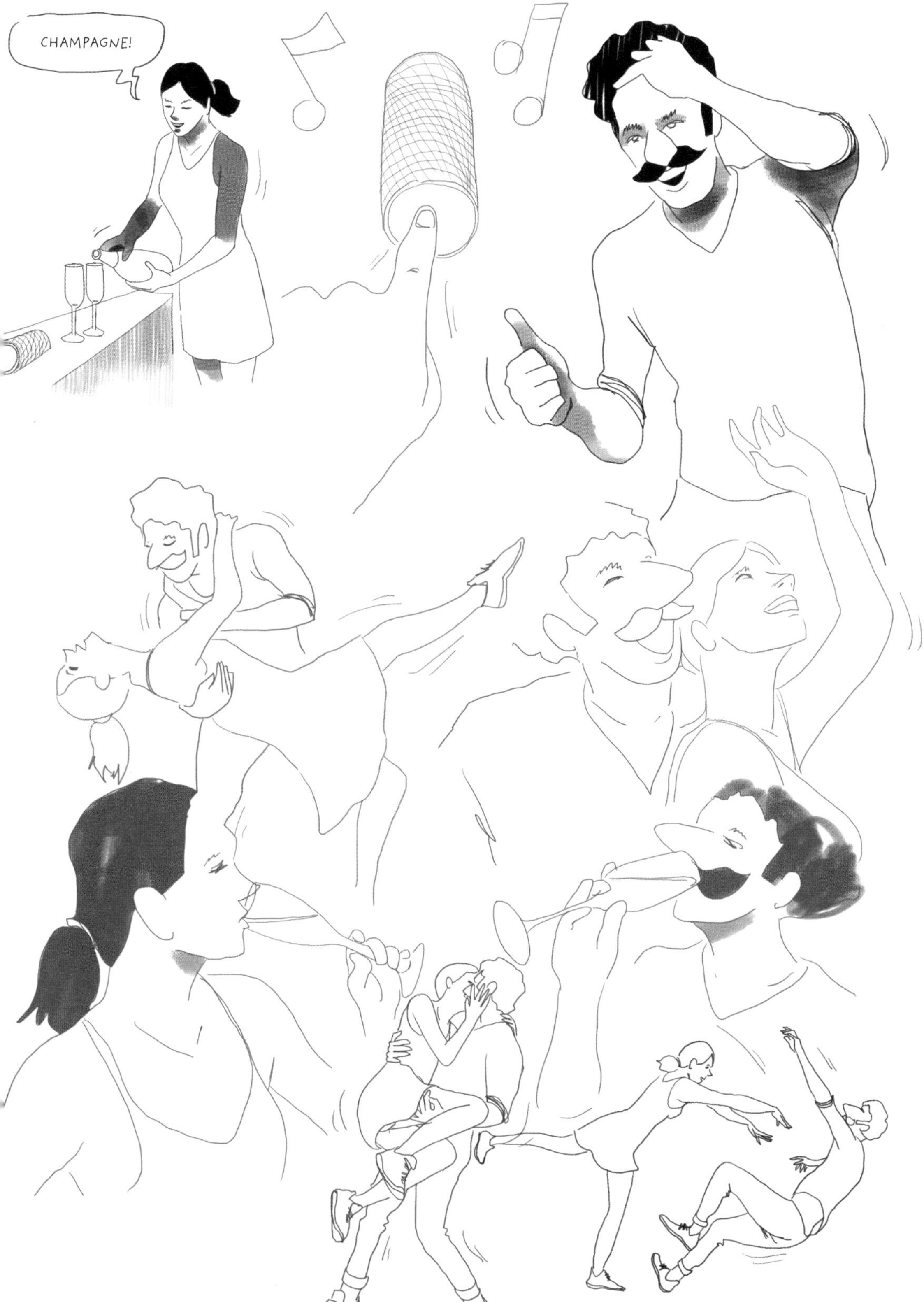
CHAMPAGNE!

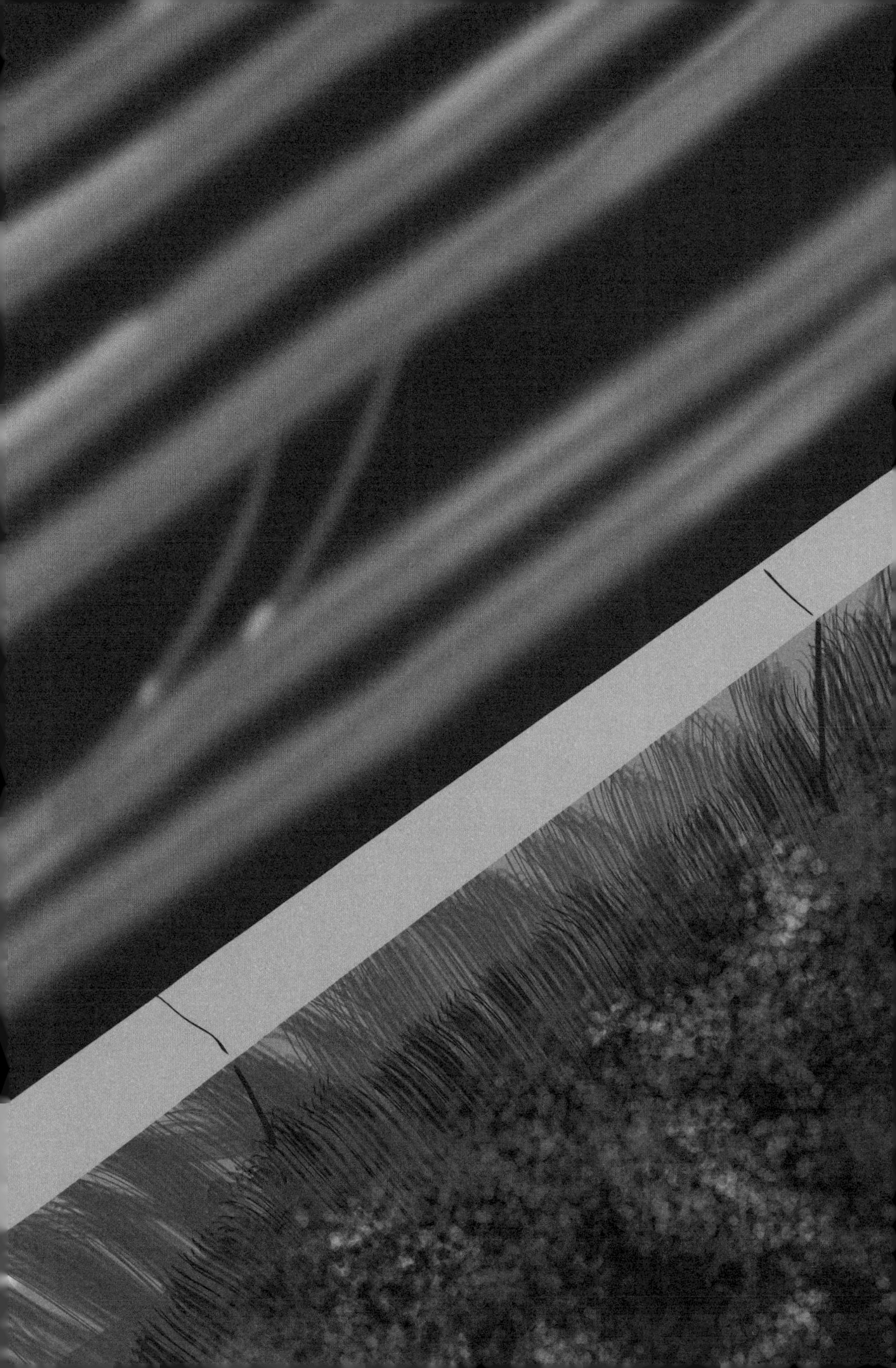

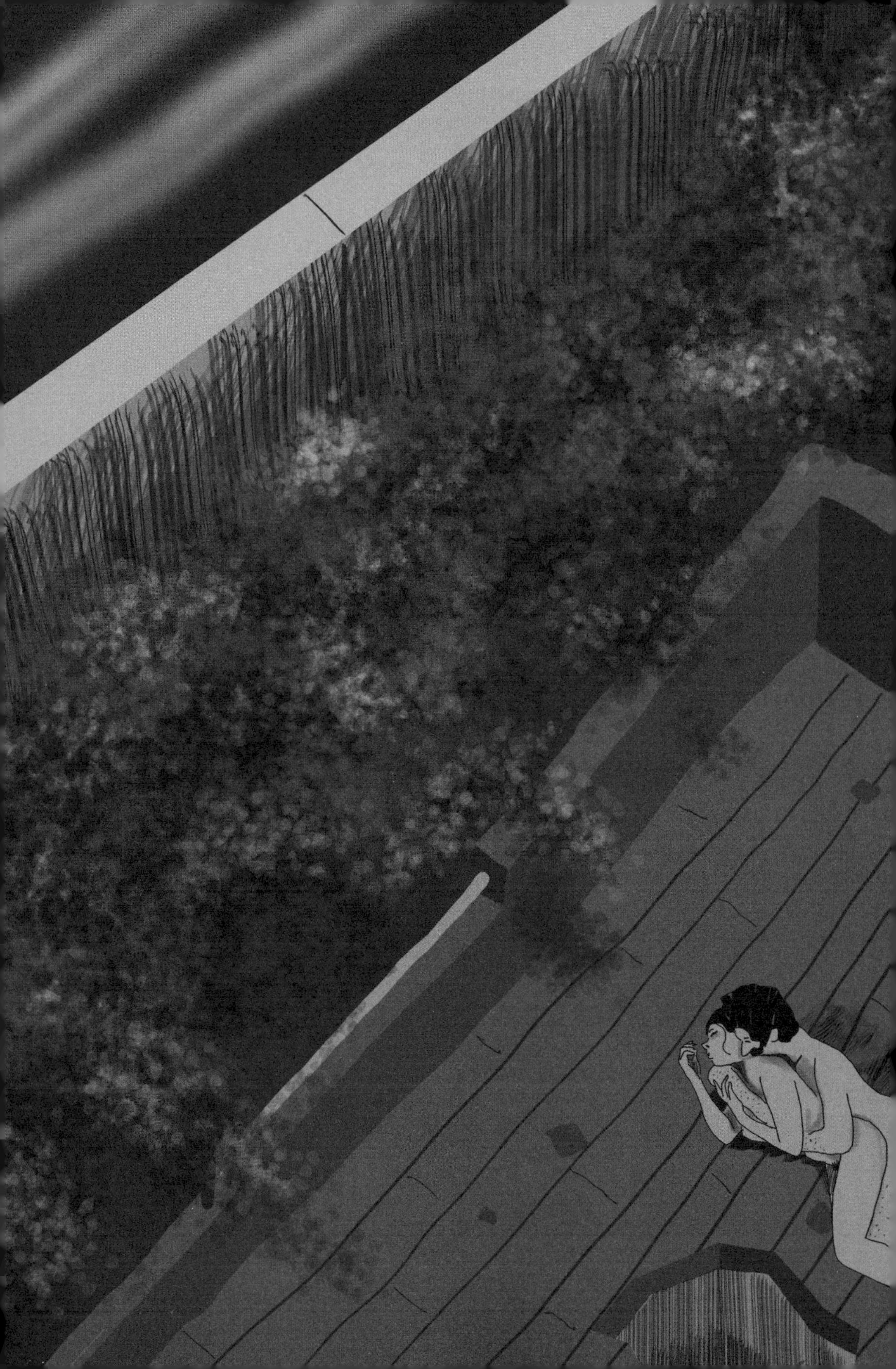

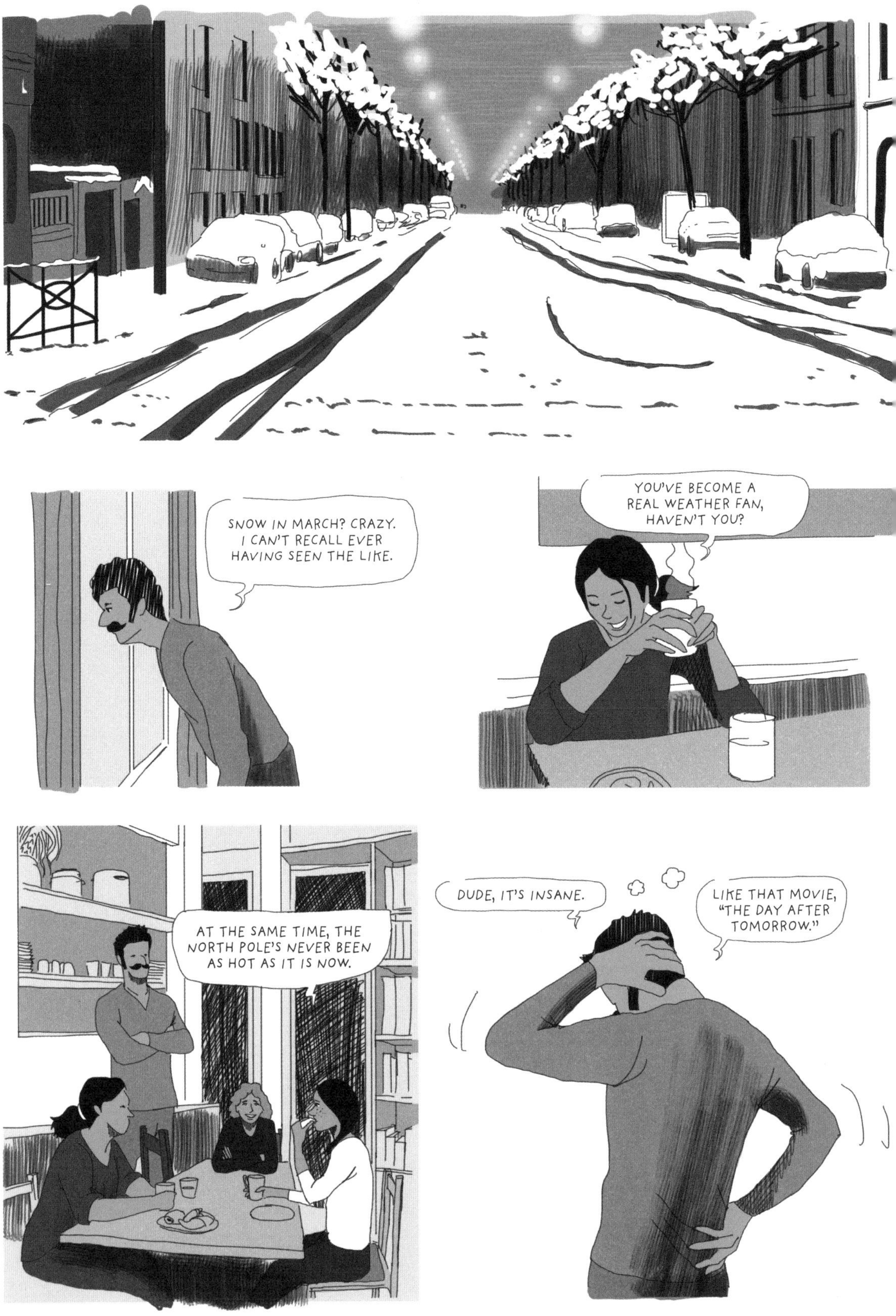

SNOW IN MARCH? CRAZY. I CAN'T RECALL EVER HAVING SEEN THE LIKE.
YOU'VE BECOME A REAL WEATHER FAN, HAVEN'T YOU?
AT THE SAME TIME, THE NORTH POLE'S NEVER BEEN AS HOT AS IT IS NOW.
DUDE, IT'S INSANE.
LIKE THAT MOVIE, "THE DAY AFTER TOMORROW."

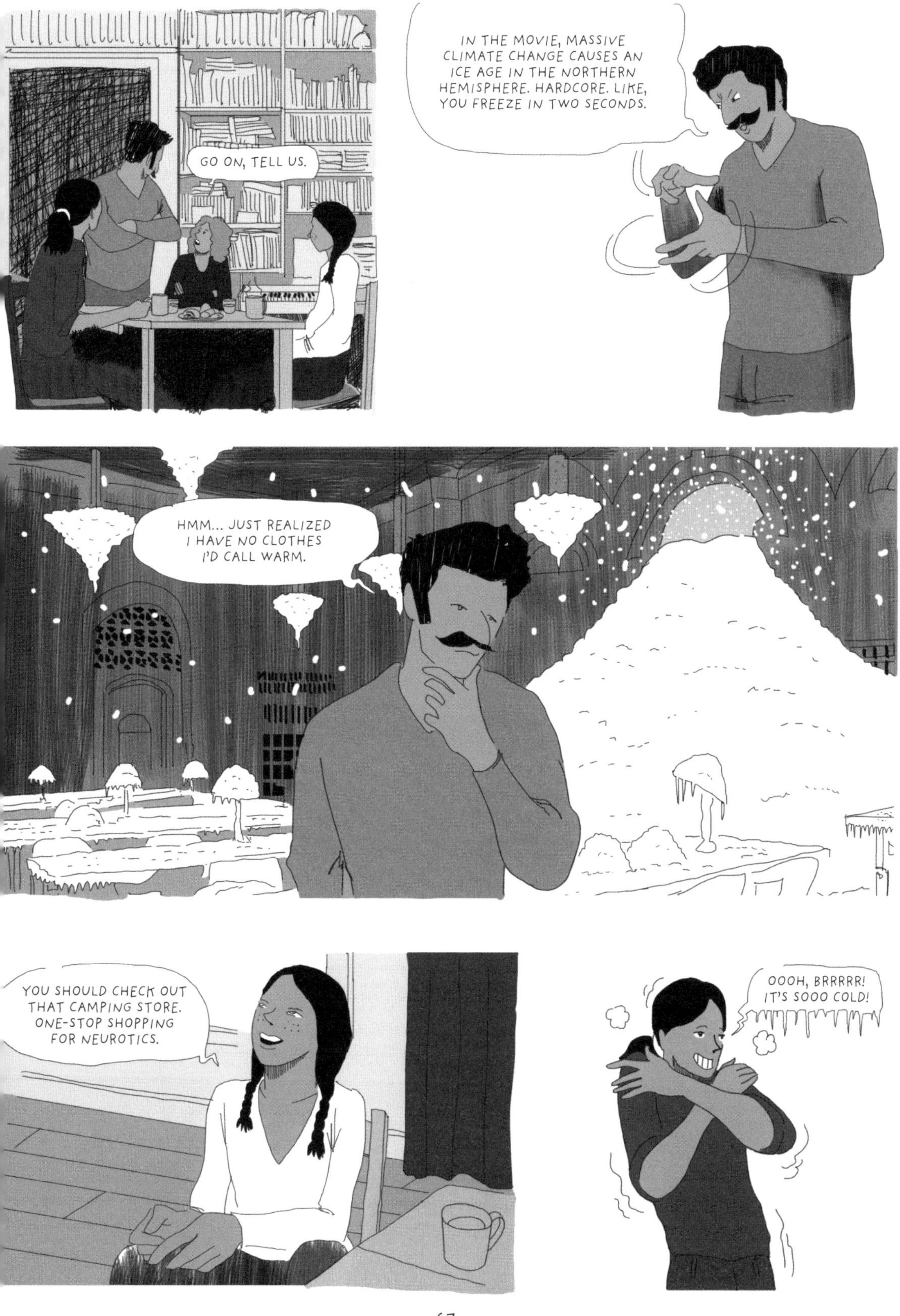
GO ON, TELL US.
IN THE MOVIE, MASSIVE CLIMATE CHANGE CAUSES AN ICE AGE IN THE NORTHERN HEMISPHERE. HARDCORE. LIKE, YOU FREEZE IN TWO SECONDS.
HMM... JUST REALIZED I HAVE NO CLOTHES I'D CALL WARM.
YOU SHOULD CHECK OUT THAT CAMPING STORE. ONE-STOP SHOPPING FOR NEUROTICS.
OOOH, BRRRRR! IT'S SOOO COLD!

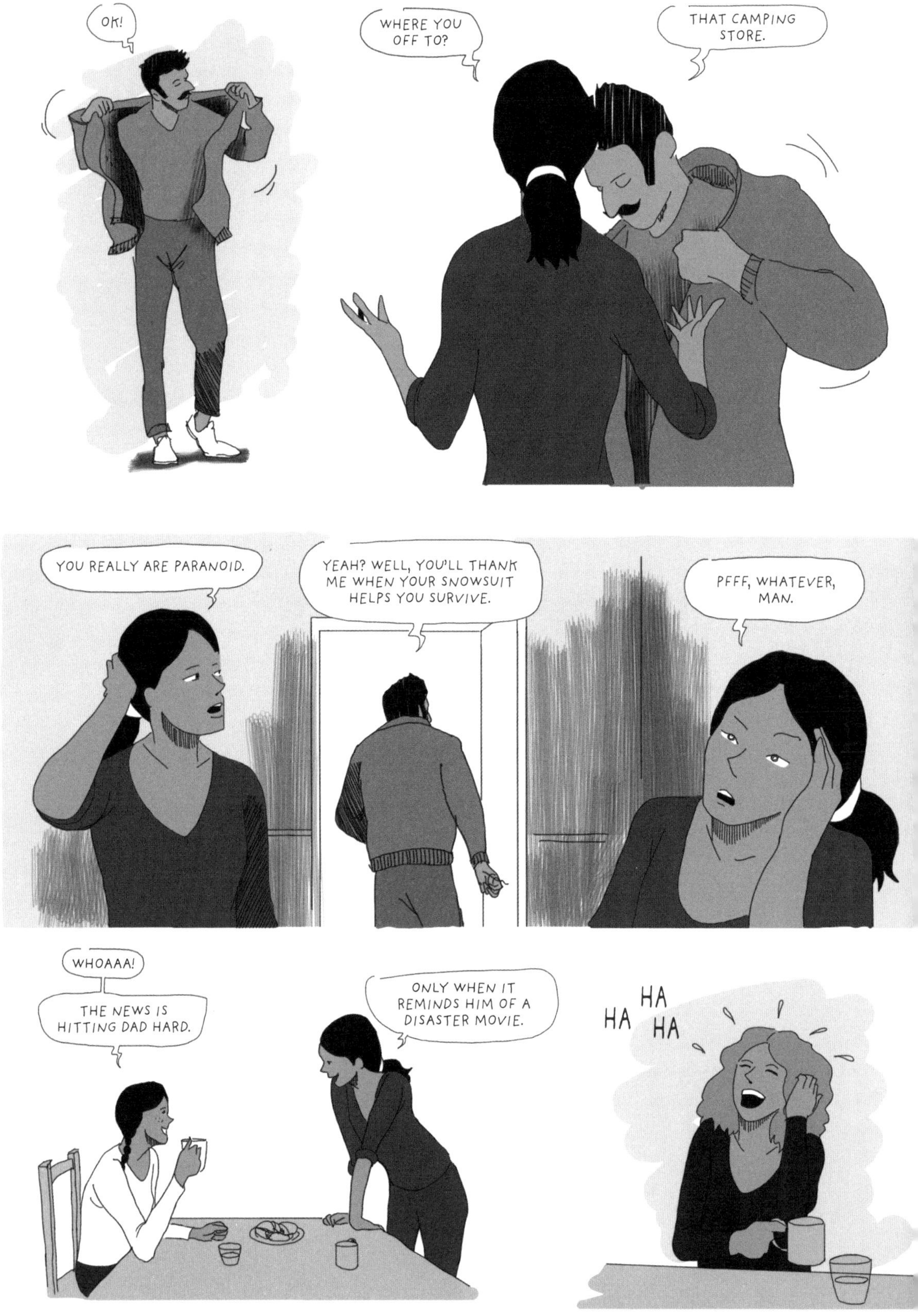
OK!
WHERE YOU OFF TO?
THAT CAMPING STORE.
YOU REALLY ARE PARANOID.
YEAH? WELL, YOU'LL THANK ME WHEN YOUR SNOWSUIT HELPS YOU SURVIVE.
PFFF, WHATEVER, MAN.
WHOAAA!
THE NEWS IS HITTING DAD HARD.
ONLY WHEN IT REMINDS HIM OF A DISASTER MOVIE.
HA HA HA

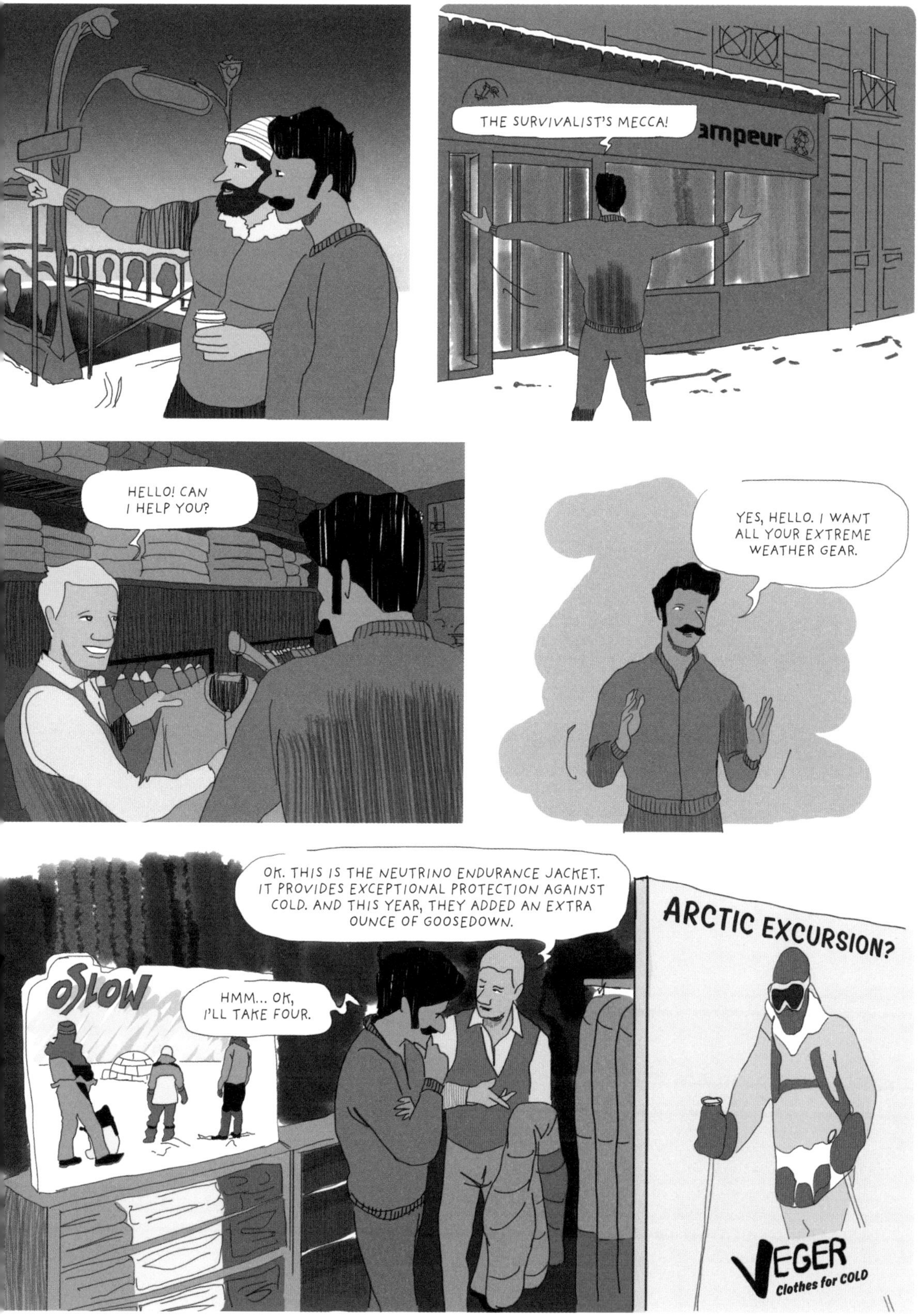
THE SURVIVALIST'S MECCA!
ampeur
HELLO! CAN I HELP YOU?
YES, HELLO. I WANT ALL YOUR EXTREME WEATHER GEAR.
OK. THIS IS THE NEUTRINO ENDURANCE JACKET. IT PROVIDES EXCEPTIONAL PROTECTION AGAINST COLD. AND THIS YEAR, THEY ADDED AN EXTRA OUNCE OF GOOSEDOWN.
OSLOW
HMM... OK, I'LL TAKE FOUR.
ARCTIC EXCURSION?
VEGER
Clothes for COLD

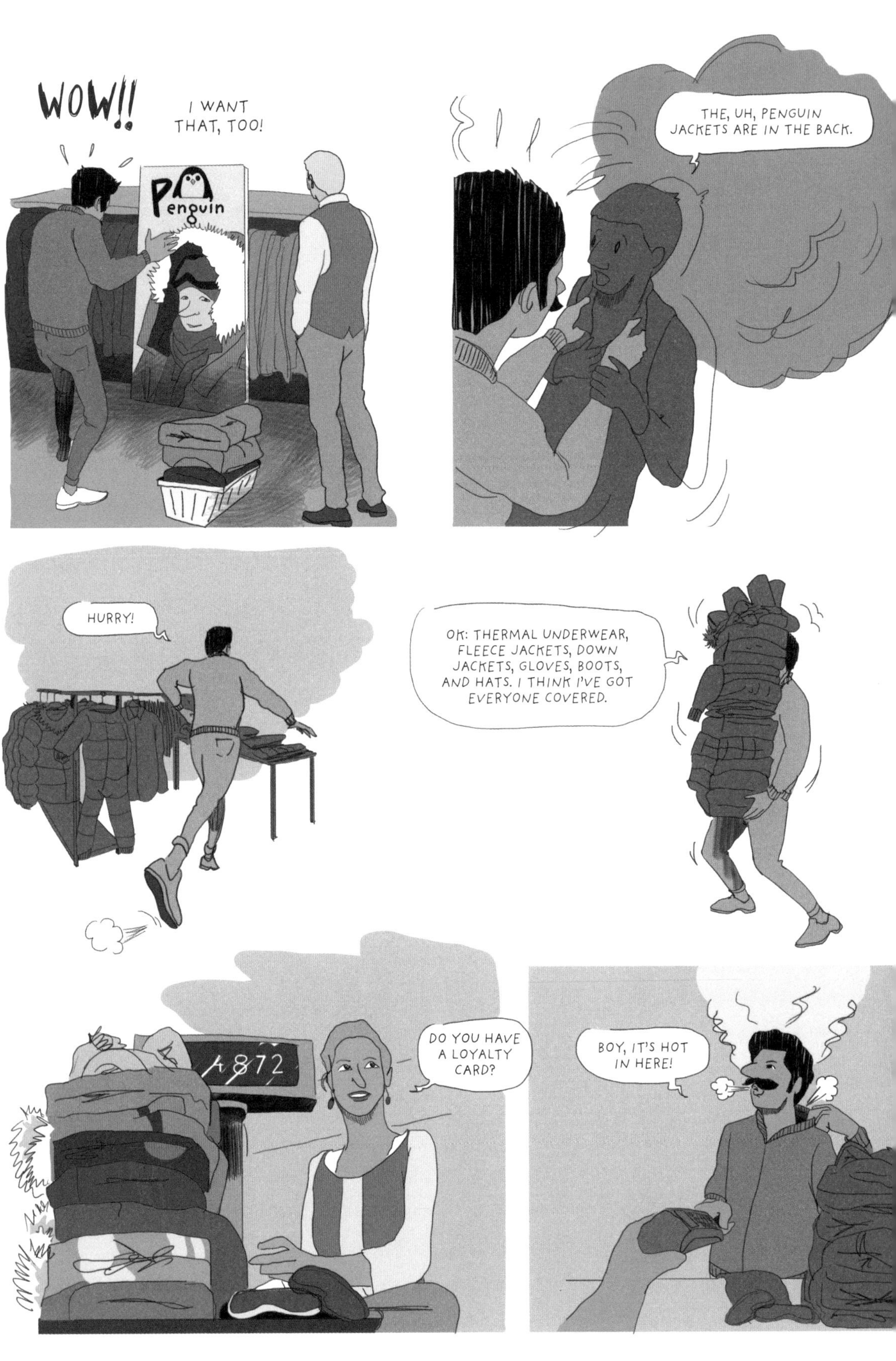
WOW!!
I WANT THAT, TOO!
Penguin
THE, UH, PENGUIN JACKETS ARE IN THE BACK.
HURRY!
OK: THERMAL UNDERWEAR, FLEECE JACKETS, DOWN JACKETS, GLOVES, BOOTS, AND HATS. I THINK I'VE GOT EVERYONE COVERED.
4872
DO YOU HAVE A LOYALTY CARD?
BOY, IT'S HOT IN HERE!

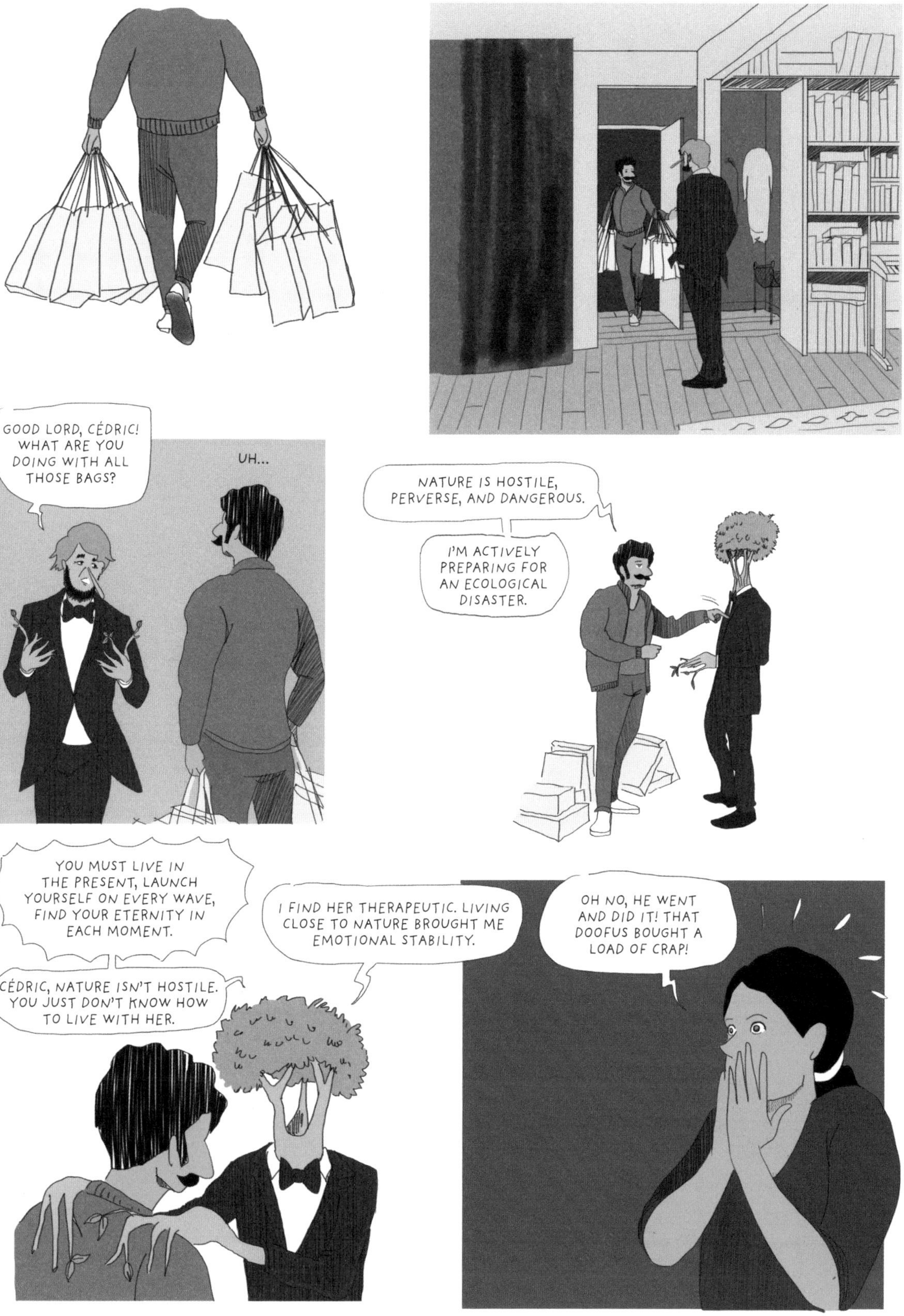
GOOD LORD, CÉDRIC! WHAT ARE YOU DOING WITH ALL THOSE BAGS?
UH...
NATURE IS HOSTILE, PERVERSE, AND DANGEROUS.
I'M ACTIVELY PREPARING FOR AN ECOLOGICAL DISASTER.
YOU MUST LIVE IN THE PRESENT, LAUNCH YOURSELF ON EVERY WAVE, FIND YOUR ETERNITY IN EACH MOMENT.
CÉDRIC, NATURE ISN'T HOSTILE. YOU JUST DON'T KNOW HOW TO LIVE WITH HER.
I FIND HER THERAPEUTIC. LIVING CLOSE TO NATURE BROUGHT ME EMOTIONAL STABILITY.
OH NO, HE WENT AND DID IT! THAT DOOFUS BOUGHT A LOAD OF CRAP!

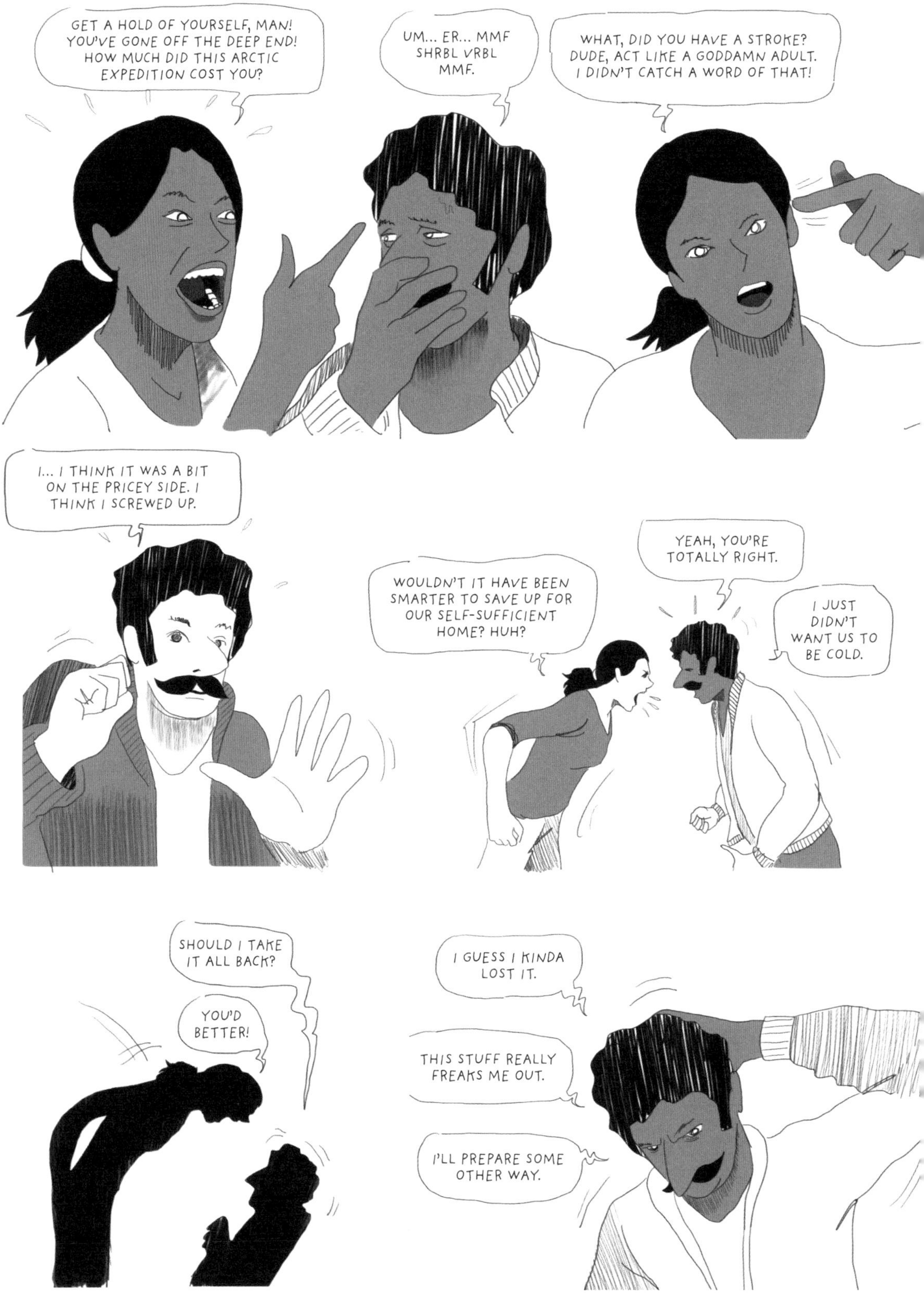
GET A HOLD OF YOURSELF, MAN! YOU'VE GONE OFF THE DEEP END! HOW MUCH DID THIS ARCTIC EXPEDITION COST YOU?
UM... ER... MMF SHRBL VRBL MMF.
WHAT, DID YOU HAVE A STROKE? DUDE, ACT LIKE A GODDAMN ADULT. I DIDN'T CATCH A WORD OF THAT!
I... I THINK IT WAS A BIT ON THE PRICEY SIDE. I THINK I SCREWED UP.
WOULDN'T IT HAVE BEEN SMARTER TO SAVE UP FOR OUR SELF-SUFFICIENT HOME? HUH?
YEAH, YOU'RE TOTALLY RIGHT.
I JUST DIDN'T WANT US TO BE COLD.
SHOULD I TAKE IT ALL BACK?
YOU'D BETTER!
I GUESS I KINDA LOST IT.
THIS STUFF REALLY FREAKS ME OUT.
I'LL PREPARE SOME OTHER WAY.

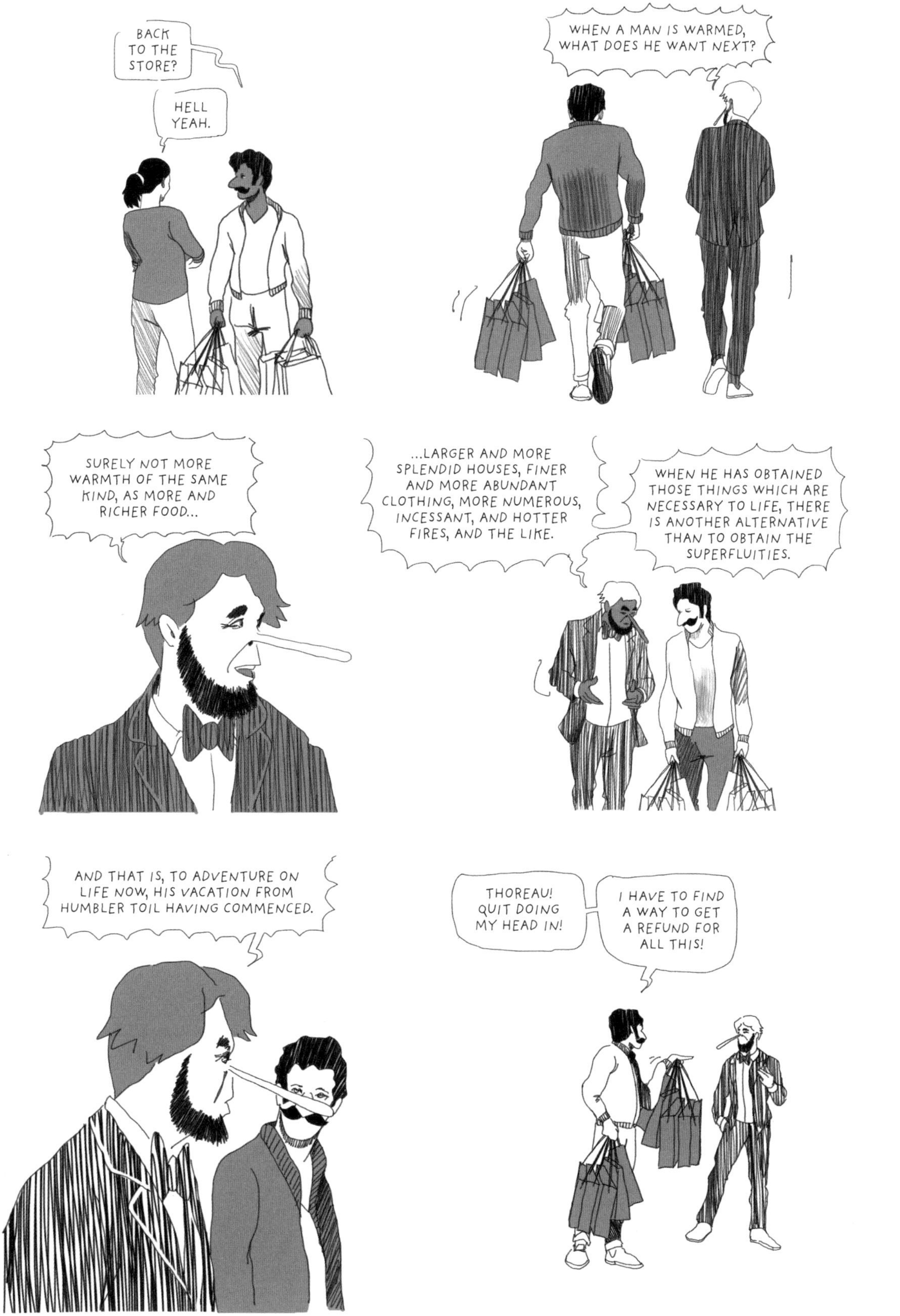

BACK TO THE STORE?
HELL YEAH.
WHEN A MAN IS WARMED, WHAT DOES HE WANT NEXT?
SURELY NOT MORE WARMTH OF THE SAME KIND, AS MORE AND RICHER FOOD...
...LARGER AND MORE SPLENDID HOUSES, FINER AND MORE ABUNDANT CLOTHING, MORE NUMEROUS, INCESSANT, AND HOTTER FIRES, AND THE LIKE.
WHEN HE HAS OBTAINED THOSE THINGS WHICH ARE NECESSARY TO LIFE, THERE IS ANOTHER ALTERNATIVE THAN TO OBTAIN THE SUPERFLUITIES.
AND THAT IS, TO ADVENTURE ON LIFE NOW, HIS VACATION FROM HUMBLER TOIL HAVING COMMENCED.
THOREAU! QUIT DOING MY HEAD IN!
I HAVE TO FIND A WAY TO GET A REFUND FOR ALL THIS!

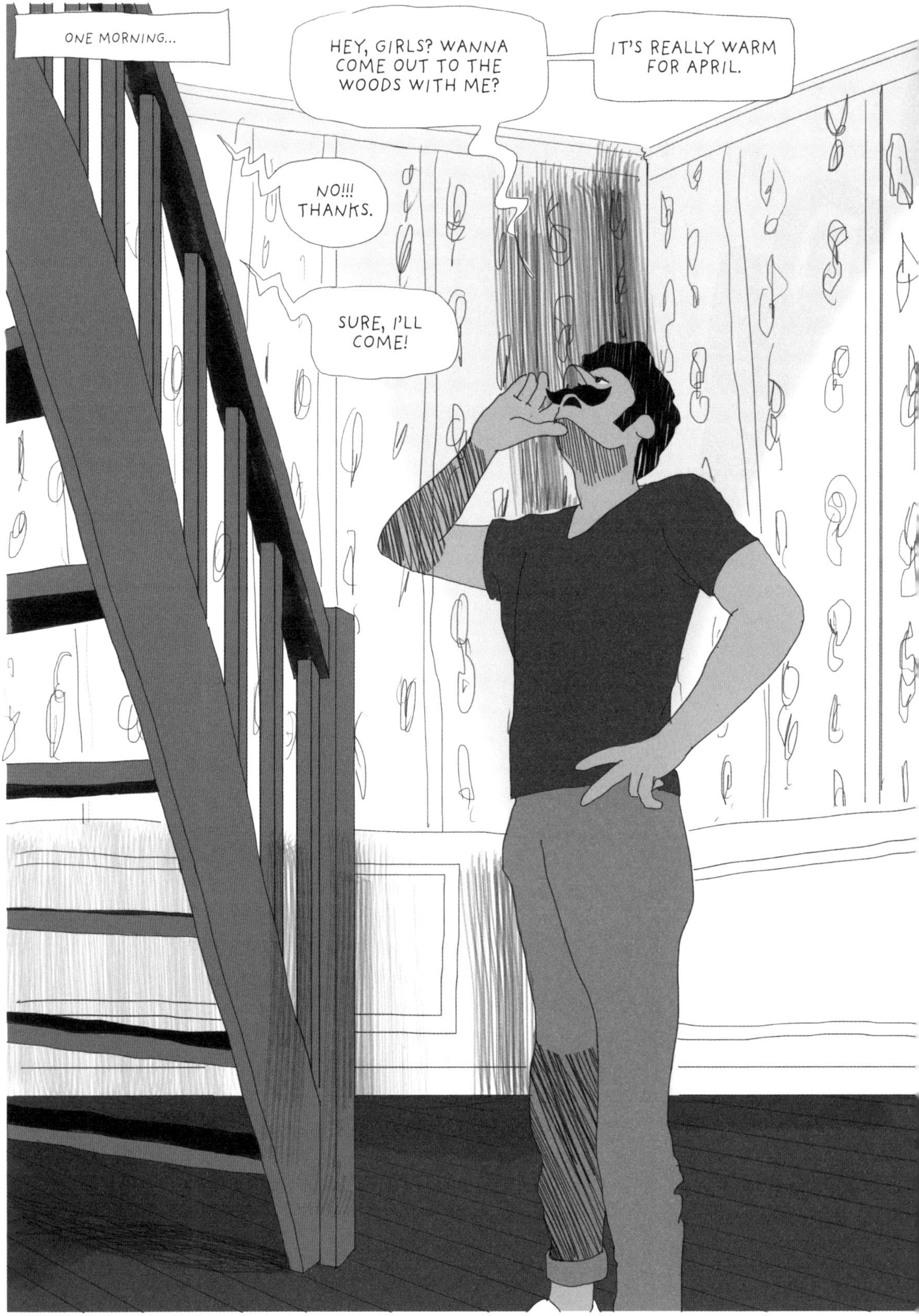
ONE MORNING...
HEY, GIRLS? WANNA COME OUT TO THE WOODS WITH ME?
IT'S REALLY WARM FOR APRIL.
NO!!! THANKS.
SURE, I'LL COME!

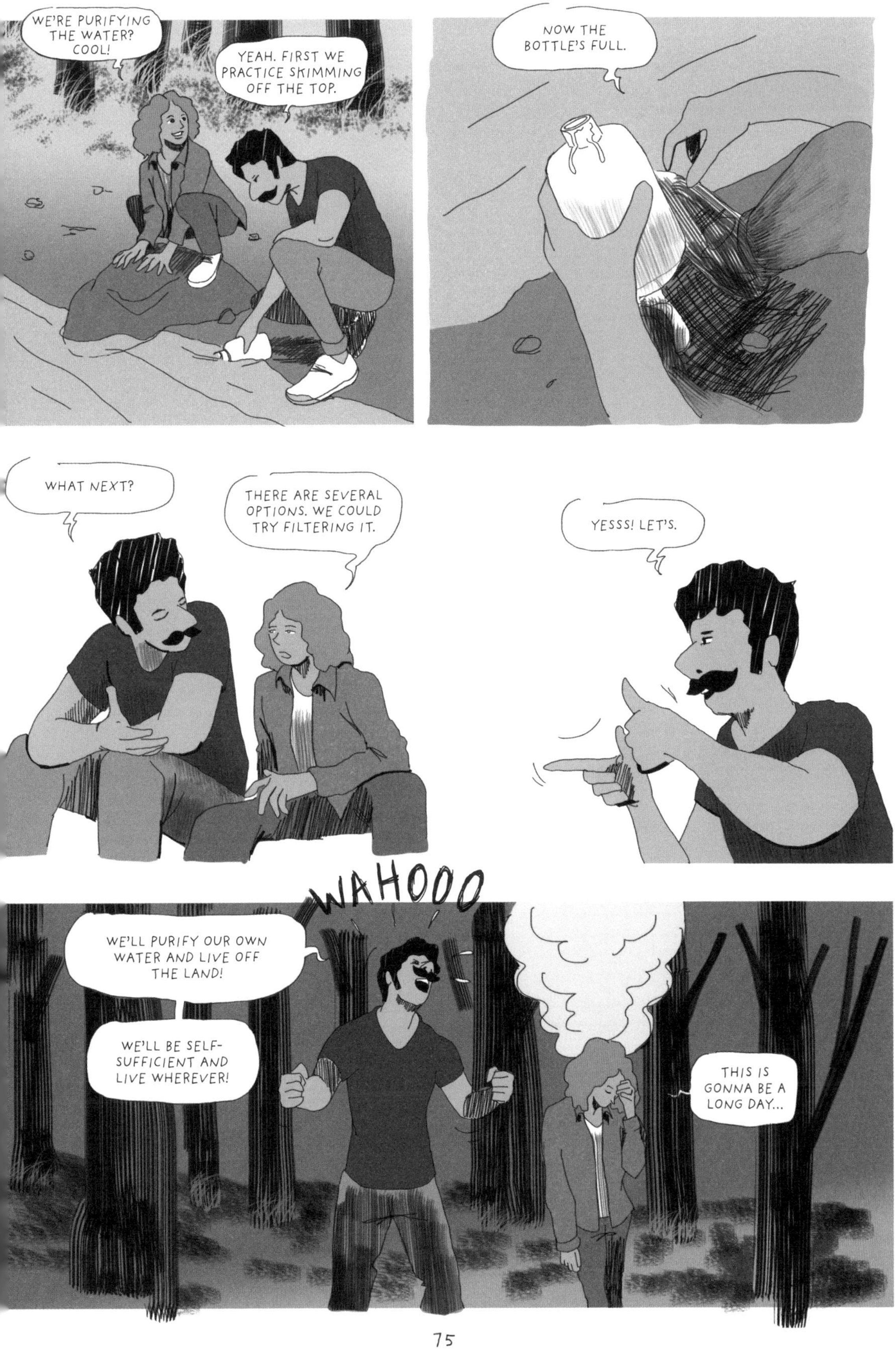
WE'RE PURIFYING THE WATER? COOL!
YEAH. FIRST WE PRACTICE SKIMMING OFF THE TOP.
NOW THE BOTTLE'S FULL.
WHAT NEXT?
THERE ARE SEVERAL OPTIONS. WE COULD TRY FILTERING IT.
YESSS! LET'S.
WAHOOO
WE'LL PURIFY OUR OWN WATER AND LIVE OFF THE LAND!
WE'LL BE SELF-SUFFICIENT AND LIVE WHEREVER!
THIS IS GONNA BE A LONG DAY...

STEP ONE: PUNCTURE THE CAP.

HERE, THREAD THE FABRIC THROUGH THE CAP.

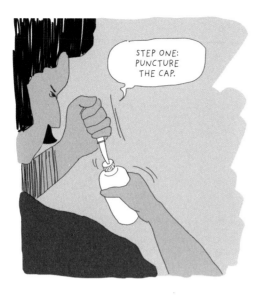

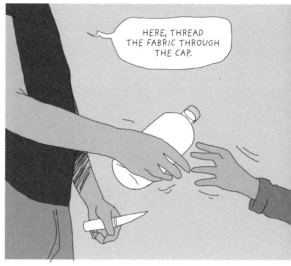

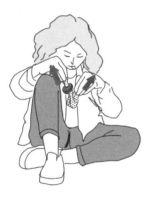

1 THREAD FABRIC THROUGH CAP OF PLASTIC BOTTLE.

2 FILL PLASTIC BOTTLE WITH COLLECTED WATER.

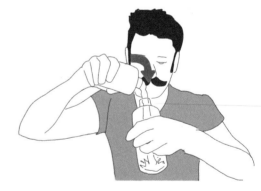

3 INSERT CLOTH INTO WATER BOTTLE AND SCREW CAP BACK ON.

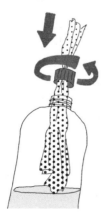

4 HANG BOTTLE UPSIDE-DOWN AND ALLOW WATER TO DRIP THROUGH FABRIC.

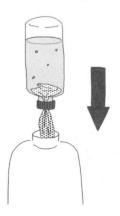

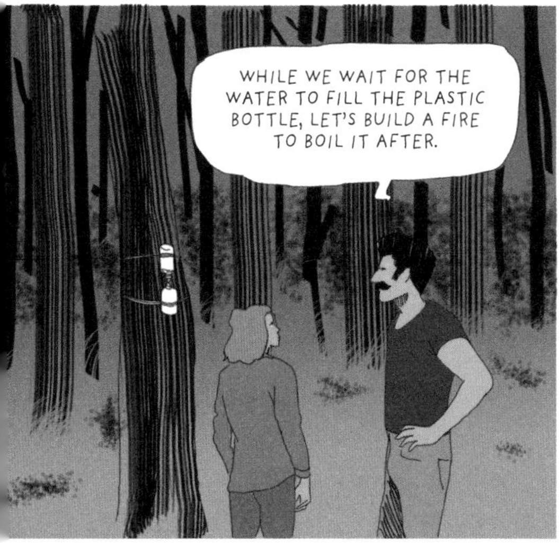
WHILE WE WAIT FOR THE WATER TO FILL THE PLASTIC BOTTLE, LET'S BUILD A FIRE TO BOIL IT AFTER.

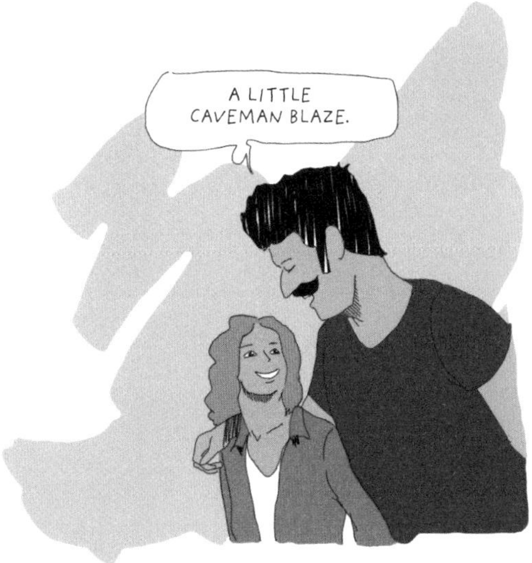
A LITTLE CAVEMAN BLAZE.

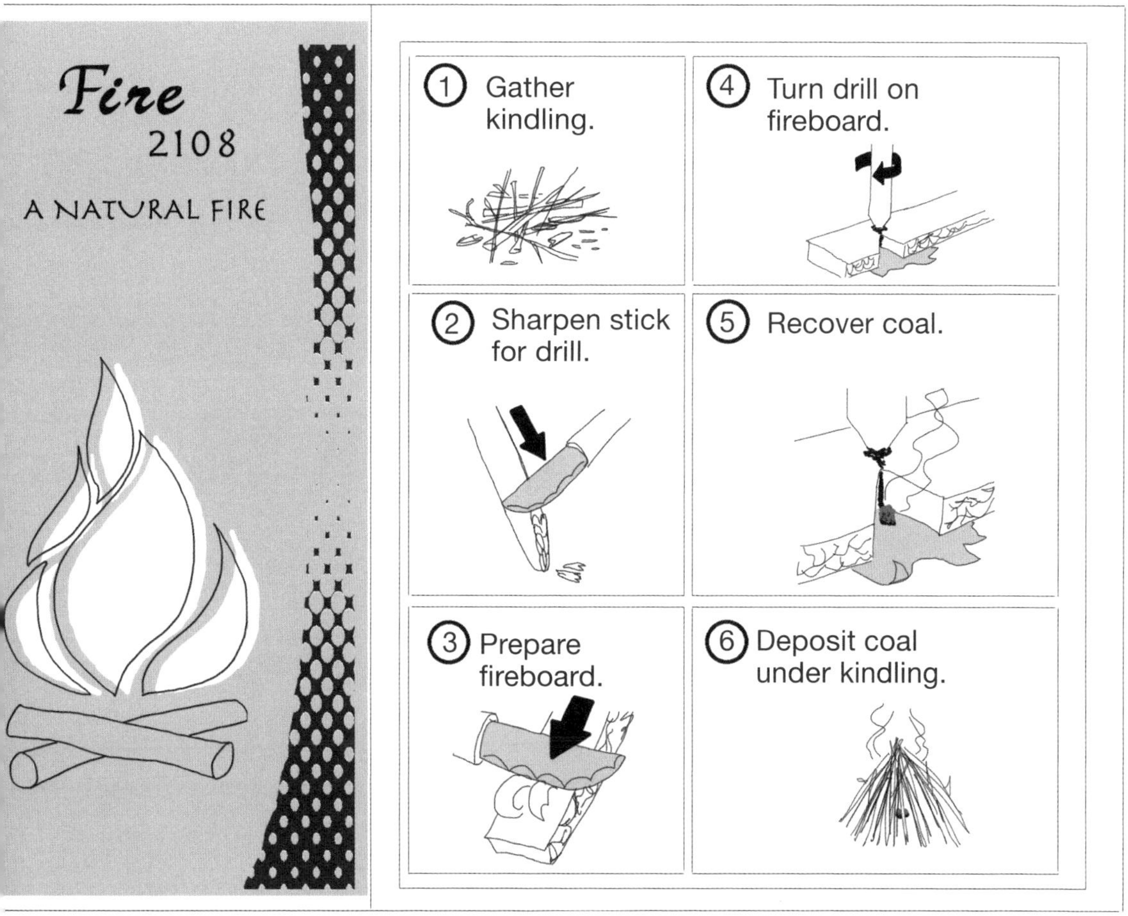
Fire
2108
A NATURAL FIRE
1 Gather kindling.
2 Sharpen stick for drill.
3 Prepare fireboard.
4 Turn drill on fireboard.
5 Recover coal.
6 Deposit coal under kindling.

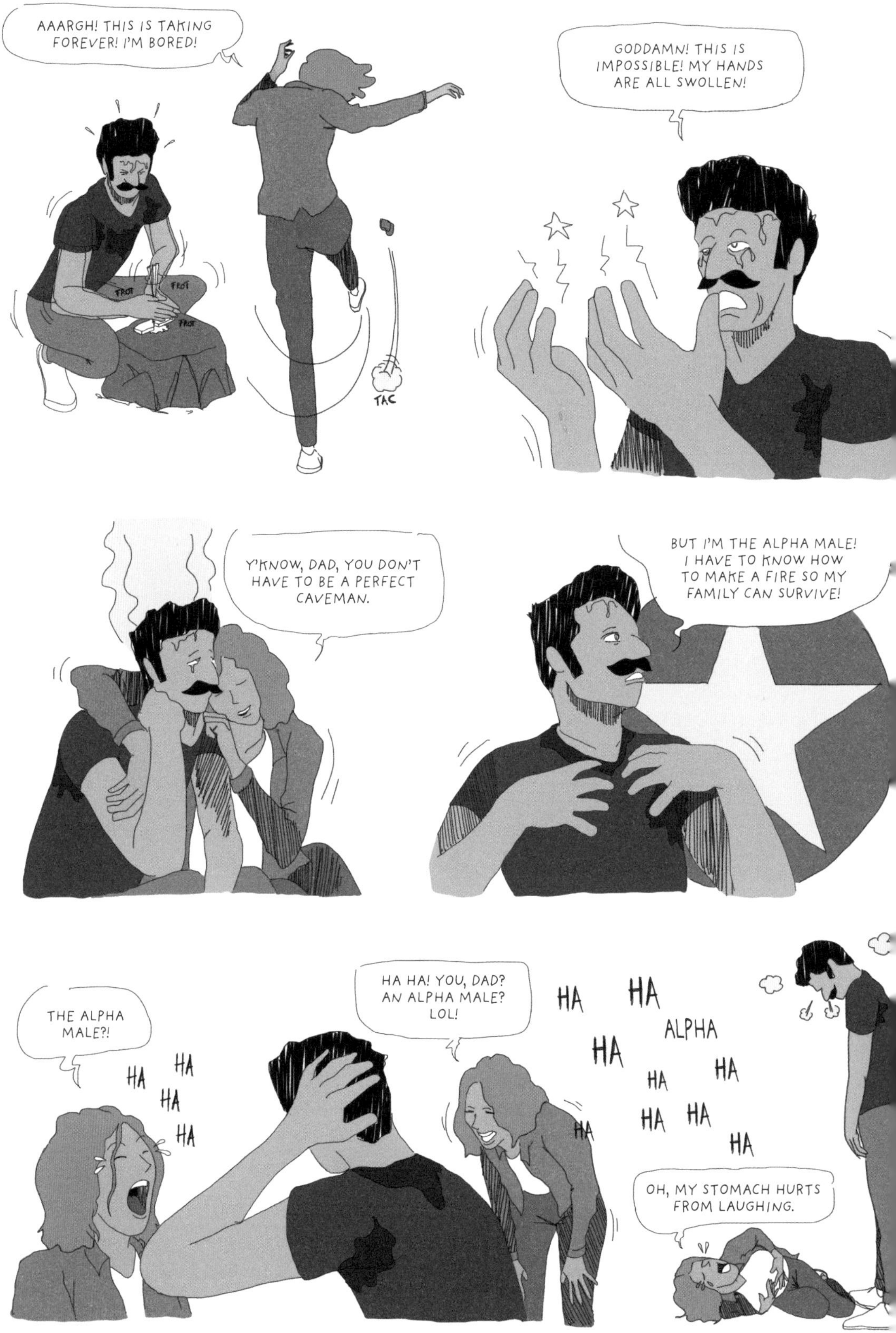
AAARGH! THIS IS TAKING FOREVER! I'M BORED!
FROT
FROT
FROT
TAC
GODDAMN! THIS IS IMPOSSIBLE! MY HANDS ARE ALL SWOLLEN!
Y'KNOW, DAD, YOU DON'T HAVE TO BE A PERFECT CAVEMAN.
BUT I'M THE ALPHA MALE! I HAVE TO KNOW HOW TO MAKE A FIRE SO MY FAMILY CAN SURVIVE!
THE ALPHA MALE?!
HA HA HA HA
HA HA! YOU, DAD? AN ALPHA MALE? LOL!
HA HA ALPHA HA HA HA HA HA HA HA
OH, MY STOMACH HURTS FROM LAUGHING.

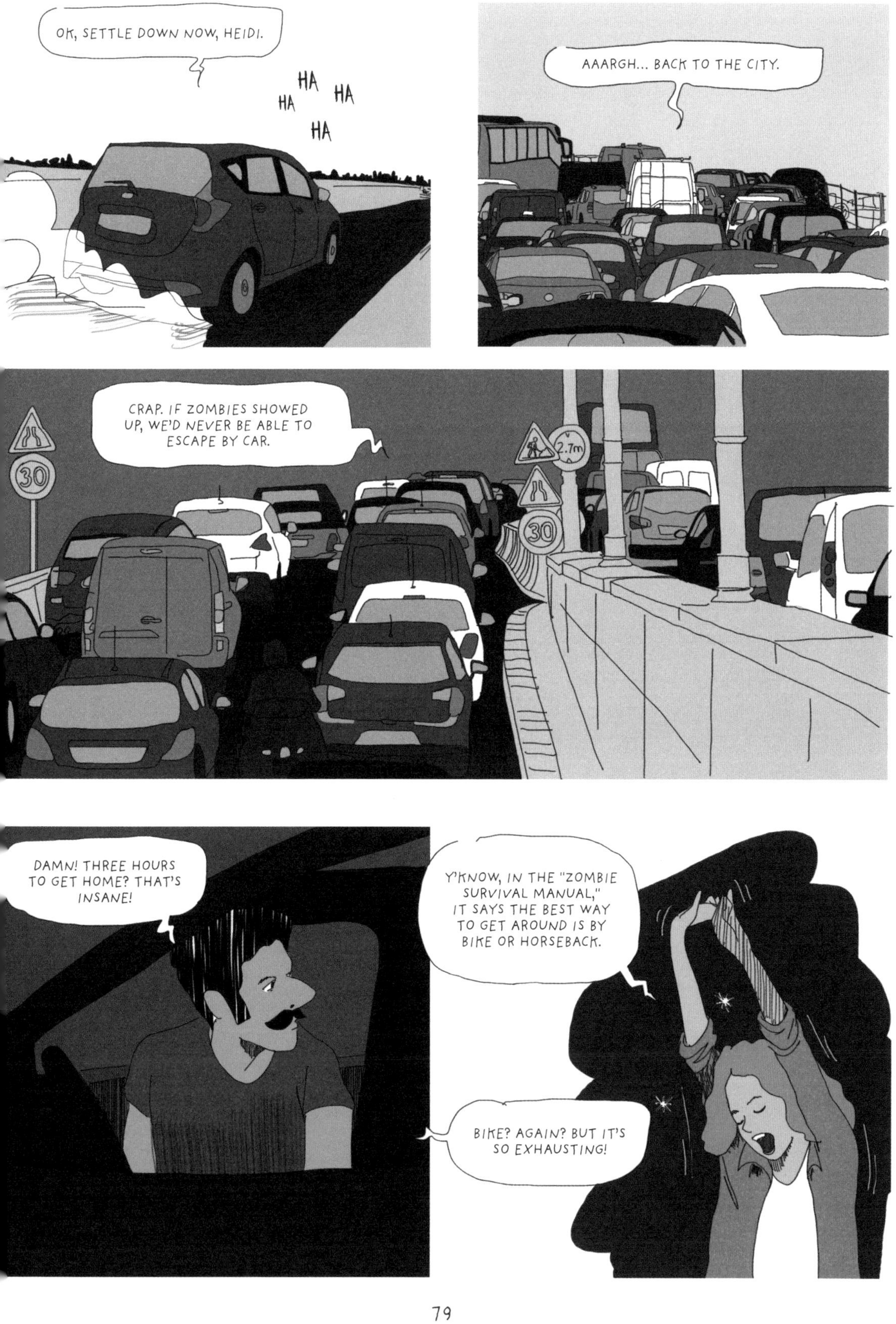
OK, SETTLE DOWN NOW, HEIDI.
HA HA HA HA
AAARGH... BACK TO THE CITY.
CRAP. IF ZOMBIES SHOWED UP, WE'D NEVER BE ABLE TO ESCAPE BY CAR.
30
2.7m
30
DAMN! THREE HOURS TO GET HOME? THAT'S INSANE!
Y'KNOW, IN THE "ZOMBIE SURVIVAL MANUAL," IT SAYS THE BEST WAY TO GET AROUND IS BY BIKE OR HORSEBACK.
BIKE? AGAIN? BUT IT'S SO EXHAUSTING!

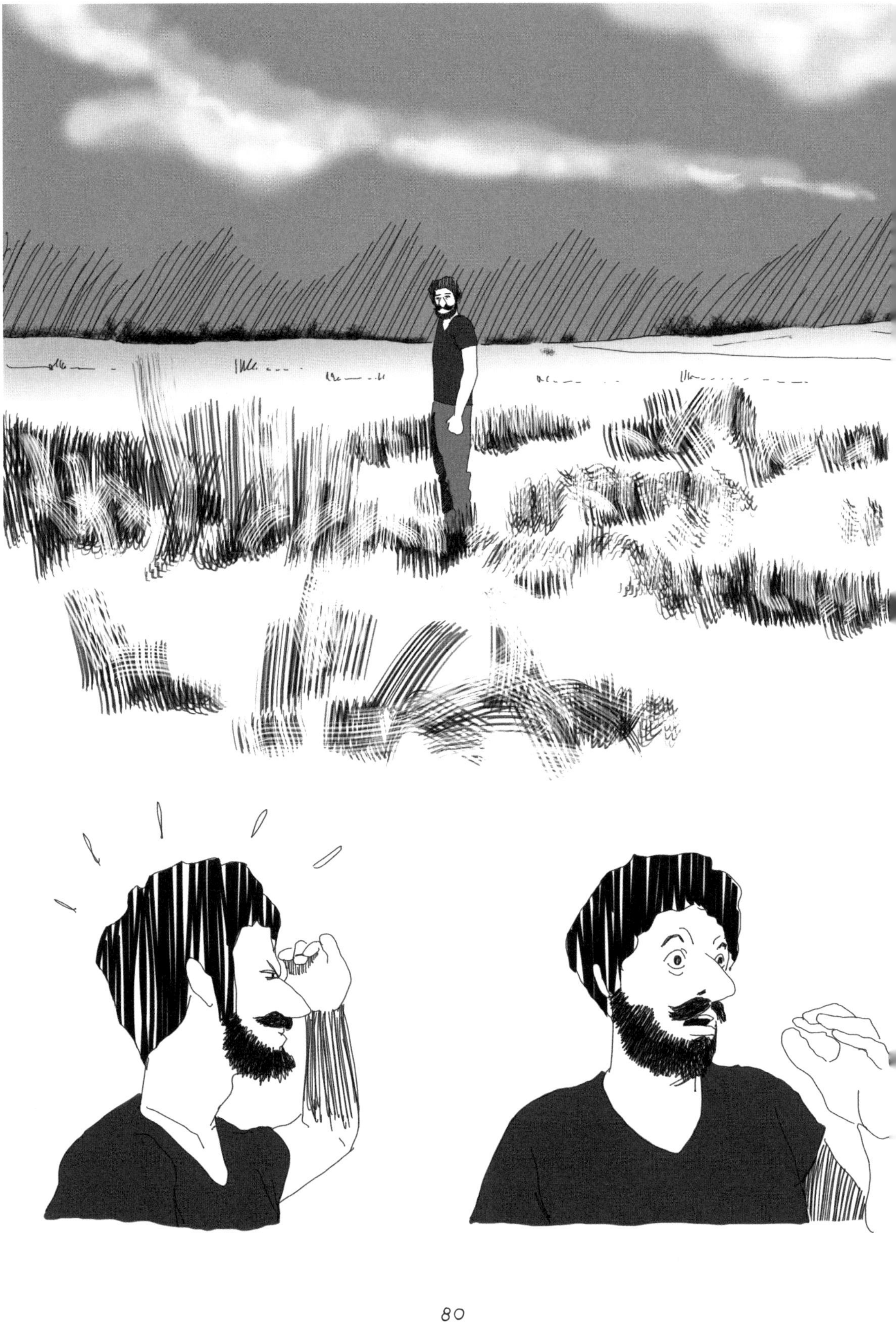

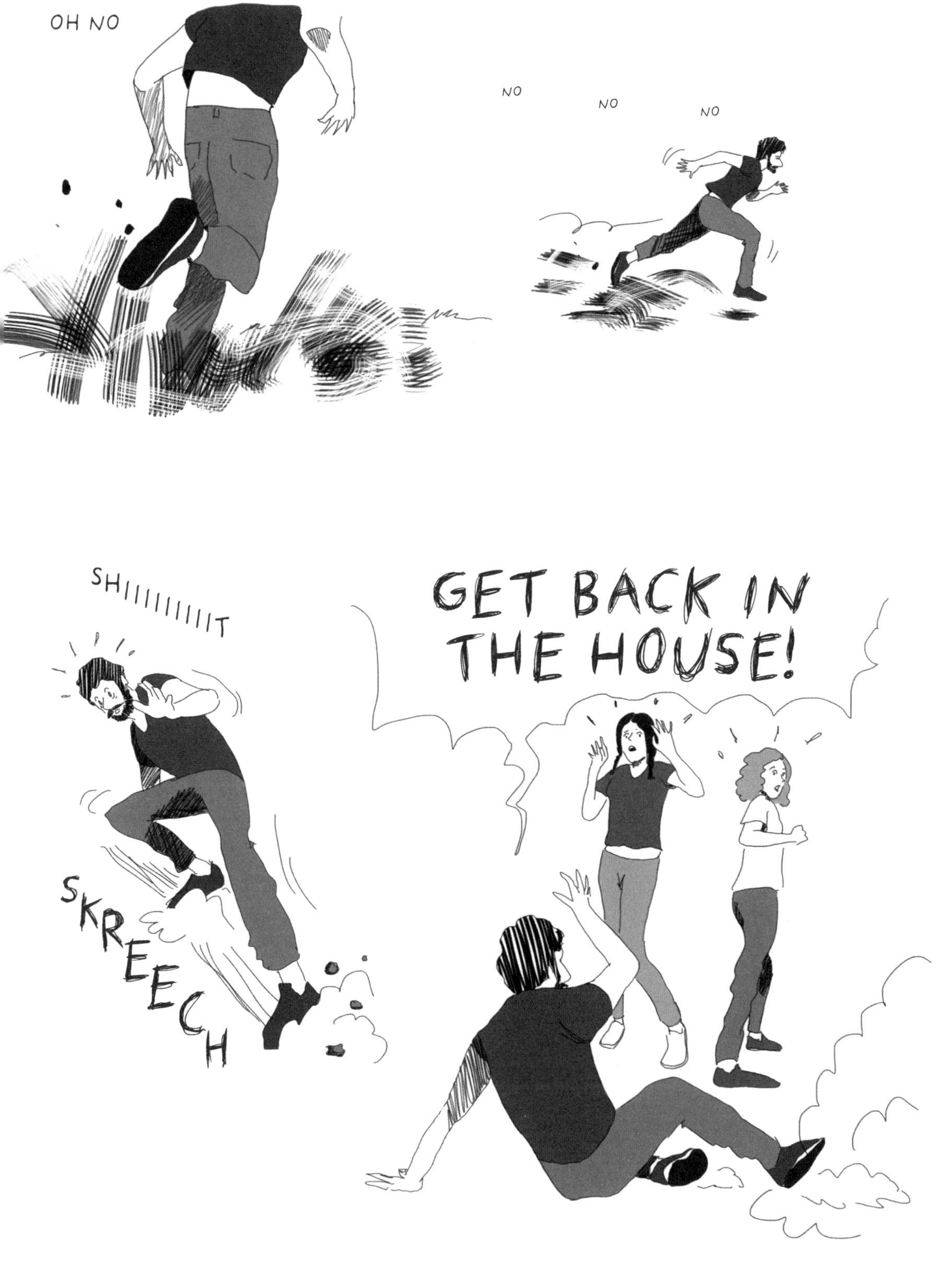
OH NO
NO
NO
NO
SHIIIIIIIIIT
SKREECH
GET BACK IN THE HOUSE!

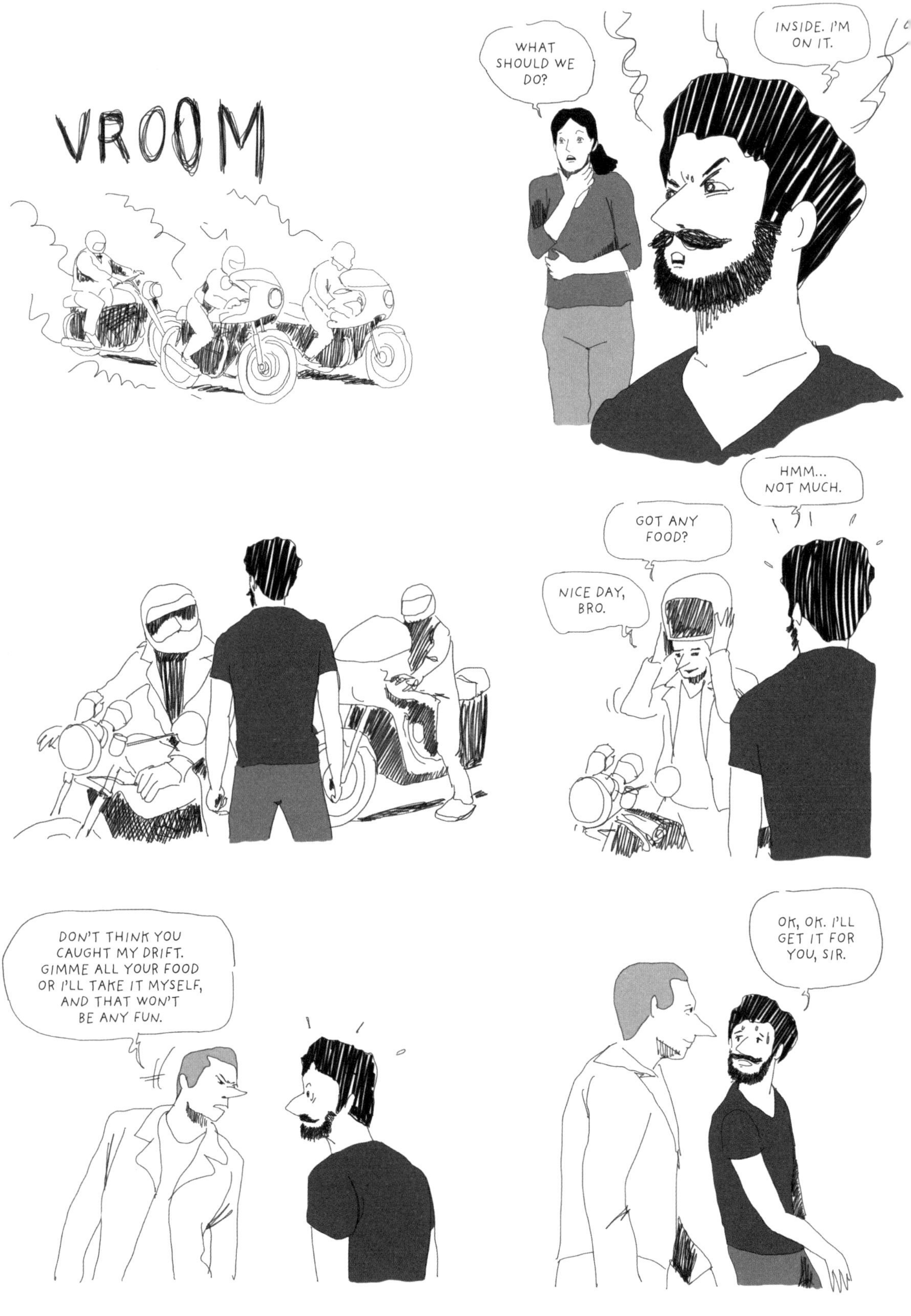
VROOM
WHAT SHOULD WE DO?
INSIDE. I'M ON IT.
NICE DAY, BRO.
GOT ANY FOOD?
HMM... NOT MUCH.
DON'T THINK YOU CAUGHT MY DRIFT. GIMME ALL YOUR FOOD OR I'LL TAKE IT MYSELF, AND THAT WON'T BE ANY FUN.
OK, OK. I'LL GET IT FOR YOU, SIR.

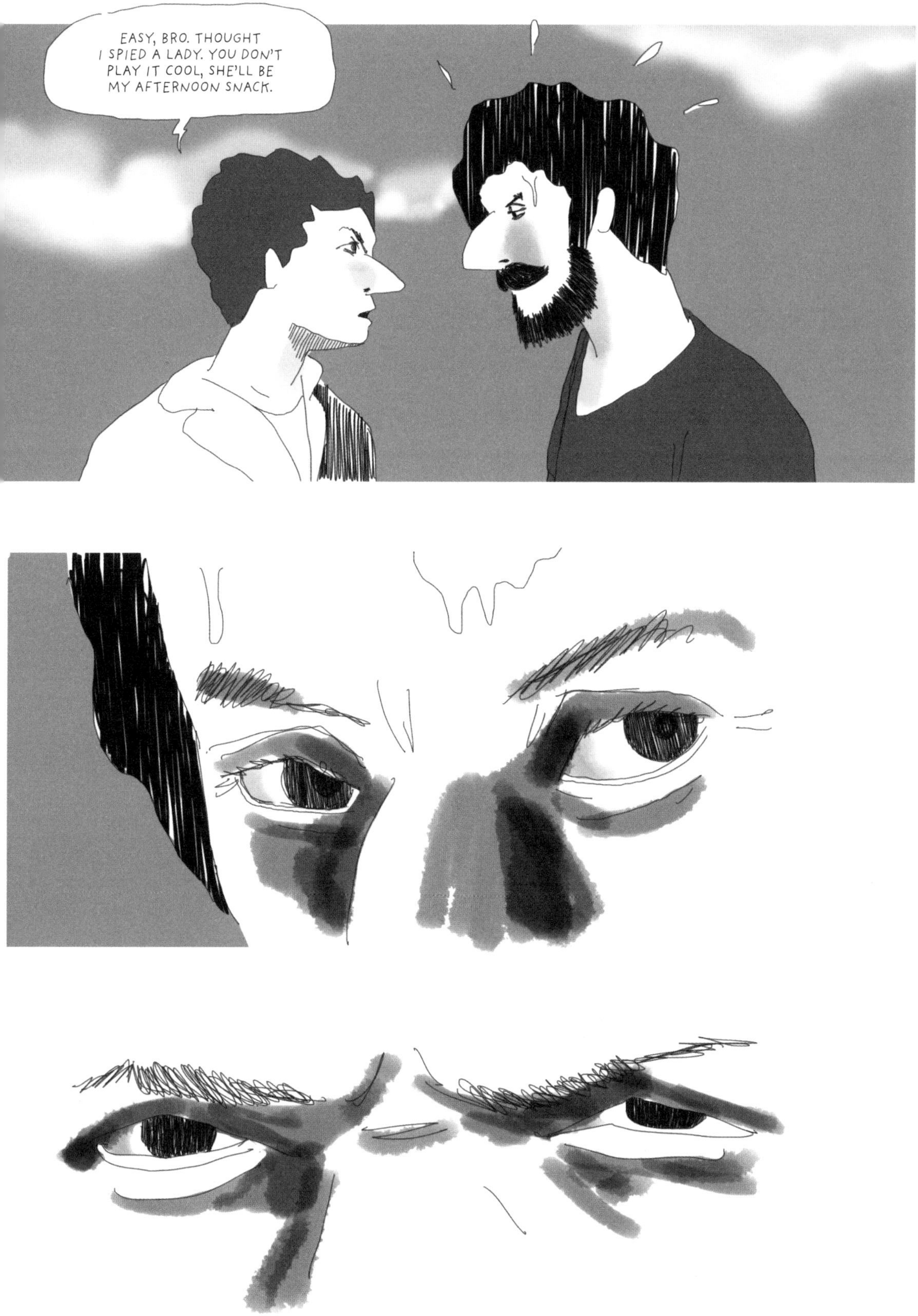
EASY, BRO. THOUGHT I SPIED A LADY. YOU DON'T PLAY IT COOL, SHE'LL BE MY AFTERNOON SNACK.

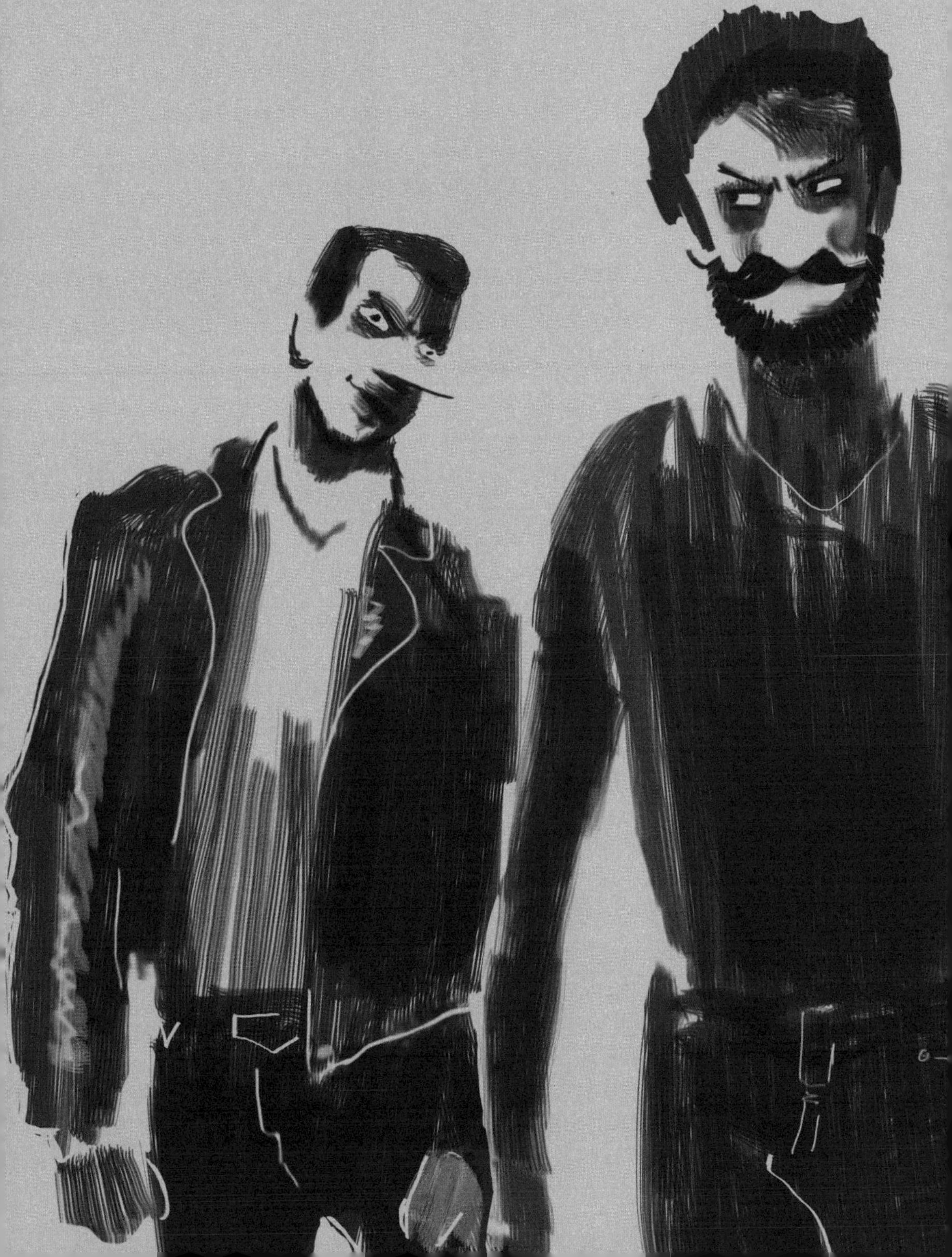

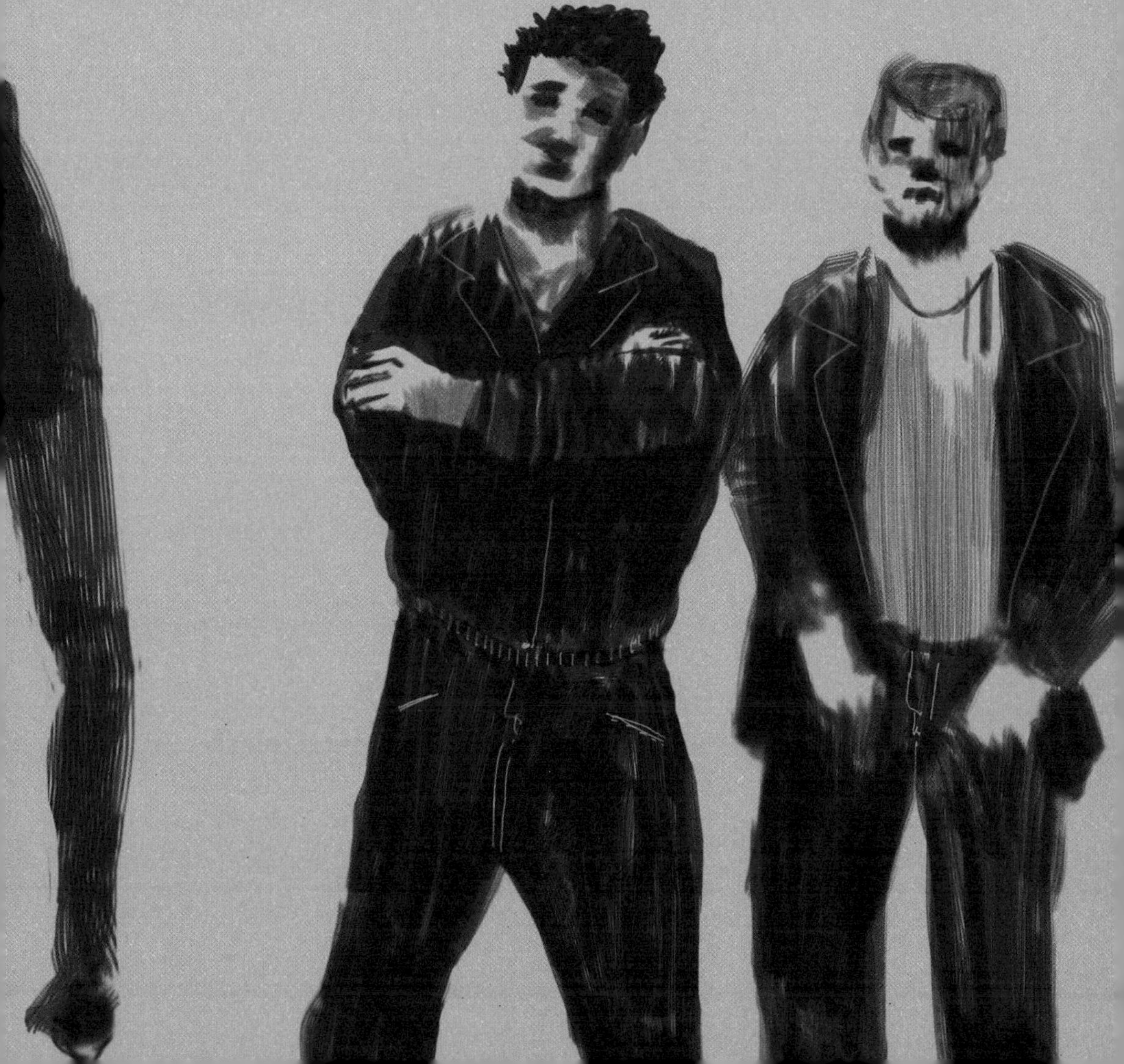

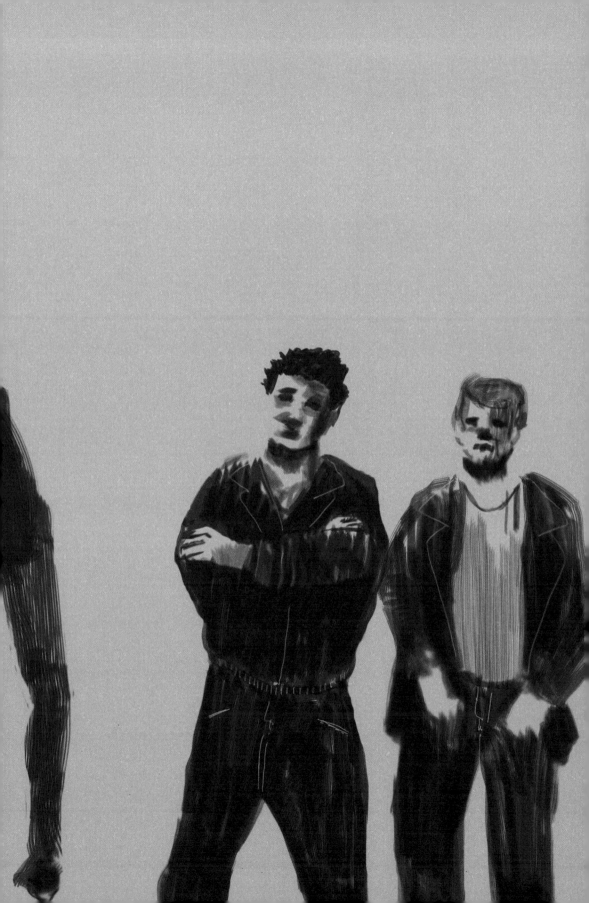

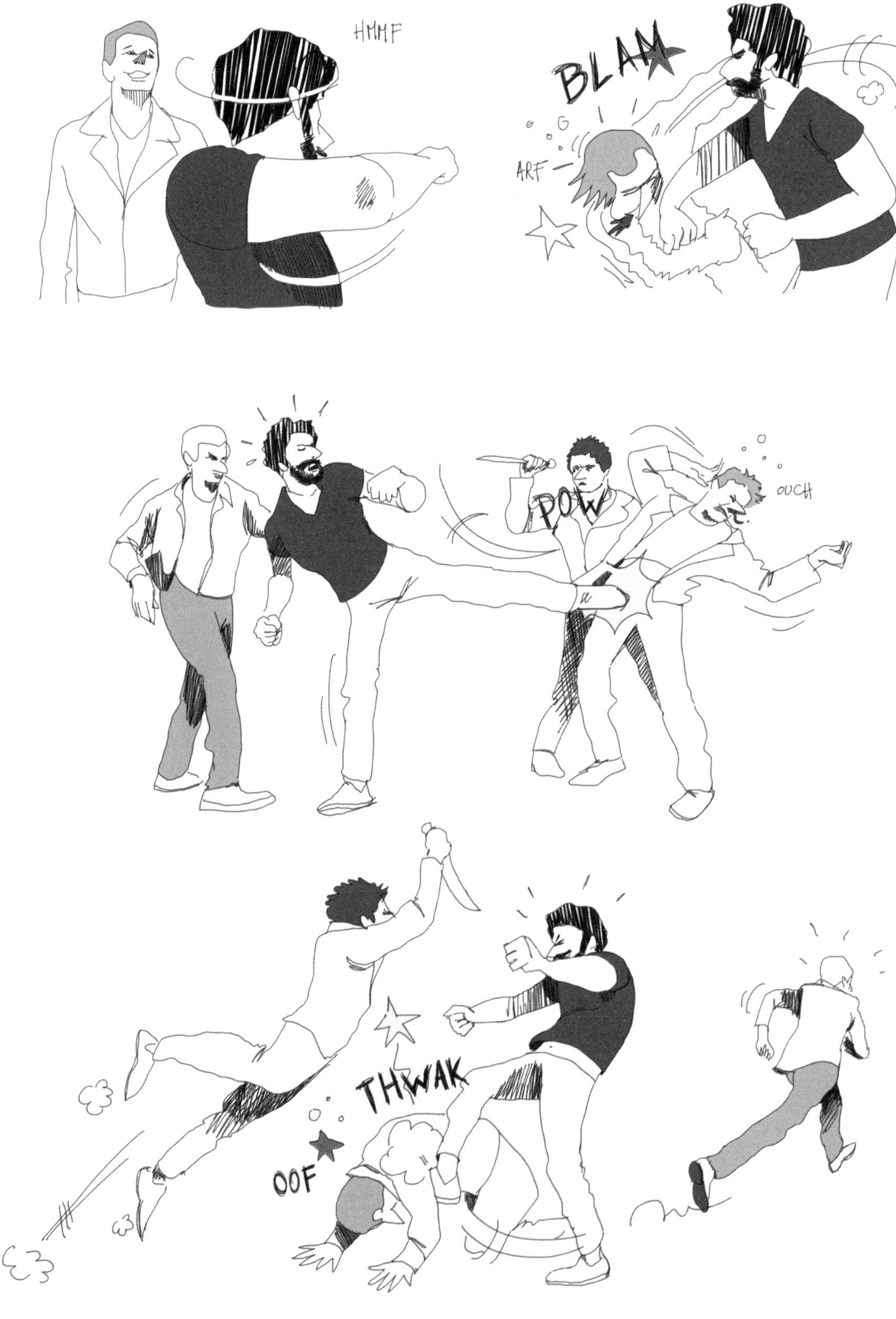
HMMF
BLAM
ARF
POW
OUCH
THWAK
OOF

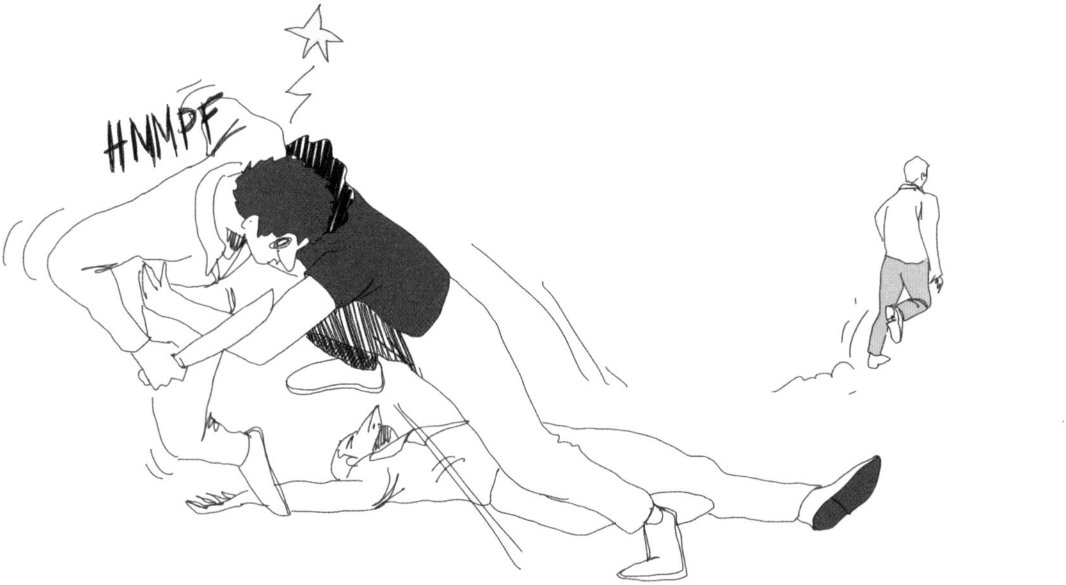
HNMPF

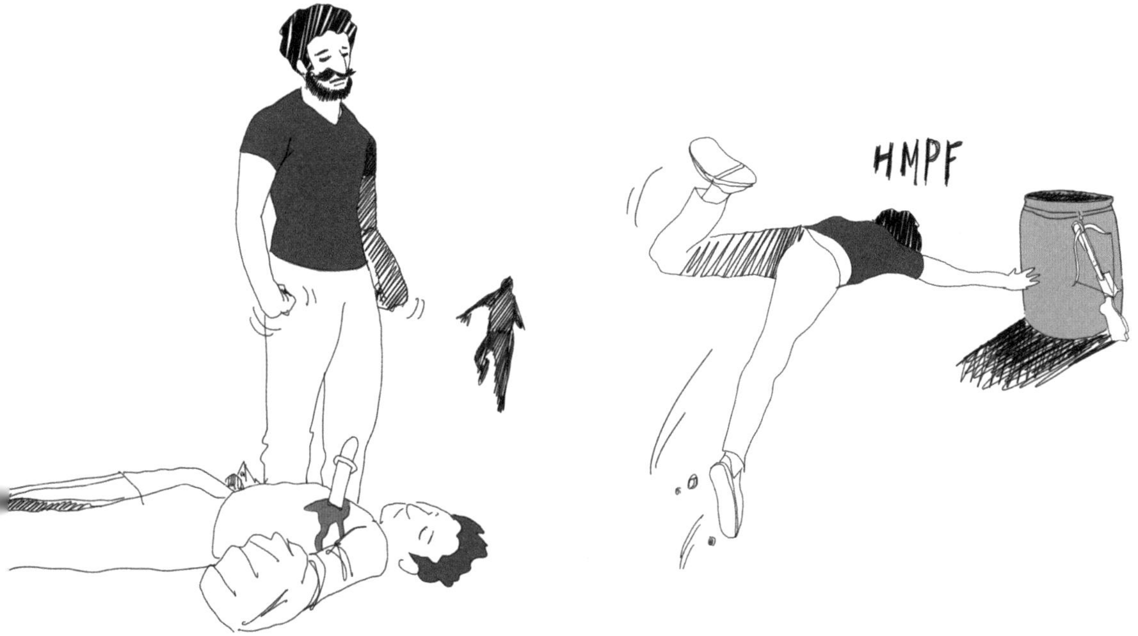
HMPF

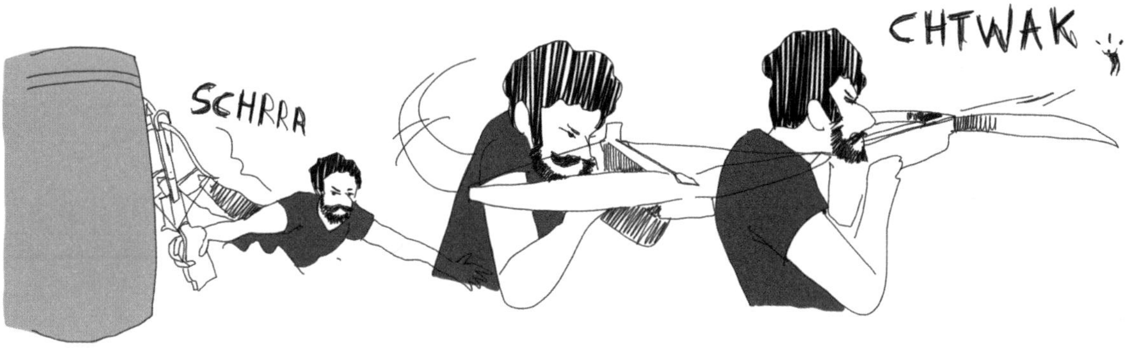
SCHRRA
CHTWAK

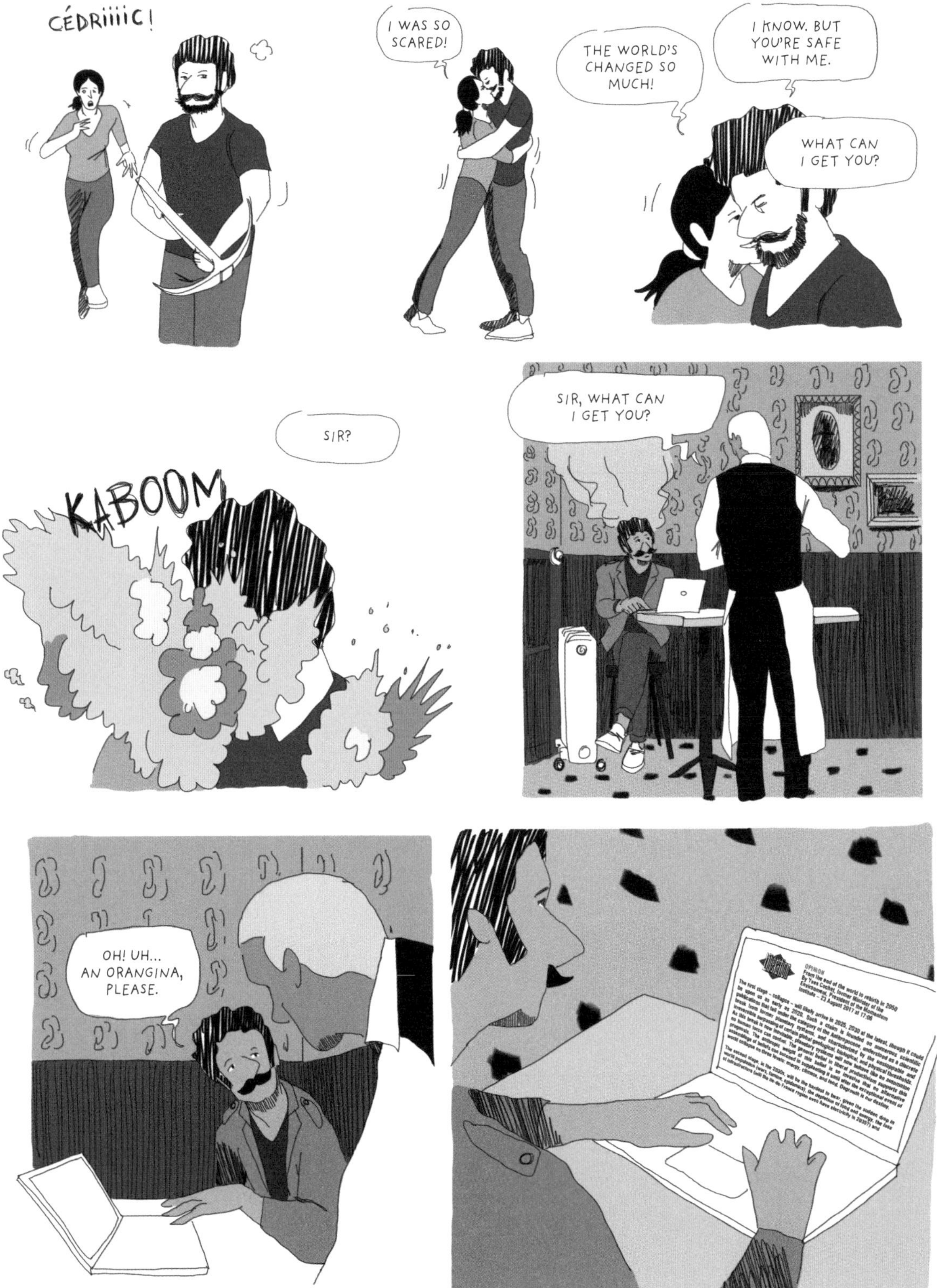

CÉDRIiiiiC!
I WAS SO SCARED!
THE WORLD'S CHANGED SO MUCH!
I KNOW. BUT YOU'RE SAFE WITH ME.
WHAT CAN I GET YOU?
SIR?
KABOOM
SIR, WHAT CAN I GET YOU?
OH! UH... AN ORANGINA, PLEASE.
OPINION
From the end of the world to rebirth in 2050
By Yves Cochet, former Minister of the Environment, President of the Momentum Institute – 23 August 2017 at 17:06
The first stage – collapse – will likely arrive in 2025, 2030 at the latest, though it could be upon us as early as 2020. Such a claim is founded on numerous scientific publications that fall under the category of the Anthropocene, understood as a discrete break from former planetary systems, and characterized by the unstoppable and irreversible surpassing of certain global geological, biological, and physical thresholds. As this break is now inevitable, planetary systems will now behave like an automaton no human force can control. The general belief in liberal productivism supports this prognosis. The anthropic weight of this belief is so invasive that no alternative assemblage of beliefs can succeed in supplanting it until after the exceptional event of world collapse on three levels: energy, climate, and food. Degrowth is our destiny.
The second stage, in the 2030s, will be the hardest to bear, given the sudden drop in world population (wars, famine, epidemics), the depletion of food and energy, the loss of infrastructure (will the Île-de-France region even have electricity in 2035?) and

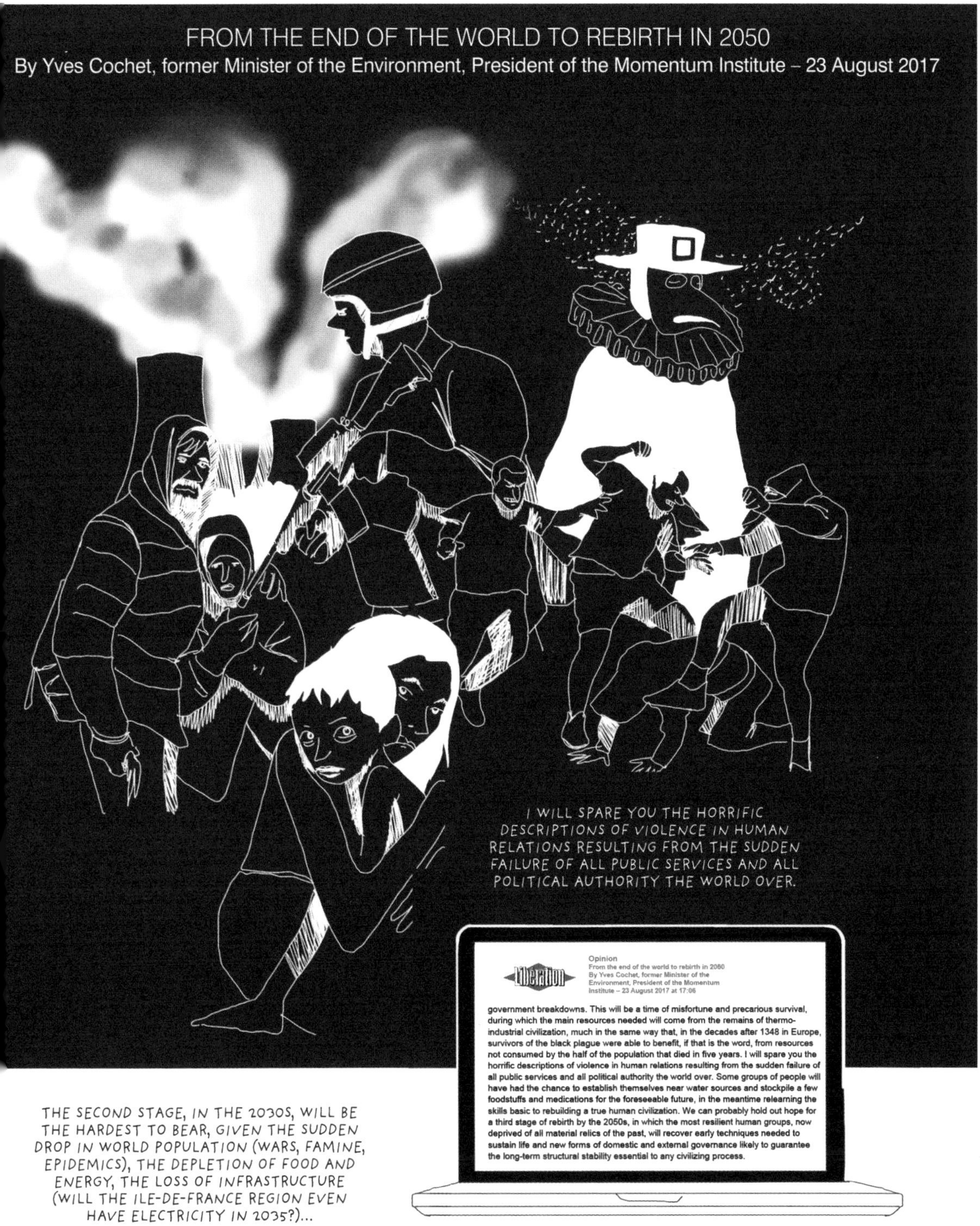
FROM THE END OF THE WORLD TO REBIRTH IN 2050
By Yves Cochet, former Minister of the Environment, President of the Momentum Institute – 23 August 2017
I WILL SPARE YOU THE HORRIFIC DESCRIPTIONS OF VIOLENCE IN HUMAN RELATIONS RESULTING FROM THE SUDDEN FAILURE OF ALL PUBLIC SERVICES AND ALL POLITICAL AUTHORITY THE WORLD OVER.
Libération
Opinion
From the end of the world to rebirth in 2050
By Yves Cochet, former Minister of the Environment, President of the Momentum Institute – 23 August 2017 at 17:06
government breakdowns. This will be a time of misfortune and precarious survival, during which the main resources needed will come from the remains of thermo-industrial civilization, much in the same way that, in the decades after 1348 in Europe, survivors of the black plague were able to benefit, if that is the word, from resources not consumed by the half of the population that died in five years. I will spare you the horrific descriptions of violence in human relations resulting from the sudden failure of all public services and all political authority the world over. Some groups of people will have had the chance to establish themselves near water sources and stockpile a few foodstuffs and medications for the foreseeable future, in the meantime relearning the skills basic to rebuilding a true human civilization. We can probably hold out hope for a third stage of rebirth by the 2050s, in which the most resilient human groups, now deprived of all material relics of the past, will recover early techniques needed to sustain life and new forms of domestic and external governance likely to guarantee the long-term structural stability essential to any civilizing process.

THE SECOND STAGE, IN THE 2030S, WILL BE THE HARDEST TO BEAR, GIVEN THE SUDDEN DROP IN WORLD POPULATION (WARS, FAMINE, EPIDEMICS), THE DEPLETION OF FOOD AND ENERGY, THE LOSS OF INFRASTRUCTURE (WILL THE ILE-DE-FRANCE REGION EVEN HAVE ELECTRICITY IN 2035?)...

THIS WILL BE A TIME OF MISFORTUNE AND PRECARIOUS SURVIVAL, DURING WHICH THE MAIN RESOURCES NEEDED WILL COME FROM THE REMAINS OF THERMO-INDUSTRIAL CIVILIZATION, MUCH IN THE SAME WAY THAT, IN THE DECADES AFTER 1348 IN EUROPE, SURVIVORS OF THE BLACK PLAGUE WERE ABLE TO BENEFIT, IF THAT IS THE WORD, FROM RESOURCES NOT CONSUMED BY THE HALF OF THE POPULATION THAT DIED IN FIVE YEARS.

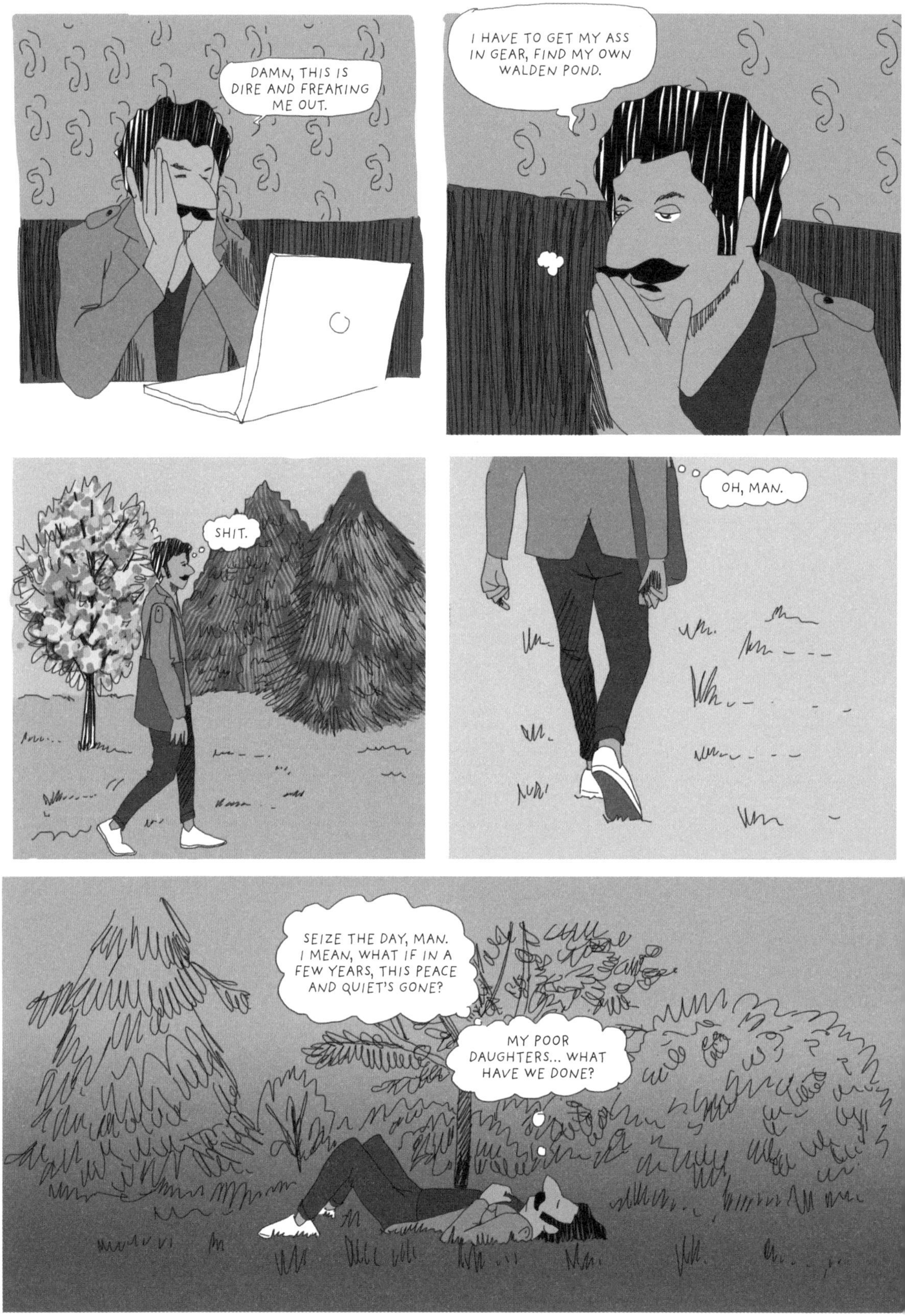
DAMN, THIS IS DIRE AND FREAKING ME OUT.
I HAVE TO GET MY ASS IN GEAR, FIND MY OWN WALDEN POND.
SHIT.
OH, MAN.
SEIZE THE DAY, MAN. I MEAN, WHAT IF IN A FEW YEARS, THIS PEACE AND QUIET'S GONE?
MY POOR DAUGHTERS... WHAT HAVE WE DONE?

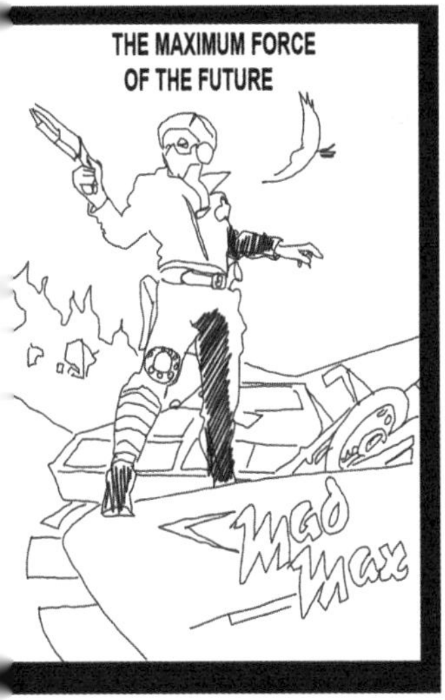
THE MAXIMUM FORCE
OF THE FUTURE
Mad Max

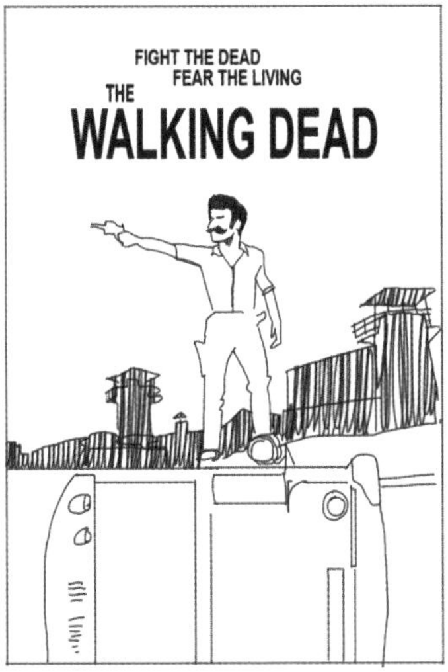
FIGHT THE DEAD
FEAR THE LIVING
THE
WALKING DEAD

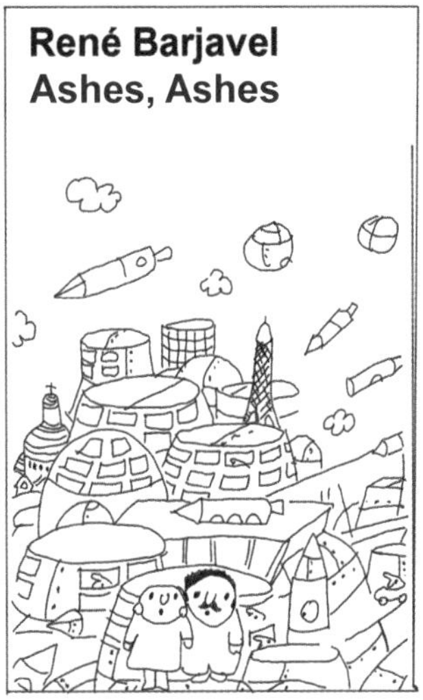
René Barjavel
Ashes, Ashes

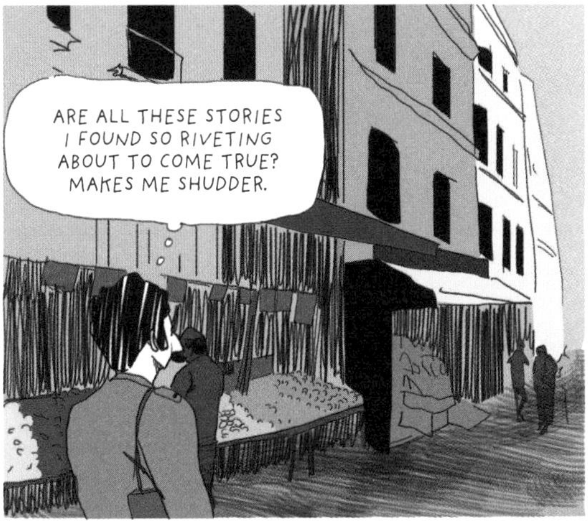
ARE ALL THESE STORIES I FOUND SO RIVETING ABOUT TO COME TRUE? MAKES ME SHUDDER.

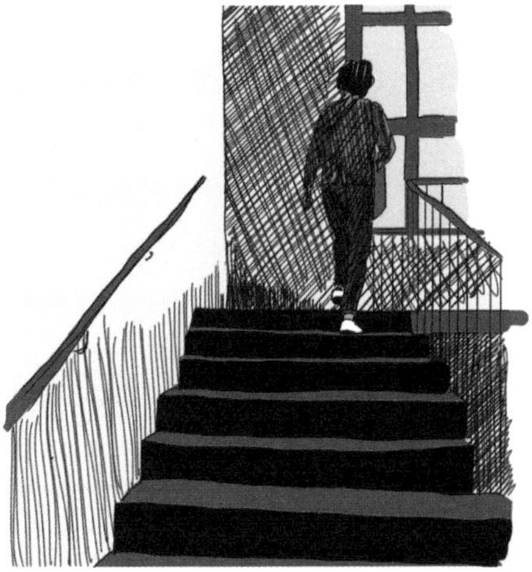

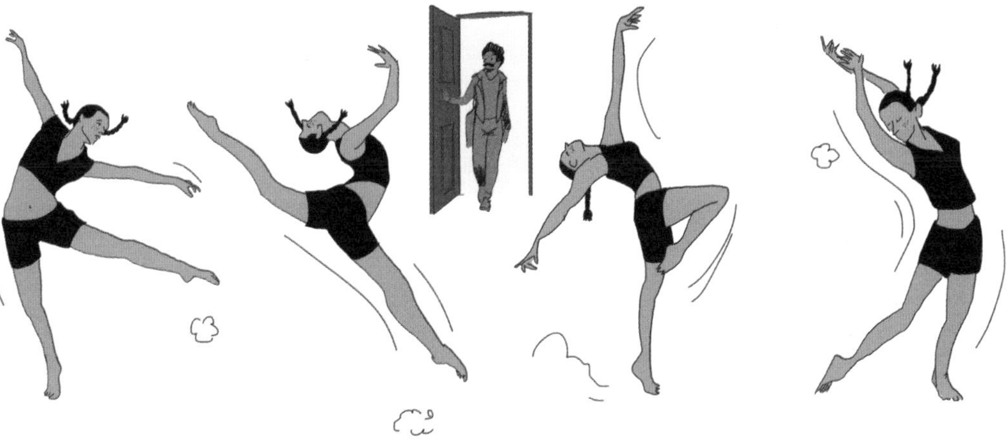

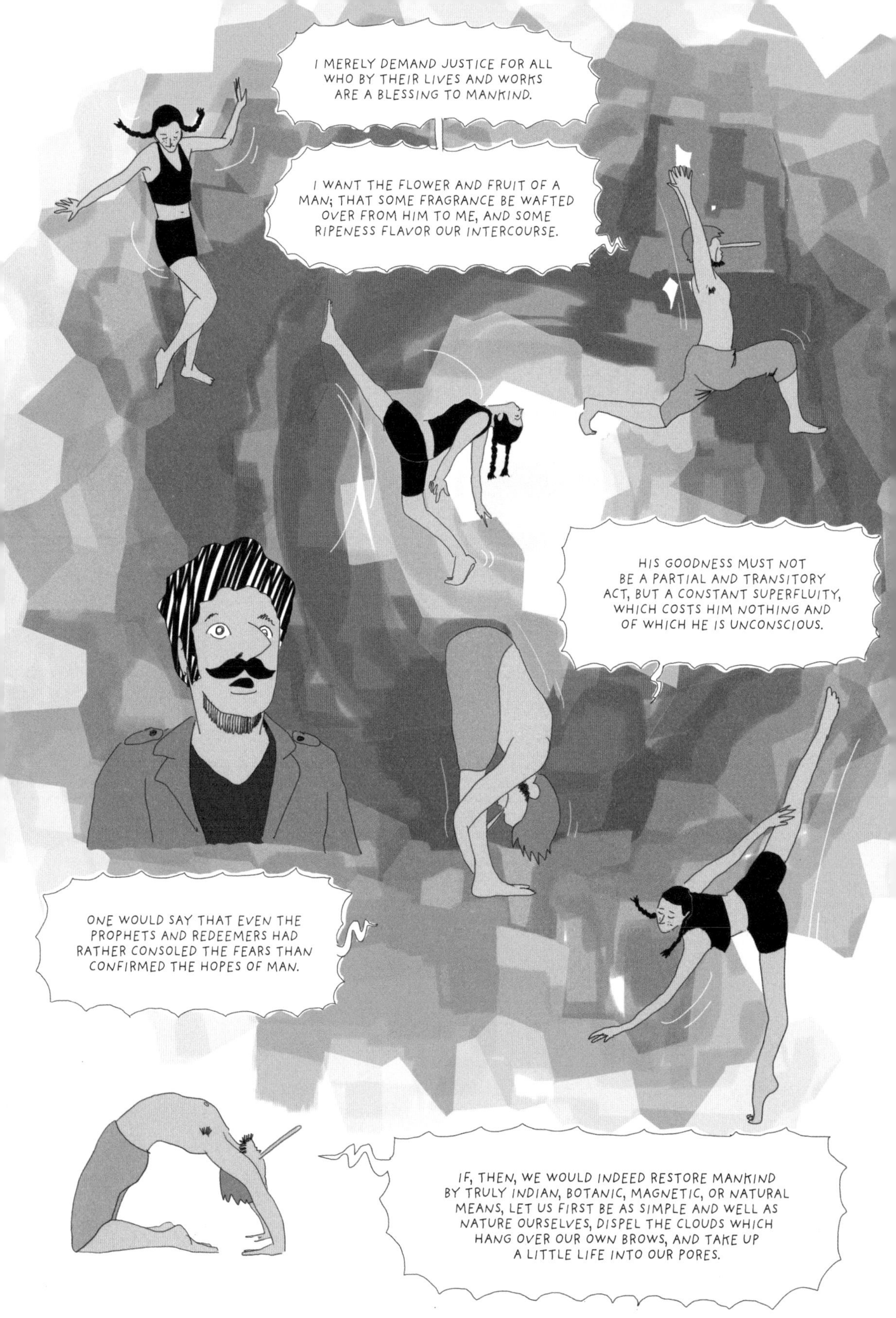
I MERELY DEMAND JUSTICE FOR ALL WHO BY THEIR LIVES AND WORKS ARE A BLESSING TO MANKIND.
I WANT THE FLOWER AND FRUIT OF A MAN; THAT SOME FRAGRANCE BE WAFTED OVER FROM HIM TO ME, AND SOME RIPENESS FLAVOR OUR INTERCOURSE.
HIS GOODNESS MUST NOT BE A PARTIAL AND TRANSITORY ACT, BUT A CONSTANT SUPERFLUITY, WHICH COSTS HIM NOTHING AND OF WHICH HE IS UNCONSCIOUS.
ONE WOULD SAY THAT EVEN THE PROPHETS AND REDEEMERS HAD RATHER CONSOLED THE FEARS THAN CONFIRMED THE HOPES OF MAN.
IF, THEN, WE WOULD INDEED RESTORE MANKIND BY TRULY INDIAN, BOTANIC, MAGNETIC, OR NATURAL MEANS, LET US FIRST BE AS SIMPLE AND WELL AS NATURE OURSELVES, DISPEL THE CLOUDS WHICH HANG OVER OUR OWN BROWS, AND TAKE UP A LITTLE LIFE INTO OUR PORES.

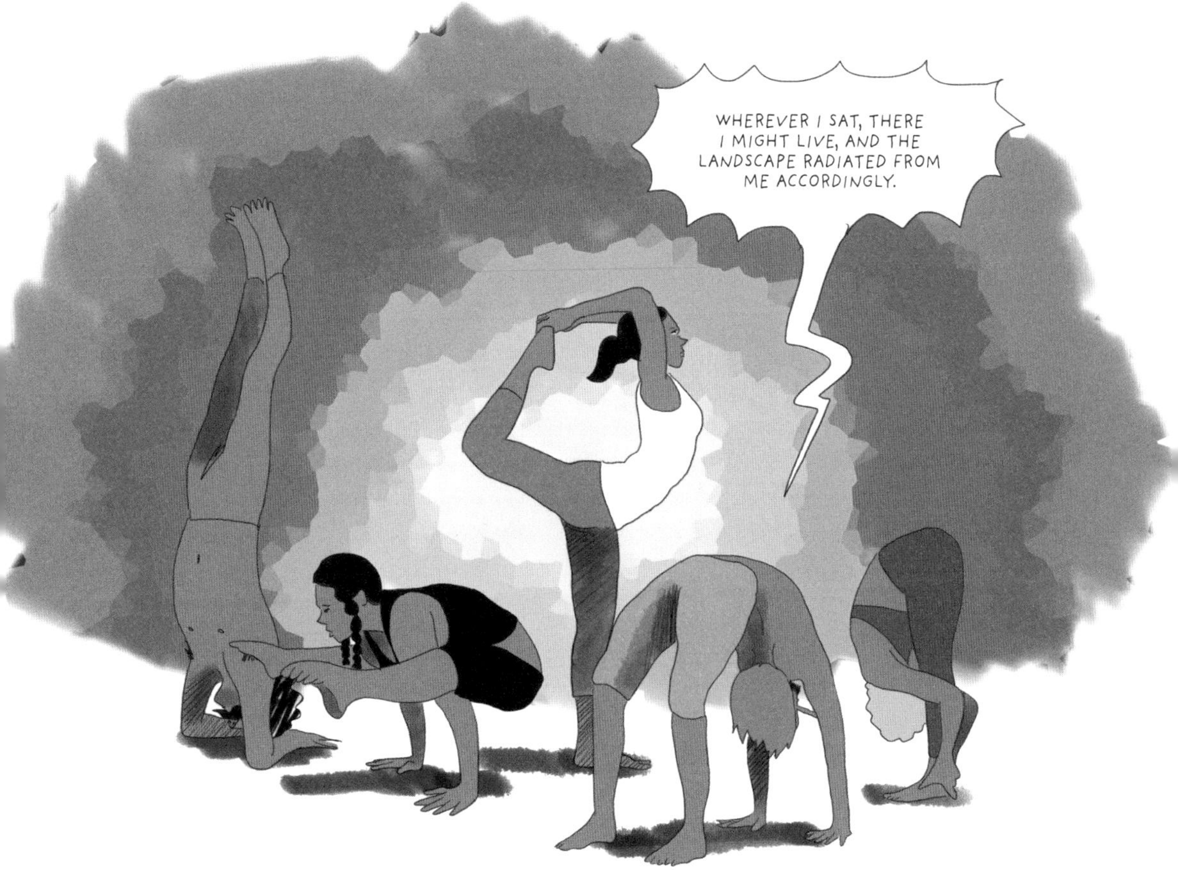
WHEREVER I SAT, THERE I MIGHT LIVE, AND THE LANDSCAPE RADIATED FROM ME ACCORDINGLY.

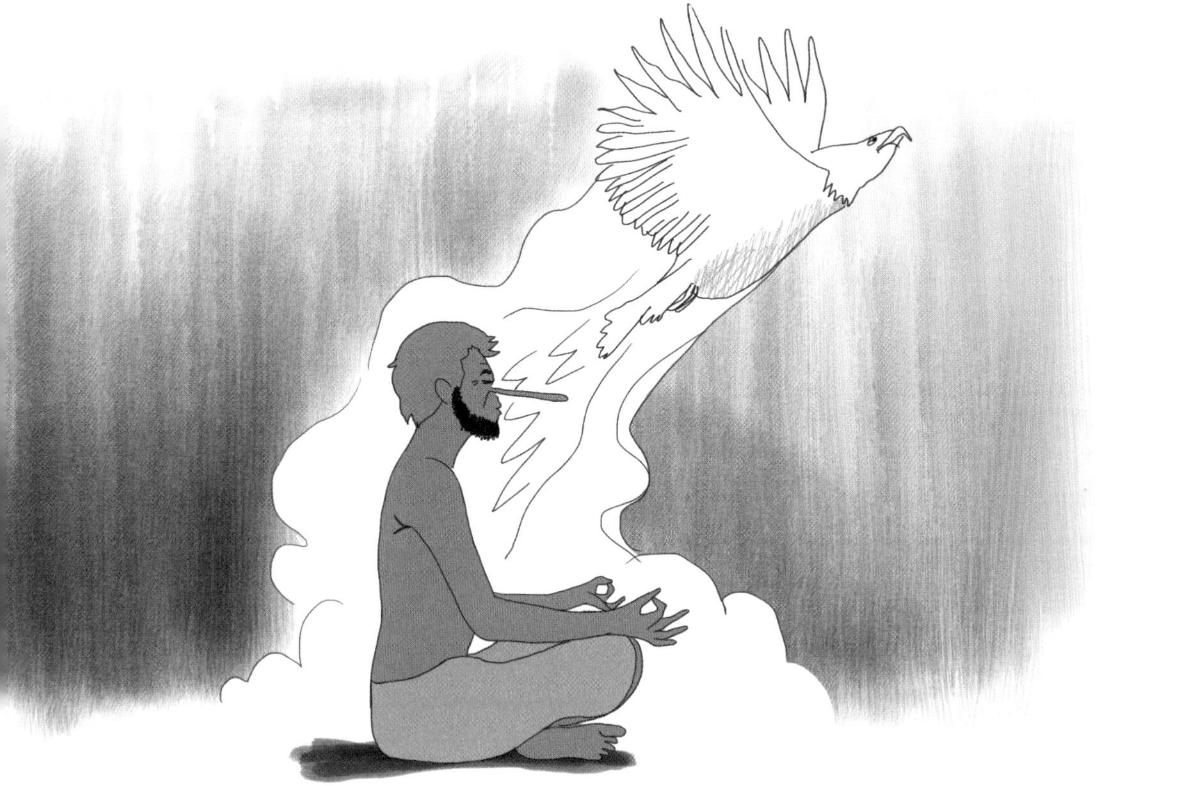

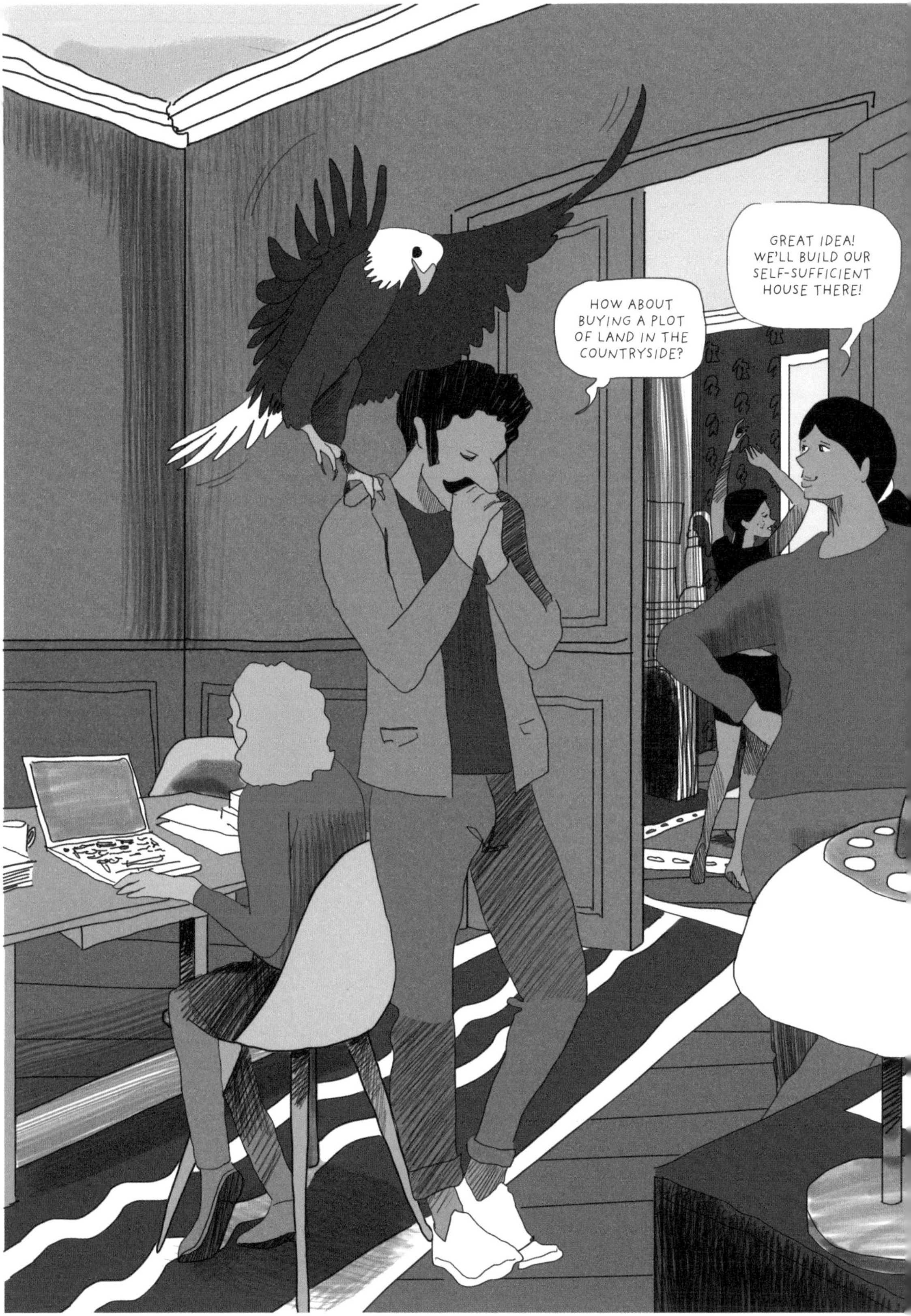
HOW ABOUT BUYING A PLOT OF LAND IN THE COUNTRYSIDE?
GREAT IDEA! WE'LL BUILD OUR SELF-SUFFICIENT HOUSE THERE!

III. Remission

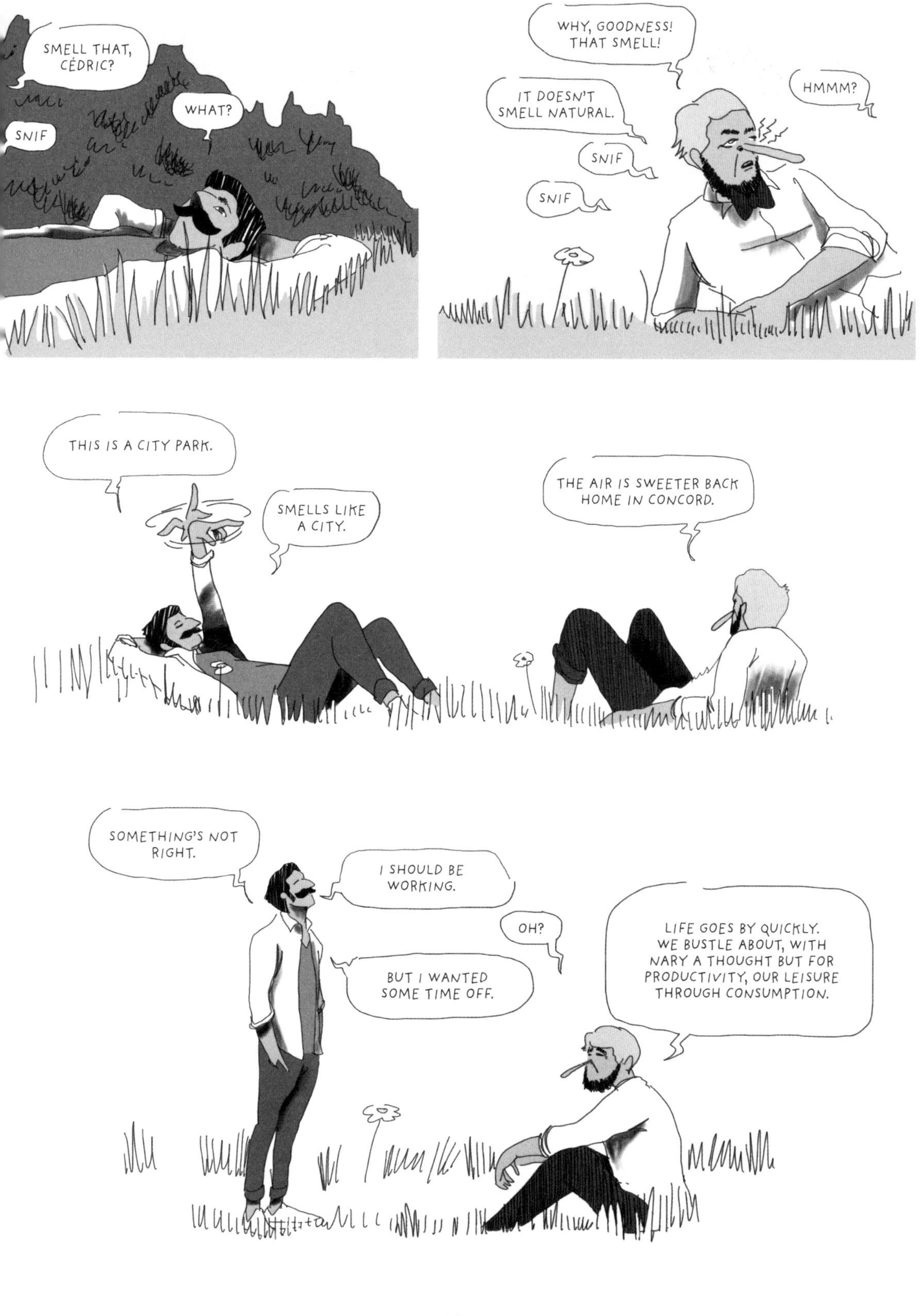
SMELL THAT, CÉDRIC?
SNIF
WHAT?
WHY, GOODNESS! THAT SMELL!
HMMM?
IT DOESN'T SMELL NATURAL.
SNIF
SNIF
THIS IS A CITY PARK.
SMELLS LIKE A CITY.
THE AIR IS SWEETER BACK HOME IN CONCORD.
SOMETHING'S NOT RIGHT.
I SHOULD BE WORKING.
BUT I WANTED SOME TIME OFF.
OH?
LIFE GOES BY QUICKLY. WE BUSTLE ABOUT, WITH NARY A THOUGHT BUT FOR PRODUCTIVITY, OUR LEISURE THROUGH CONSUMPTION.

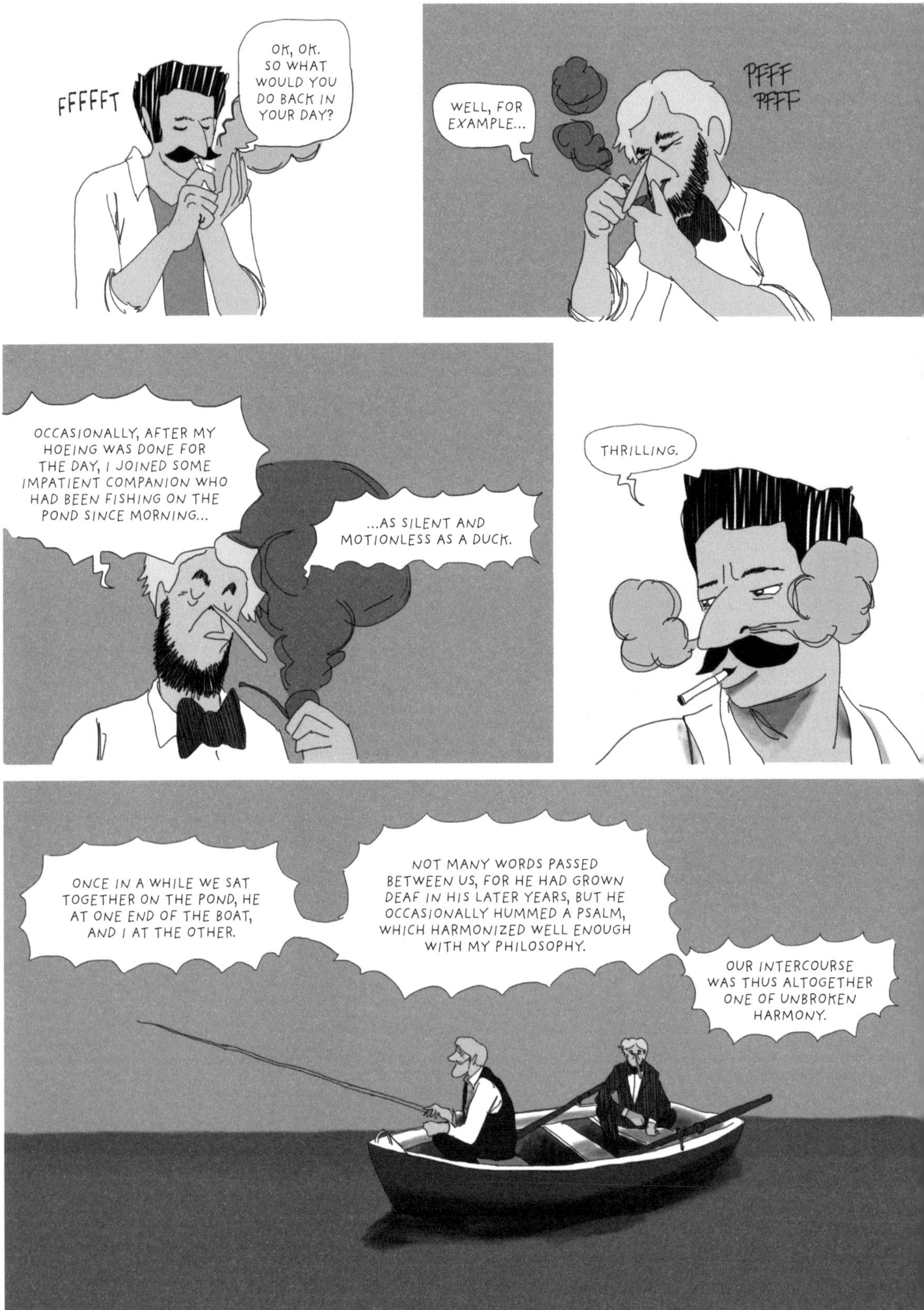
FFFFFT
OK, OK. SO WHAT WOULD YOU DO BACK IN YOUR DAY?
WELL, FOR EXAMPLE...
PFFF PFFF
OCCASIONALLY, AFTER MY HOEING WAS DONE FOR THE DAY, I JOINED SOME IMPATIENT COMPANION WHO HAD BEEN FISHING ON THE POND SINCE MORNING...
...AS SILENT AND MOTIONLESS AS A DUCK.
THRILLING.
ONCE IN A WHILE WE SAT TOGETHER ON THE POND, HE AT ONE END OF THE BOAT, AND I AT THE OTHER.
NOT MANY WORDS PASSED BETWEEN US, FOR HE HAD GROWN DEAF IN HIS LATER YEARS, BUT HE OCCASIONALLY HUMMED A PSALM, WHICH HARMONIZED WELL ENOUGH WITH MY PHILOSOPHY.
OUR INTERCOURSE WAS THUS ALTOGETHER ONE OF UNBROKEN HARMONY.

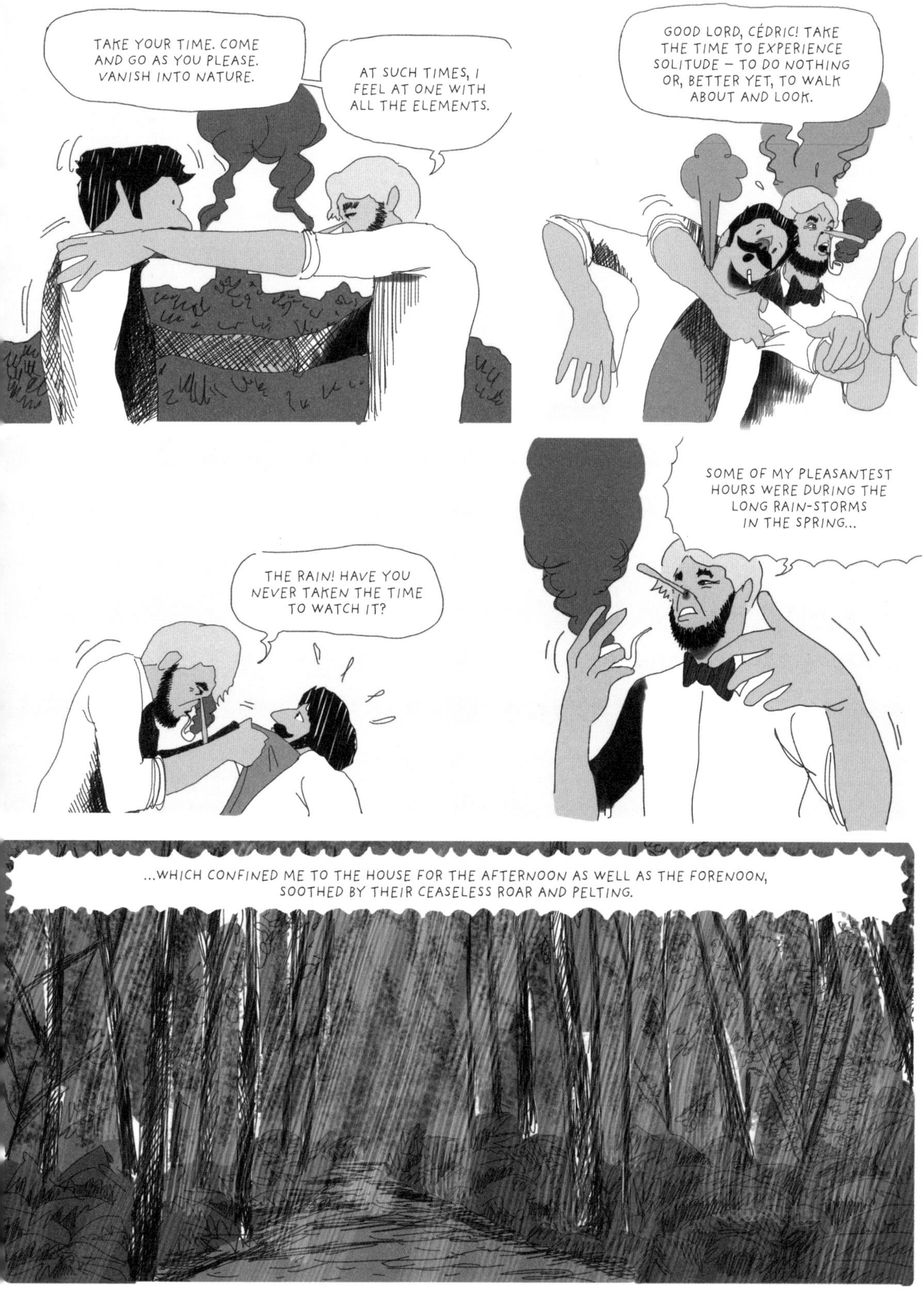
TAKE YOUR TIME. COME AND GO AS YOU PLEASE. VANISH INTO NATURE.
AT SUCH TIMES, I FEEL AT ONE WITH ALL THE ELEMENTS.
GOOD LORD, CÉDRIC! TAKE THE TIME TO EXPERIENCE SOLITUDE – TO DO NOTHING OR, BETTER YET, TO WALK ABOUT AND LOOK.
THE RAIN! HAVE YOU NEVER TAKEN THE TIME TO WATCH IT?
SOME OF MY PLEASANTEST HOURS WERE DURING THE LONG RAIN-STORMS IN THE SPRING...
...WHICH CONFINED ME TO THE HOUSE FOR THE AFTERNOON AS WELL AS THE FORENOON, SOOTHED BY THEIR CEASELESS ROAR AND PELTING.

I SAT BEHIND MY DOOR IN MY LITTLE HOUSE...

...WHICH WAS ALL ENTRY...

...AND THOROUGHLY ENJOYED ITS PROTECTION.

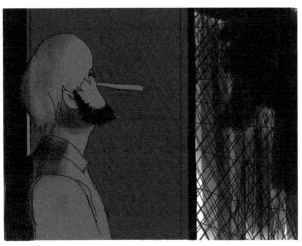

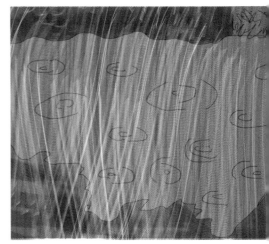

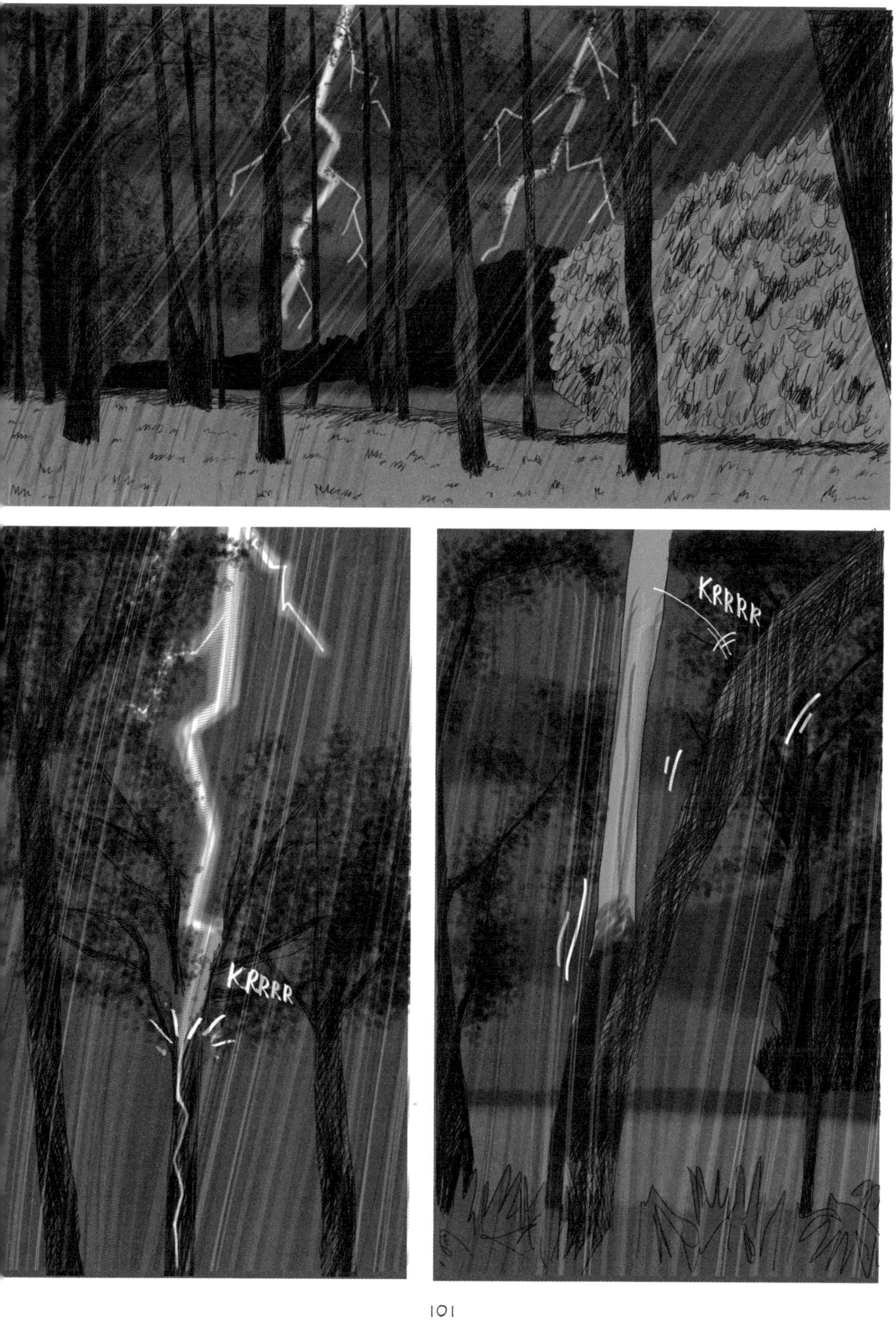
KRRRR
KRRRR

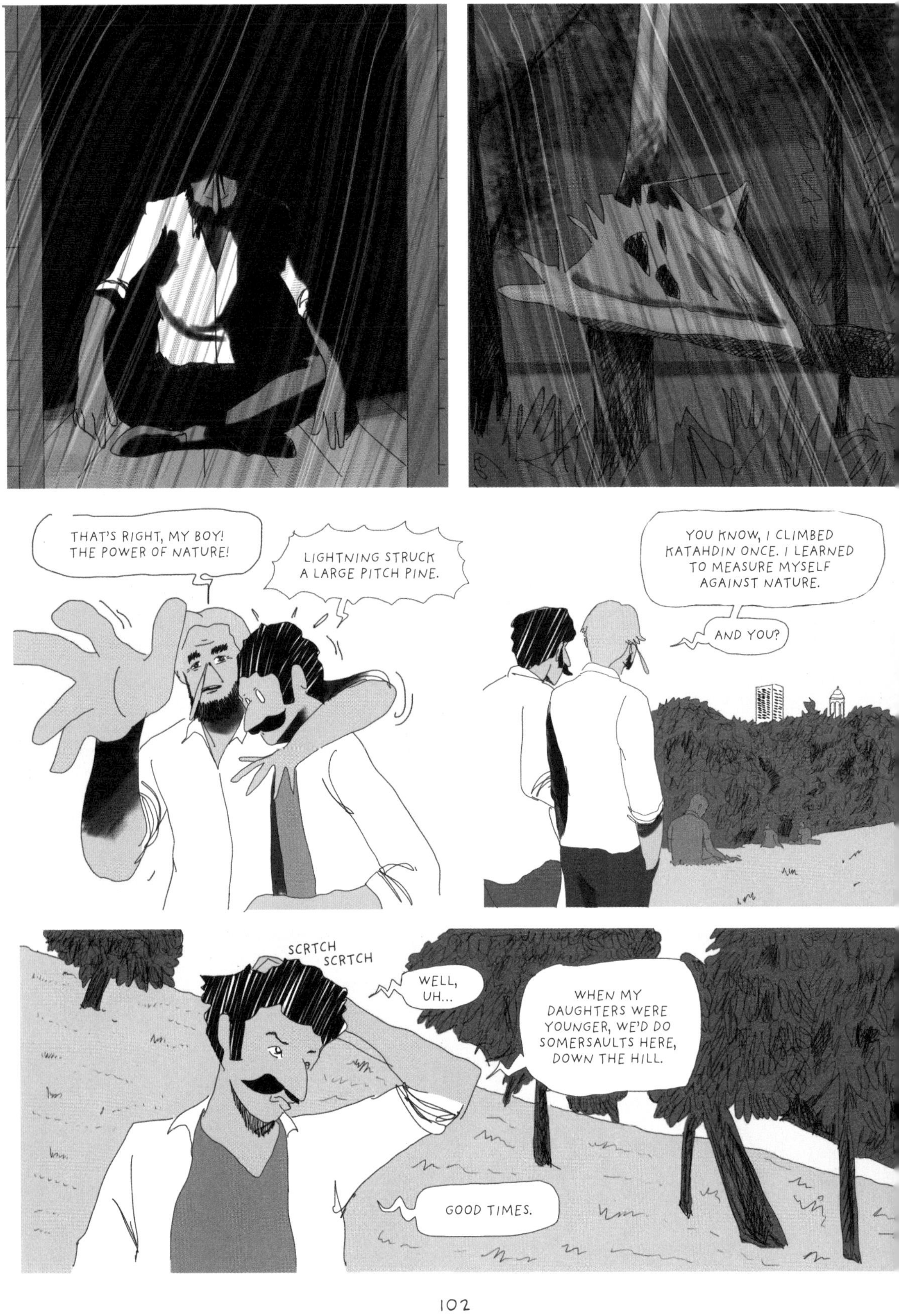
THAT'S RIGHT, MY BOY! THE POWER OF NATURE!
LIGHTNING STRUCK A LARGE PITCH PINE.
YOU KNOW, I CLIMBED KATAHDIN ONCE. I LEARNED TO MEASURE MYSELF AGAINST NATURE.
AND YOU?
SCRTCH SCRTCH
WELL, UH...
WHEN MY DAUGHTERS WERE YOUNGER, WE'D DO SOMERSAULTS HERE, DOWN THE HILL.
GOOD TIMES.

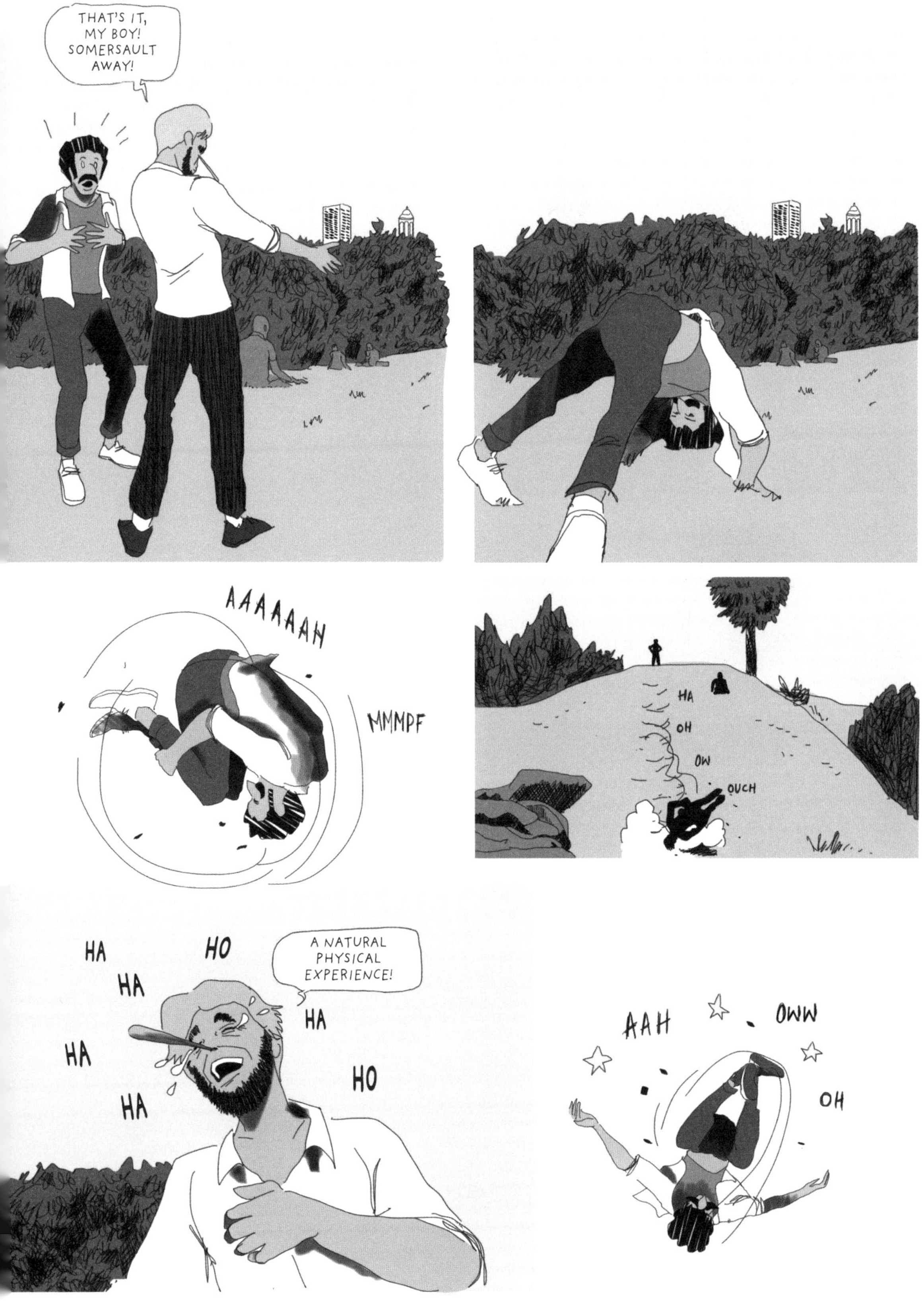
THAT'S IT, MY BOY! SOMERSAULT AWAY!
AAAAAAH
MMMPF
HA
OH
OW
OUCH
HA
HO
HA
HA
HA
A NATURAL PHYSICAL EXPERIENCE!
HA
HO
AAH
OWW
OH

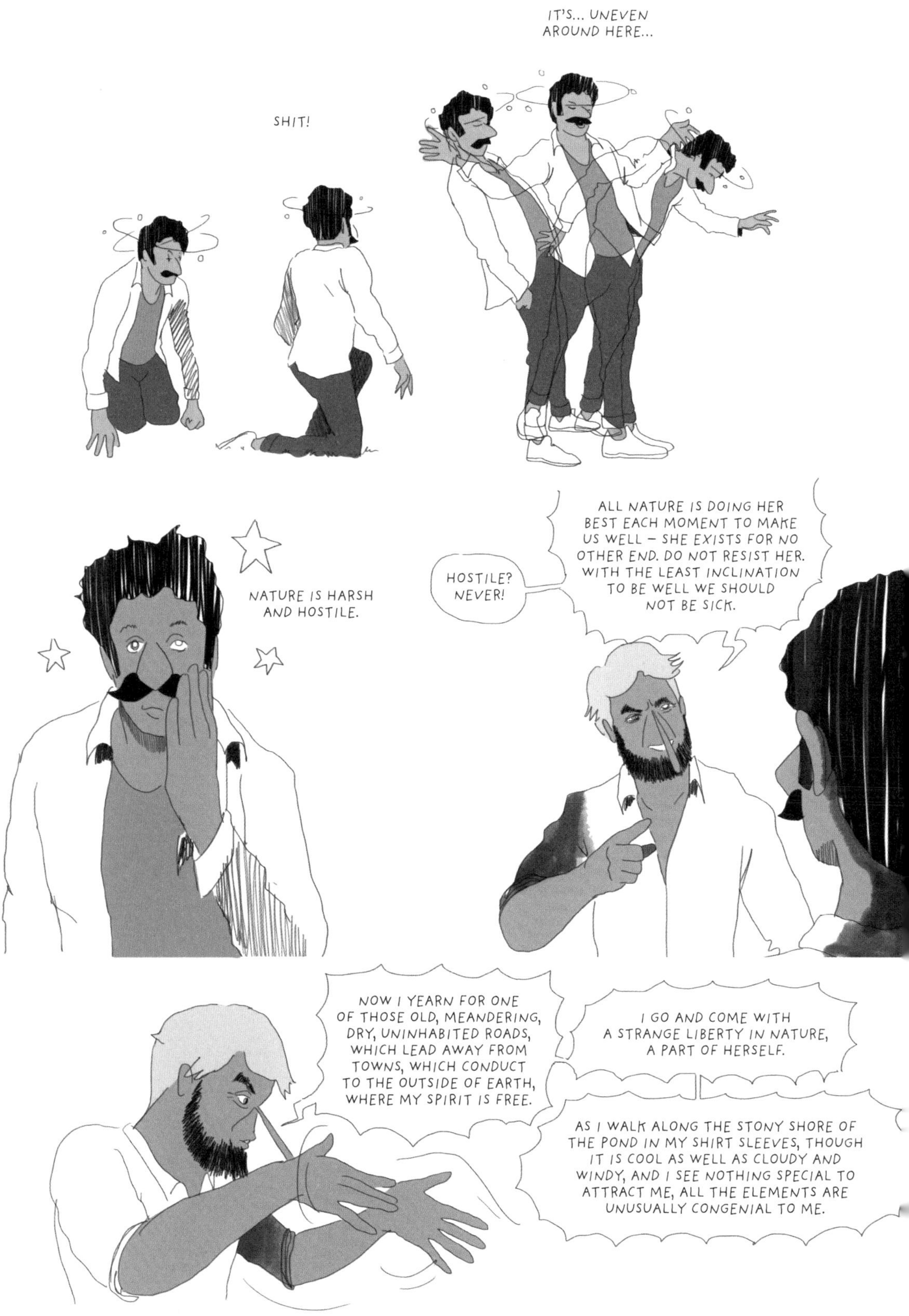

SHIT!
IT'S... UNEVEN AROUND HERE...
NATURE IS HARSH AND HOSTILE.
HOSTILE? NEVER!
ALL NATURE IS DOING HER BEST EACH MOMENT TO MAKE US WELL – SHE EXISTS FOR NO OTHER END. DO NOT RESIST HER. WITH THE LEAST INCLINATION TO BE WELL WE SHOULD NOT BE SICK.
NOW I YEARN FOR ONE OF THOSE OLD, MEANDERING, DRY, UNINHABITED ROADS, WHICH LEAD AWAY FROM TOWNS, WHICH CONDUCT TO THE OUTSIDE OF EARTH, WHERE MY SPIRIT IS FREE.
I GO AND COME WITH A STRANGE LIBERTY IN NATURE, A PART OF HERSELF.
AS I WALK ALONG THE STONY SHORE OF THE POND IN MY SHIRT SLEEVES, THOUGH IT IS COOL AS WELL AS CLOUDY AND WINDY, AND I SEE NOTHING SPECIAL TO ATTRACT ME, ALL THE ELEMENTS ARE UNUSUALLY CONGENIAL TO ME.

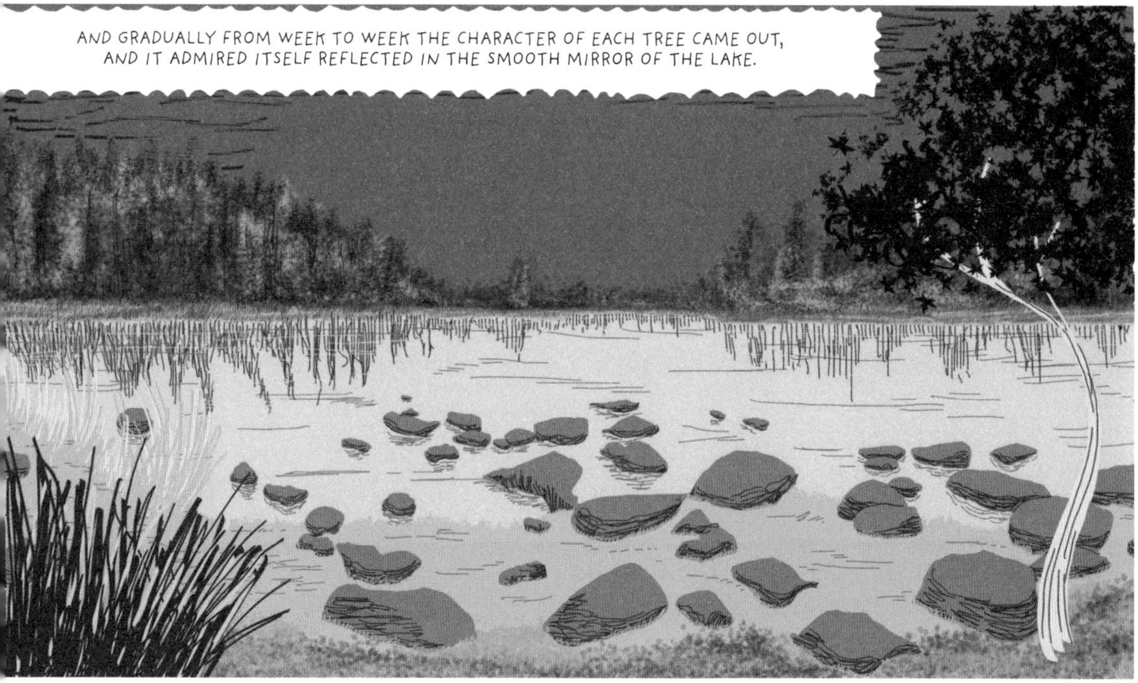
AND GRADUALLY FROM WEEK TO WEEK THE CHARACTER OF EACH TREE CAME OUT, AND IT ADMIRED ITSELF REFLECTED IN THE SMOOTH MIRROR OF THE LAKE.

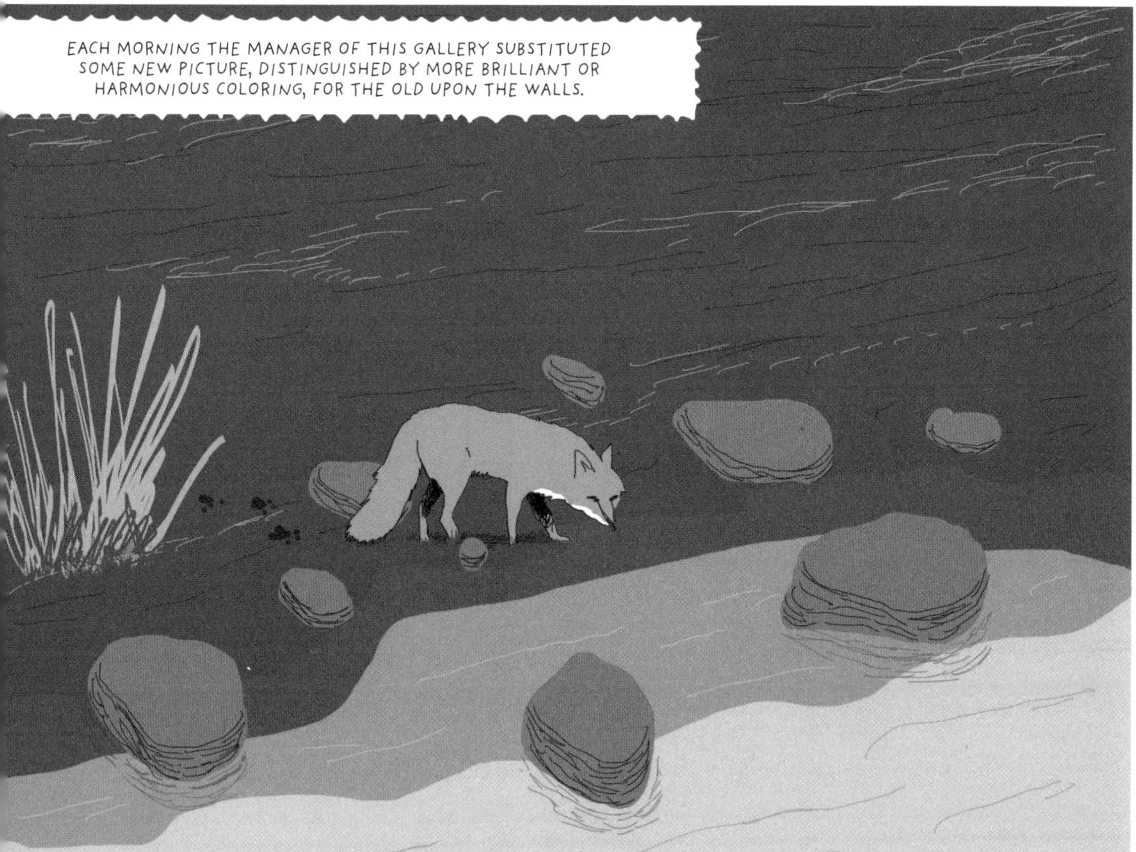
EACH MORNING THE MANAGER OF THIS GALLERY SUBSTITUTED SOME NEW PICTURE, DISTINGUISHED BY MORE BRILLIANT OR HARMONIOUS COLORING, FOR THE OLD UPON THE WALLS.

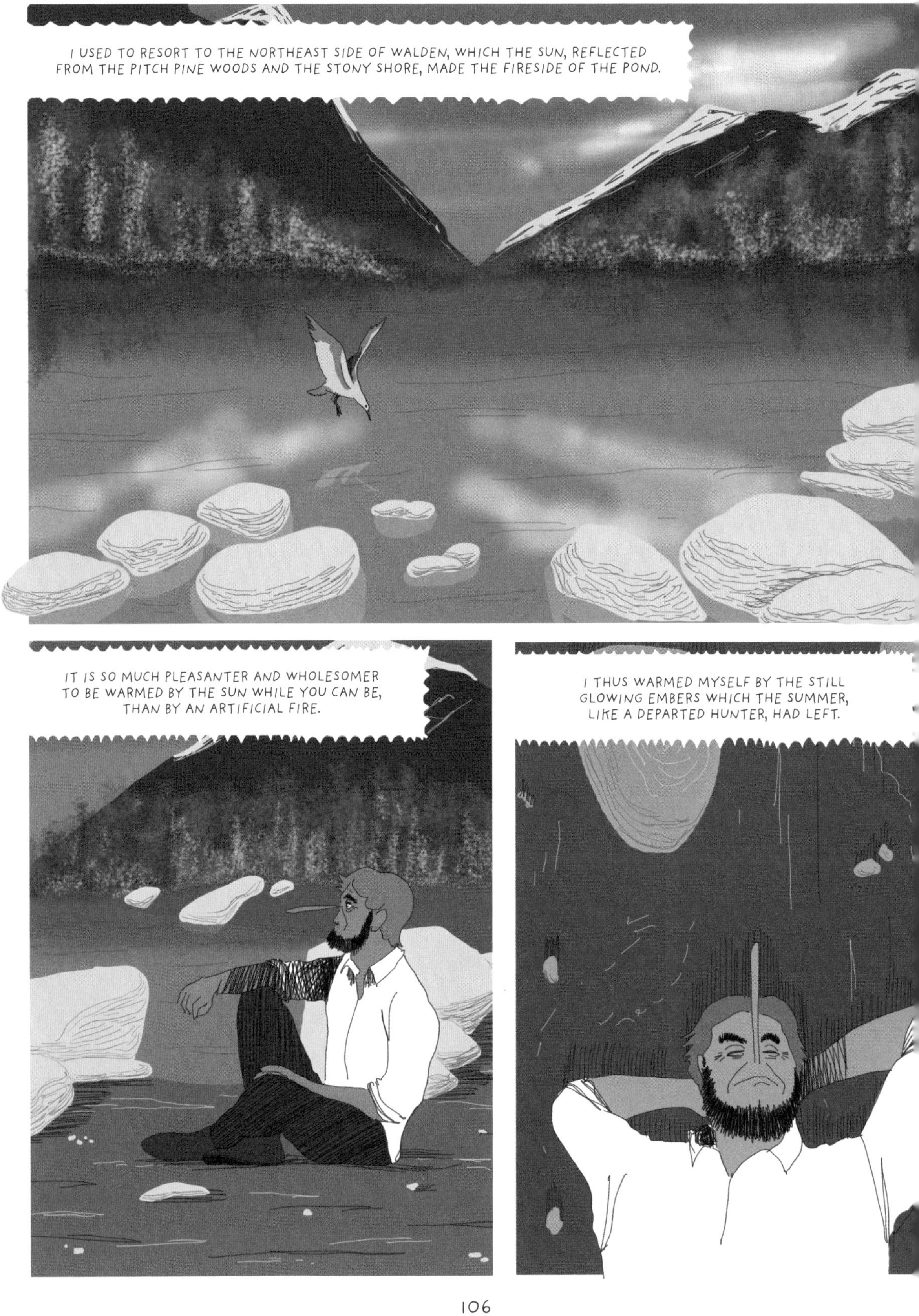
I USED TO RESORT TO THE NORTHEAST SIDE OF WALDEN, WHICH THE SUN, REFLECTED FROM THE PITCH PINE WOODS AND THE STONY SHORE, MADE THE FIRESIDE OF THE POND.
IT IS SO MUCH PLEASANTER AND WHOLESOMER TO BE WARMED BY THE SUN WHILE YOU CAN BE, THAN BY AN ARTIFICIAL FIRE.
I THUS WARMED MYSELF BY THE STILL GLOWING EMBERS WHICH THE SUMMER, LIKE A DEPARTED HUNTER, HAD LEFT.

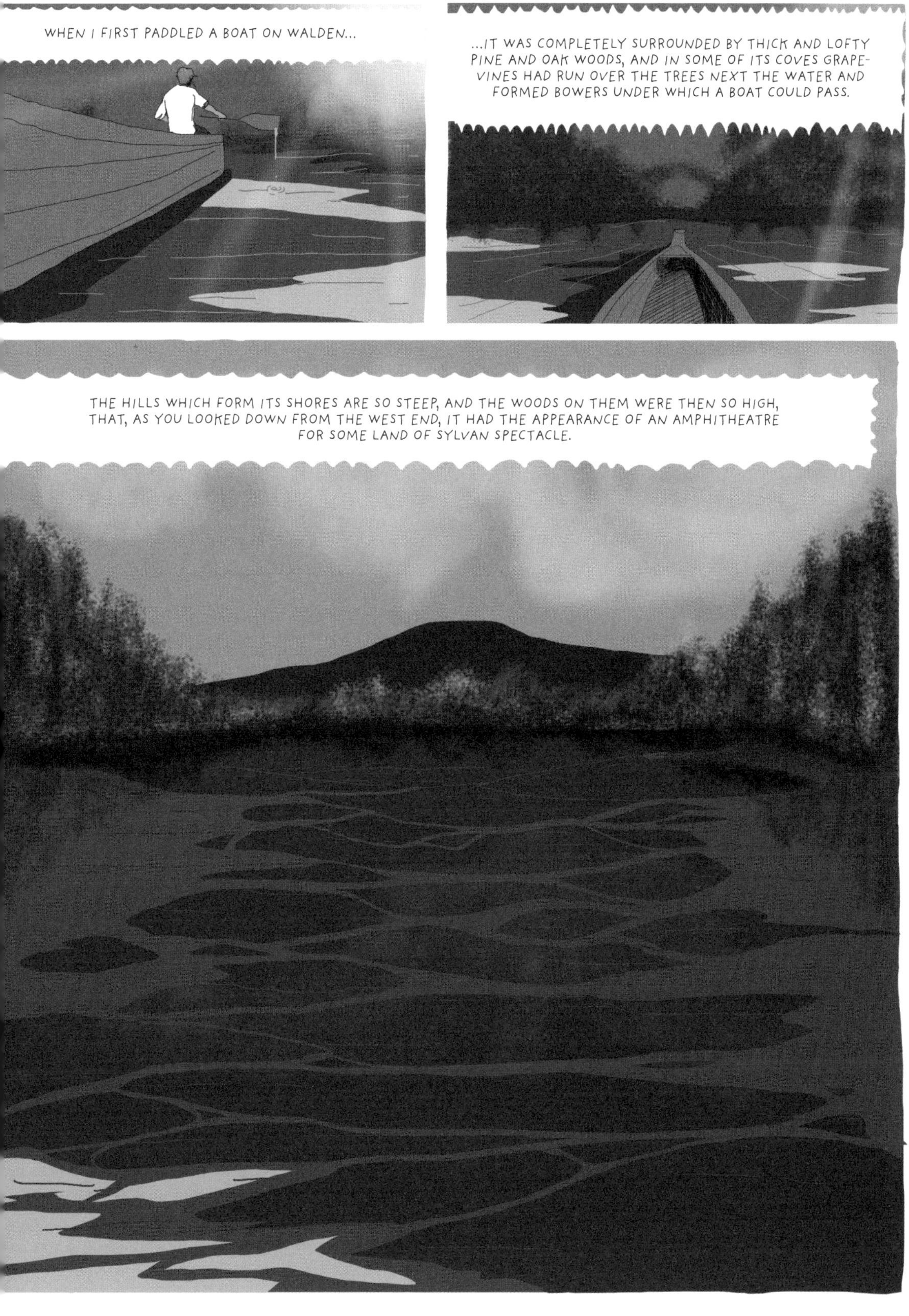
WHEN I FIRST PADDLED A BOAT ON WALDEN...
...IT WAS COMPLETELY SURROUNDED BY THICK AND LOFTY PINE AND OAK WOODS, AND IN SOME OF ITS COVES GRAPE-VINES HAD RUN OVER THE TREES NEXT THE WATER AND FORMED BOWERS UNDER WHICH A BOAT COULD PASS.
THE HILLS WHICH FORM ITS SHORES ARE SO STEEP, AND THE WOODS ON THEM WERE THEN SO HIGH, THAT, AS YOU LOOKED DOWN FROM THE WEST END, IT HAD THE APPEARANCE OF AN AMPHITHEATRE FOR SOME LAND OF SYLVAN SPECTACLE.

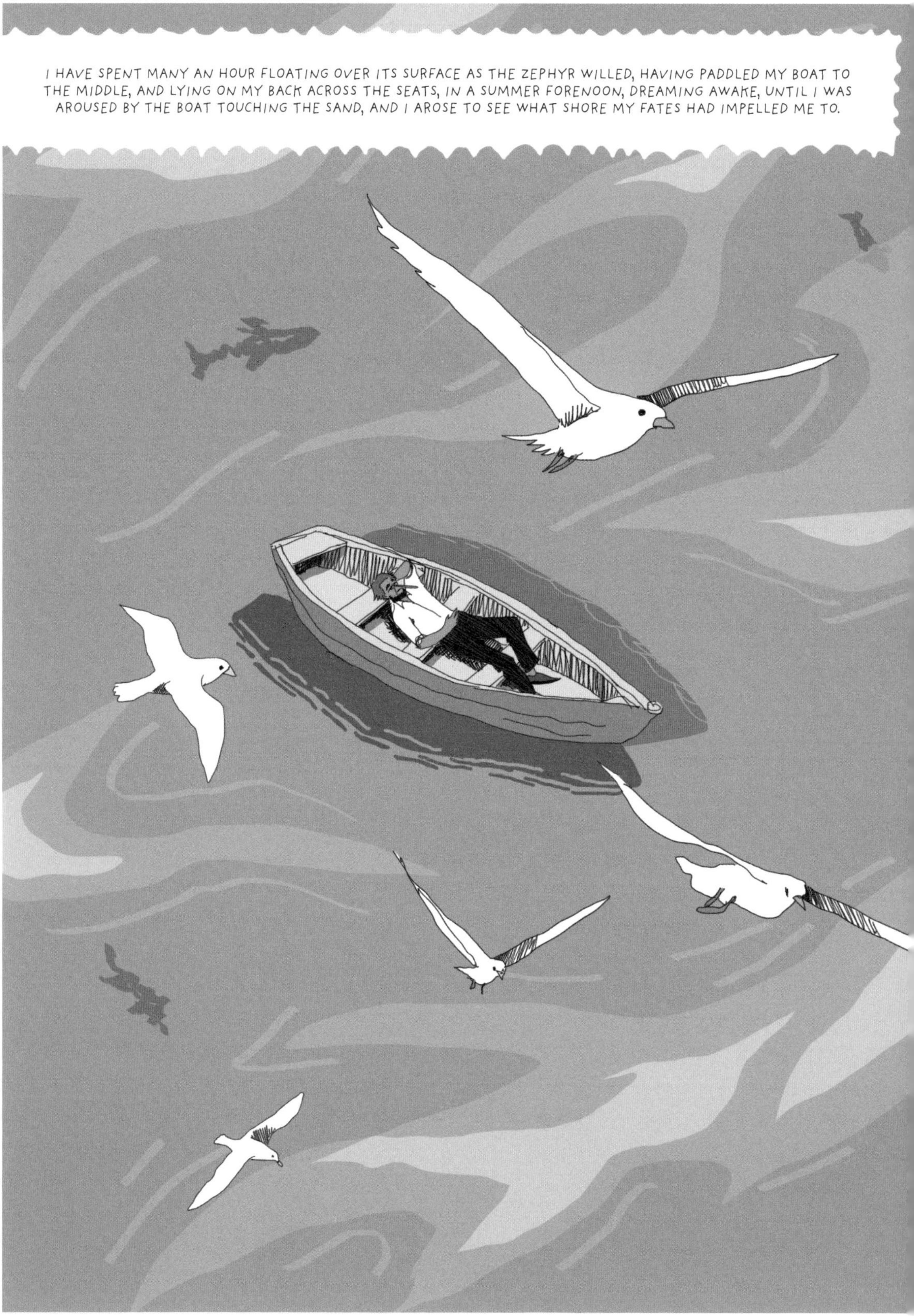
I HAVE SPENT MANY AN HOUR FLOATING OVER ITS SURFACE AS THE ZEPHYR WILLED, HAVING PADDLED MY BOAT TO THE MIDDLE, AND LYING ON MY BACK ACROSS THE SEATS, IN A SUMMER FORENOON, DREAMING AWAKE, UNTIL I WAS AROUSED BY THE BOAT TOUCHING THE SAND, AND I AROSE TO SEE WHAT SHORE MY FATES HAD IMPELLED ME TO.

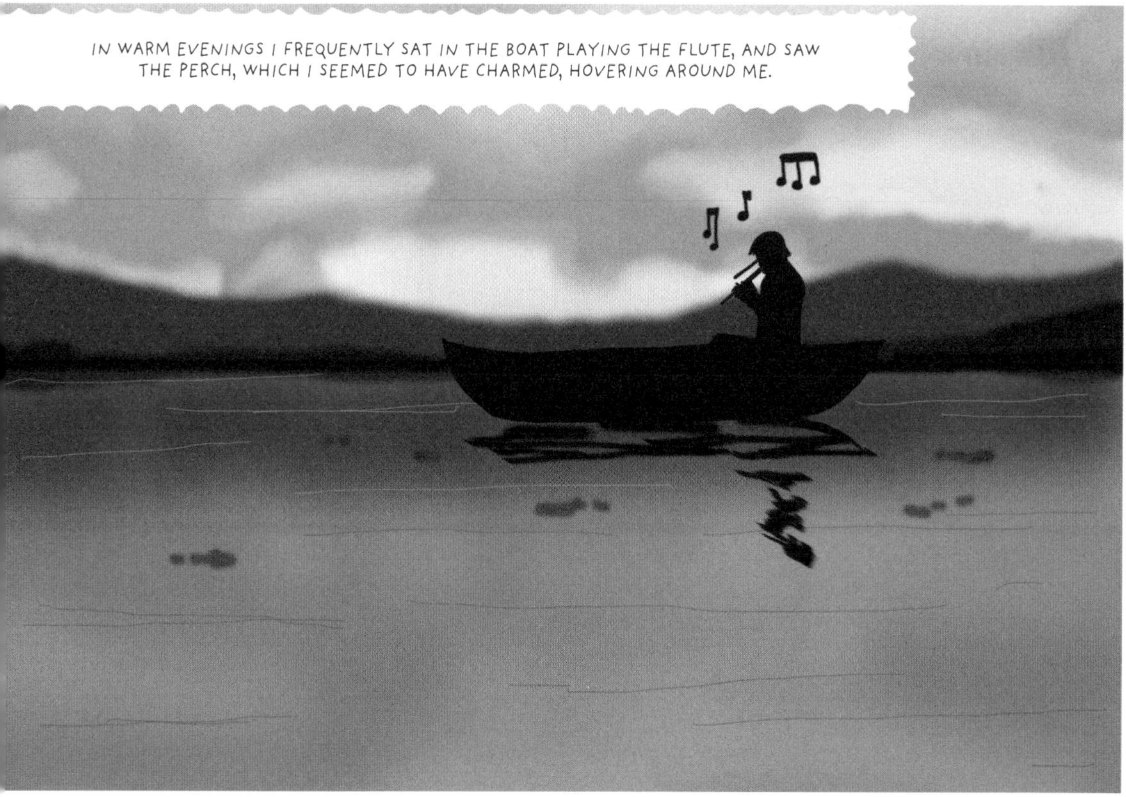
IN WARM EVENINGS I FREQUENTLY SAT IN THE BOAT PLAYING THE FLUTE, AND SAW THE PERCH, WHICH I SEEMED TO HAVE CHARMED, HOVERING AROUND ME.

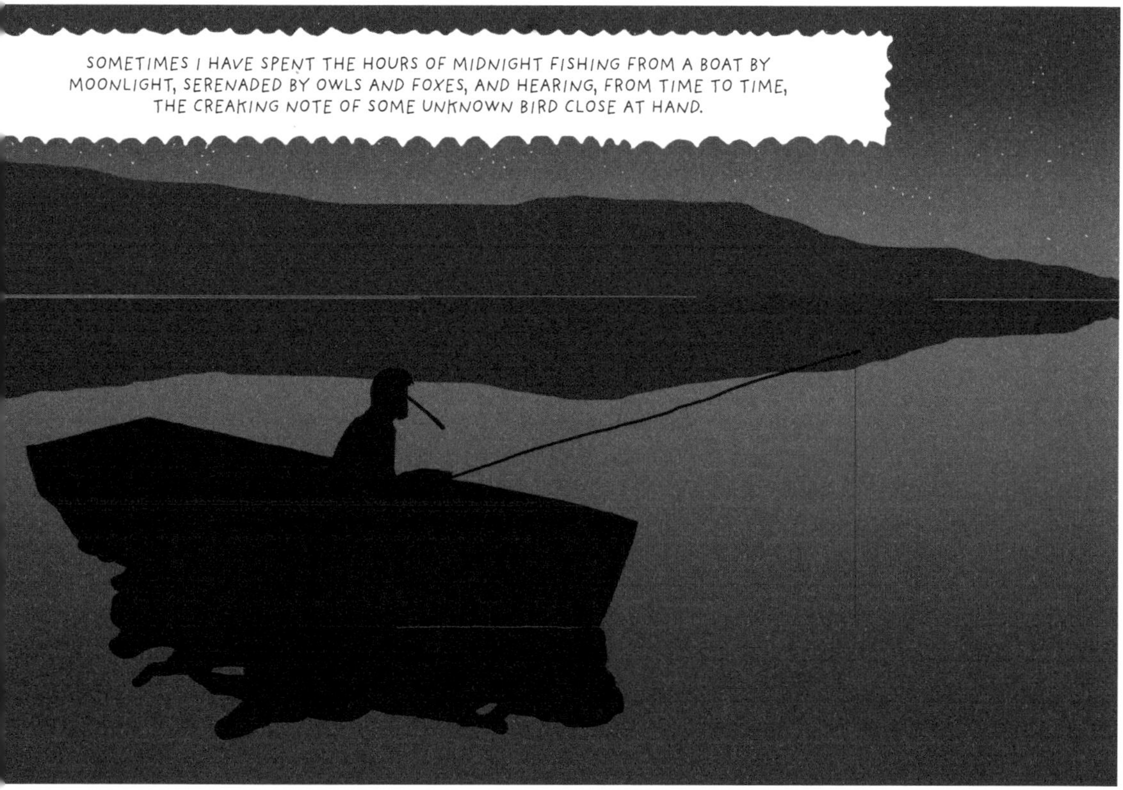
SOMETIMES I HAVE SPENT THE HOURS OF MIDNIGHT FISHING FROM A BOAT BY MOONLIGHT, SERENADED BY OWLS AND FOXES, AND HEARING, FROM TIME TO TIME, THE CREAKING NOTE OF SOME UNKNOWN BIRD CLOSE AT HAND.

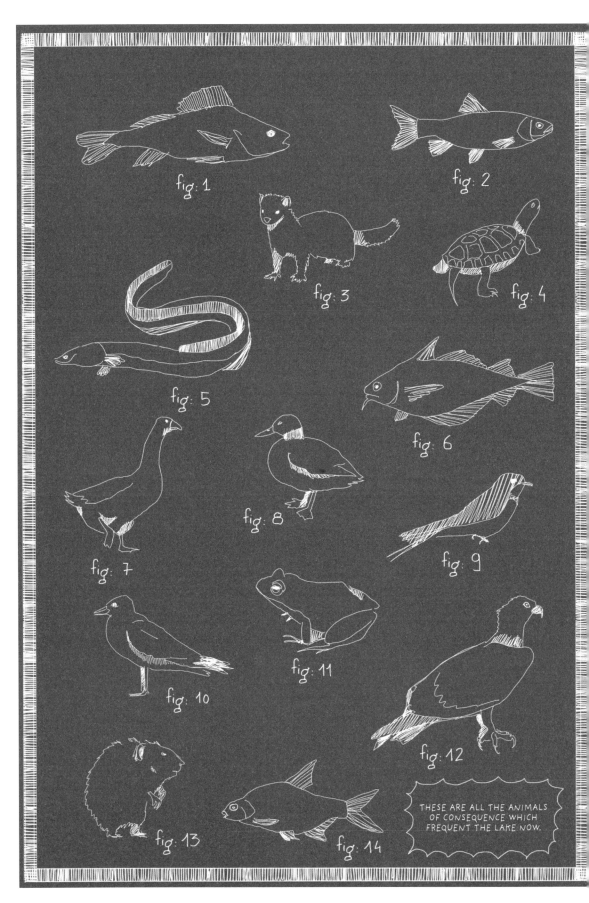

fig: 1

fig: 2

fig: 3

fig: 4

fig: 5

fig: 6

fig: 7

fig: 8

fig: 9

fig: 10

fig: 11

fig: 12

fig: 13

fig: 14

THESE ARE ALL THE ANIMALS OF CONSEQUENCE WHICH FREQUENT THE LAKE NOW.

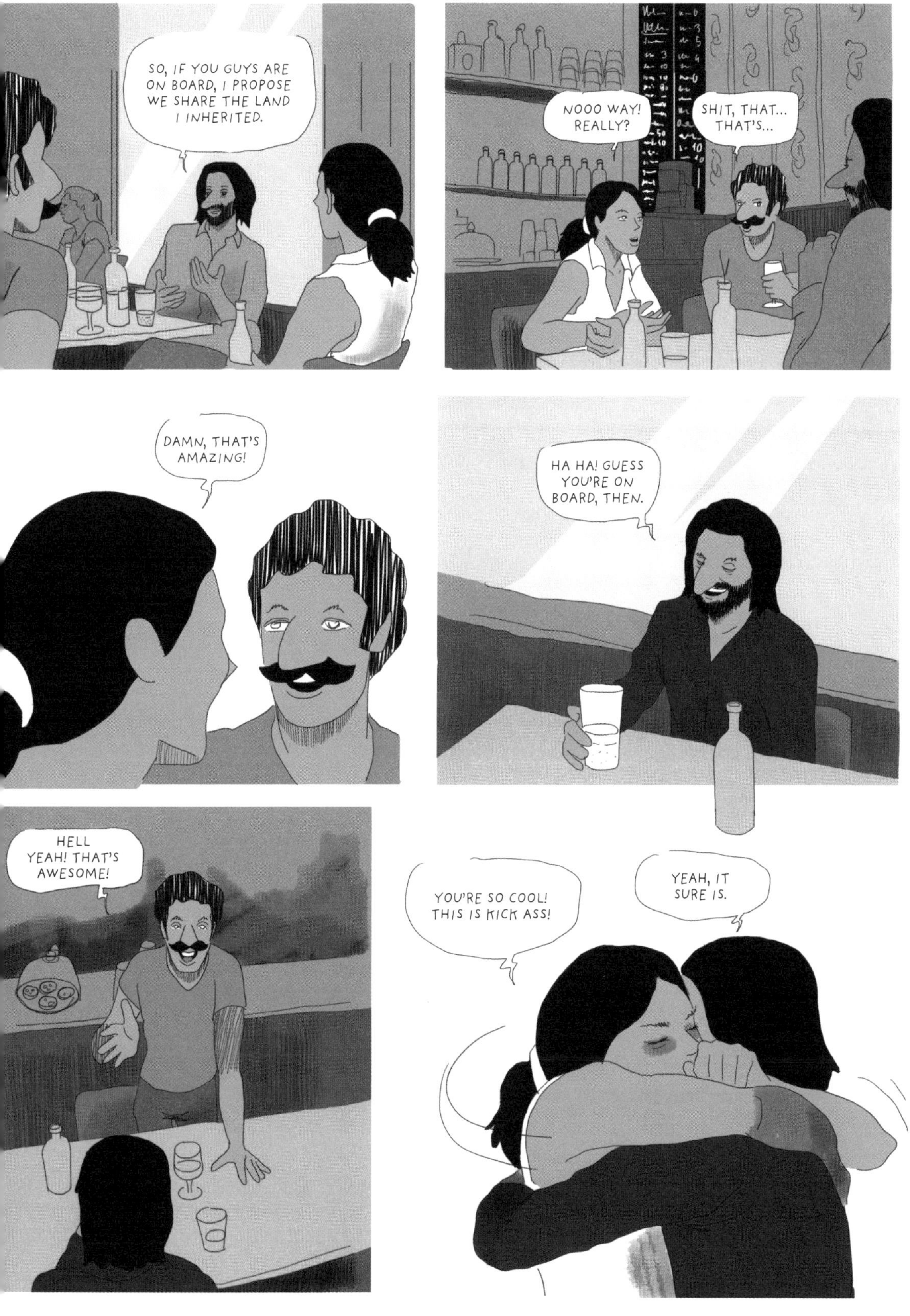
SO, IF YOU GUYS ARE ON BOARD, I PROPOSE WE SHARE THE LAND I INHERITED.
NOOO WAY! REALLY?
SHIT, THAT... THAT'S...
DAMN, THAT'S AMAZING!
HA HA! GUESS YOU'RE ON BOARD, THEN.
HELL YEAH! THAT'S AWESOME!
YOU'RE SO COOL! THIS IS KICK ASS!
YEAH, IT SURE IS.

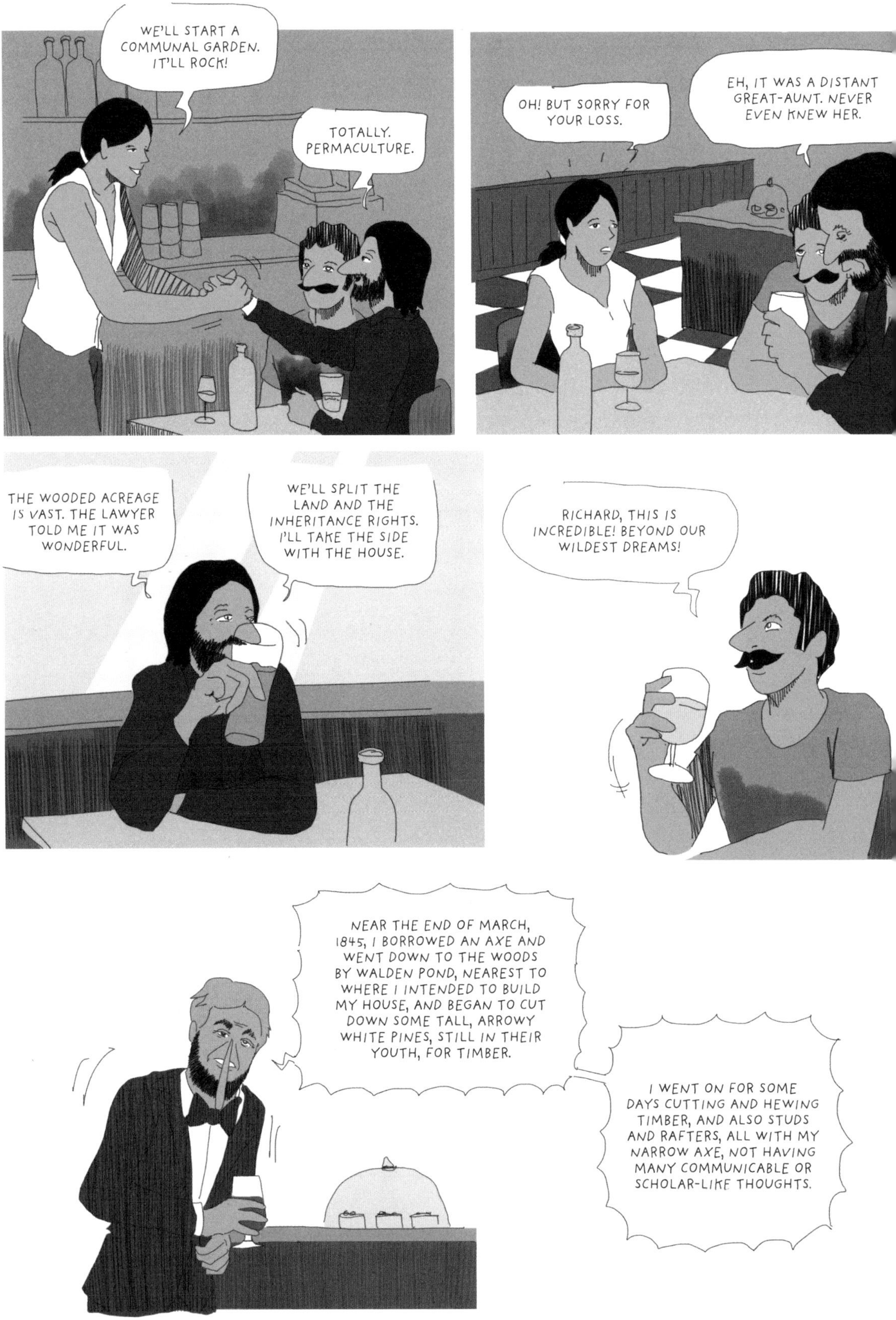
WE'LL START A COMMUNAL GARDEN. IT'LL ROCK!
TOTALLY. PERMACULTURE.
OH! BUT SORRY FOR YOUR LOSS.
EH, IT WAS A DISTANT GREAT-AUNT. NEVER EVEN KNEW HER.
THE WOODED ACREAGE IS VAST. THE LAWYER TOLD ME IT WAS WONDERFUL.
WE'LL SPLIT THE LAND AND THE INHERITANCE RIGHTS. I'LL TAKE THE SIDE WITH THE HOUSE.
RICHARD, THIS IS INCREDIBLE! BEYOND OUR WILDEST DREAMS!
NEAR THE END OF MARCH, 1845, I BORROWED AN AXE AND WENT DOWN TO THE WOODS BY WALDEN POND, NEAREST TO WHERE I INTENDED TO BUILD MY HOUSE, AND BEGAN TO CUT DOWN SOME TALL, ARROWY WHITE PINES, STILL IN THEIR YOUTH, FOR TIMBER.
I WENT ON FOR SOME DAYS CUTTING AND HEWING TIMBER, AND ALSO STUDS AND RAFTERS, ALL WITH MY NARROW AXE, NOT HAVING MANY COMMUNICABLE OR SCHOLAR-LIKE THOUGHTS.

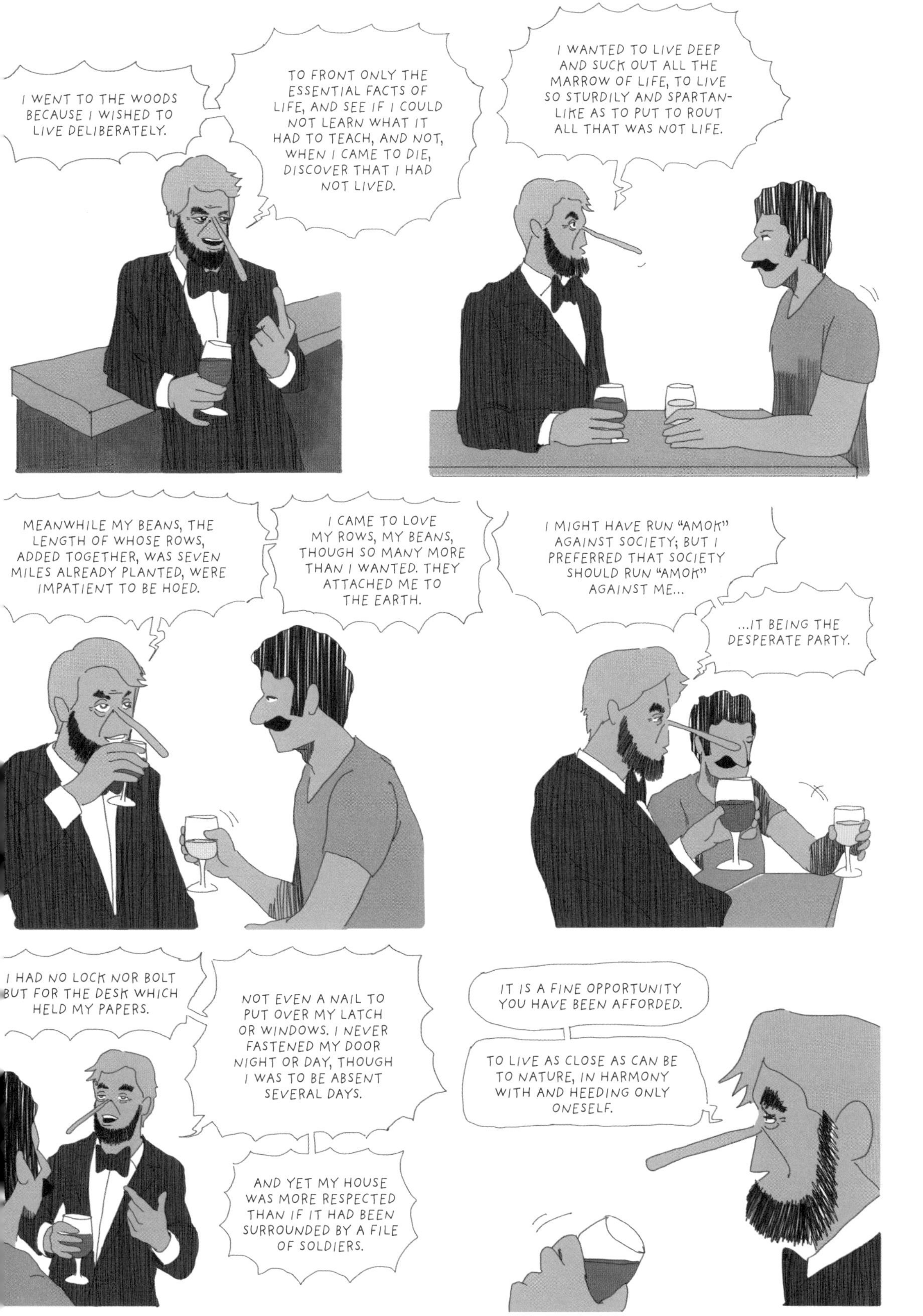
I WENT TO THE WOODS BECAUSE I WISHED TO LIVE DELIBERATELY.
TO FRONT ONLY THE ESSENTIAL FACTS OF LIFE, AND SEE IF I COULD NOT LEARN WHAT IT HAD TO TEACH, AND NOT, WHEN I CAME TO DIE, DISCOVER THAT I HAD NOT LIVED.
I WANTED TO LIVE DEEP AND SUCK OUT ALL THE MARROW OF LIFE, TO LIVE SO STURDILY AND SPARTAN-LIKE AS TO PUT TO ROUT ALL THAT WAS NOT LIFE.
MEANWHILE MY BEANS, THE LENGTH OF WHOSE ROWS, ADDED TOGETHER, WAS SEVEN MILES ALREADY PLANTED, WERE IMPATIENT TO BE HOED.
I CAME TO LOVE MY ROWS, MY BEANS, THOUGH SO MANY MORE THAN I WANTED. THEY ATTACHED ME TO THE EARTH.
I MIGHT HAVE RUN "AMOK" AGAINST SOCIETY; BUT I PREFERRED THAT SOCIETY SHOULD RUN "AMOK" AGAINST ME...
...IT BEING THE DESPERATE PARTY.
I HAD NO LOCK NOR BOLT BUT FOR THE DESK WHICH HELD MY PAPERS.
NOT EVEN A NAIL TO PUT OVER MY LATCH OR WINDOWS. I NEVER FASTENED MY DOOR NIGHT OR DAY, THOUGH I WAS TO BE ABSENT SEVERAL DAYS.
AND YET MY HOUSE WAS MORE RESPECTED THAN IF IT HAD BEEN SURROUNDED BY A FILE OF SOLDIERS.
IT IS A FINE OPPORTUNITY YOU HAVE BEEN AFFORDED.
TO LIVE AS CLOSE AS CAN BE TO NATURE, IN HARMONY WITH AND HEEDING ONLY ONESELF.

LATER...

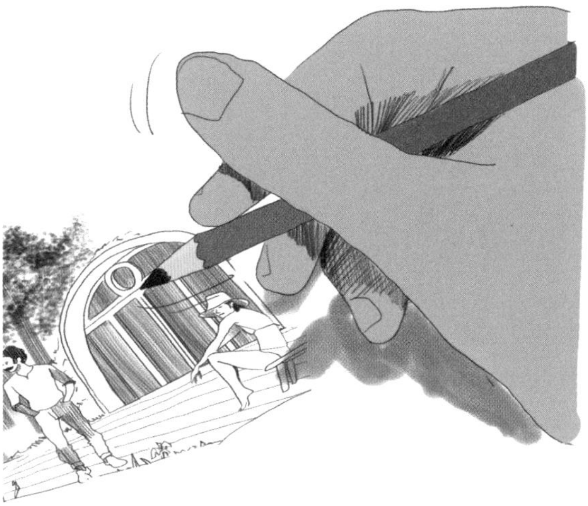

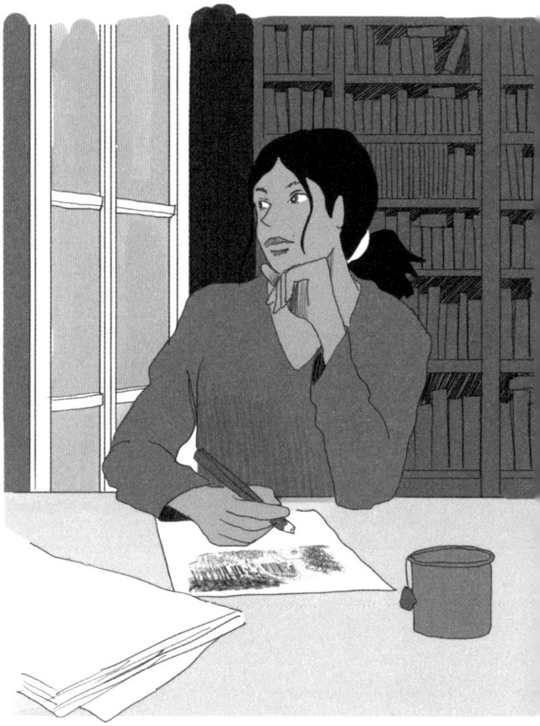

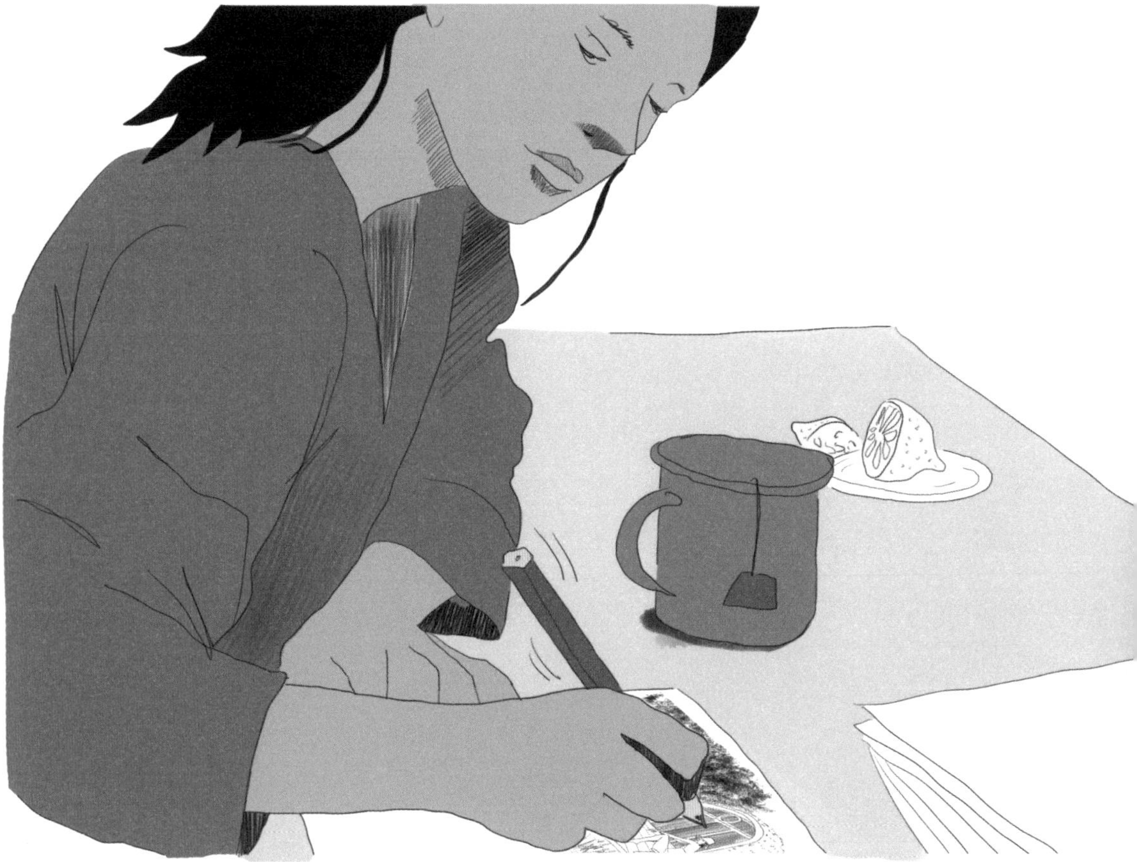

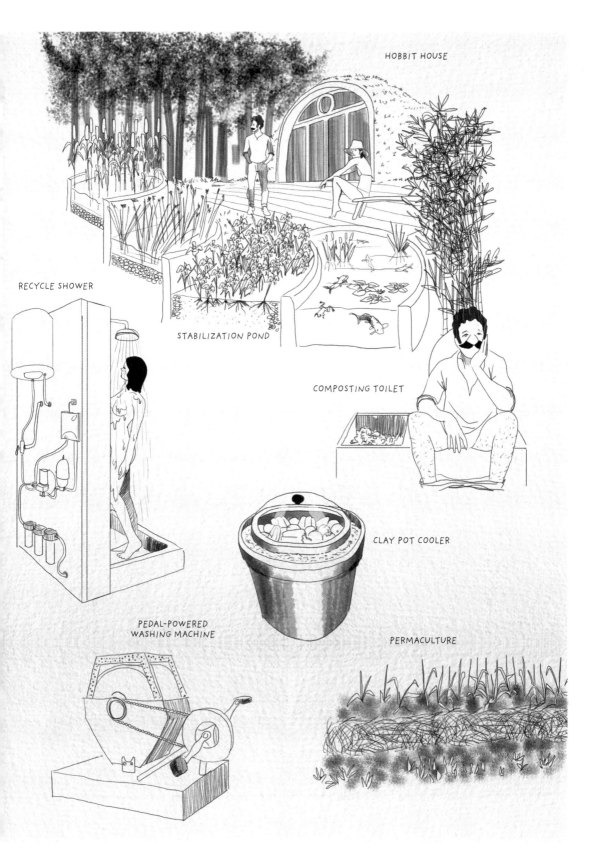

HOBBIT HOUSE

RECYCLE SHOWER

STABILIZATION POND

COMPOSTING TOILET

CLAY POT COOLER

PEDAL-POWERED
WASHING MACHINE

PERMACULTURE

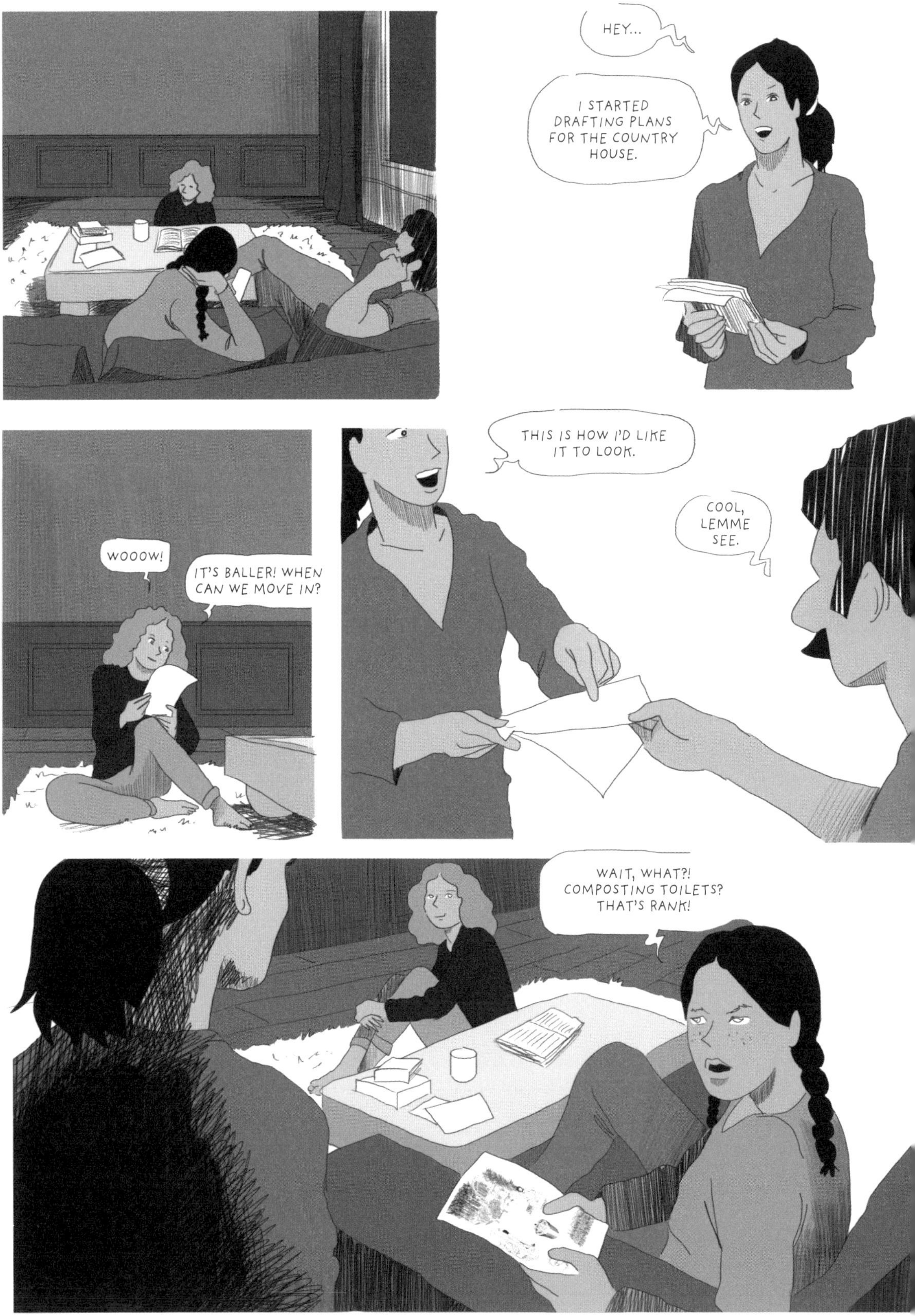
HEY...
I STARTED DRAFTING PLANS FOR THE COUNTRY HOUSE.
WOOOW!
IT'S BALLER! WHEN CAN WE MOVE IN?
THIS IS HOW I'D LIKE IT TO LOOK.
COOL, LEMME SEE.
WAIT, WHAT?! COMPOSTING TOILETS? THAT'S RANK!

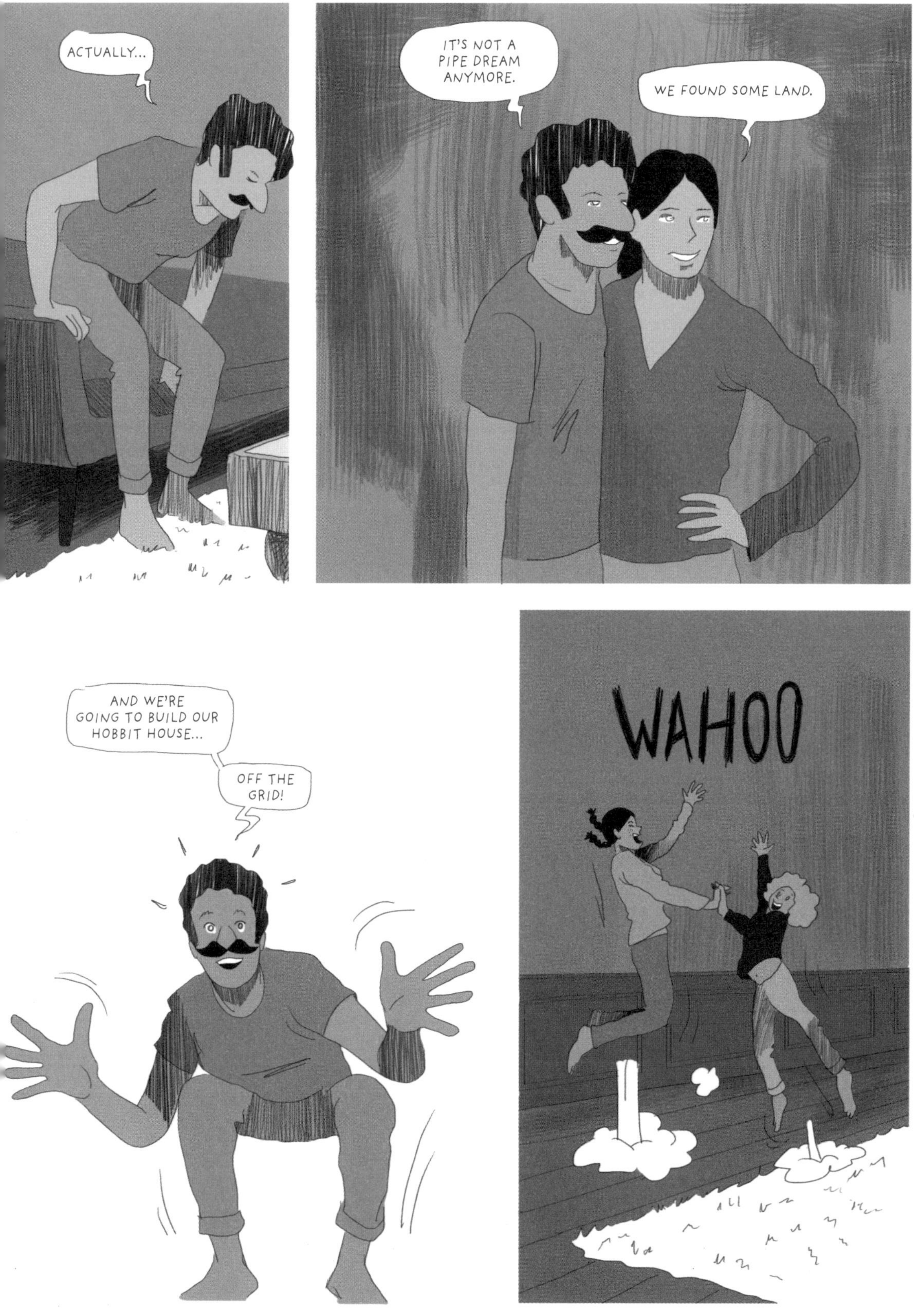
ACTUALLY...
IT'S NOT A PIPE DREAM ANYMORE.
WE FOUND SOME LAND.
AND WE'RE GOING TO BUILD OUR HOBBIT HOUSE...
OFF THE GRID!
WAHOO

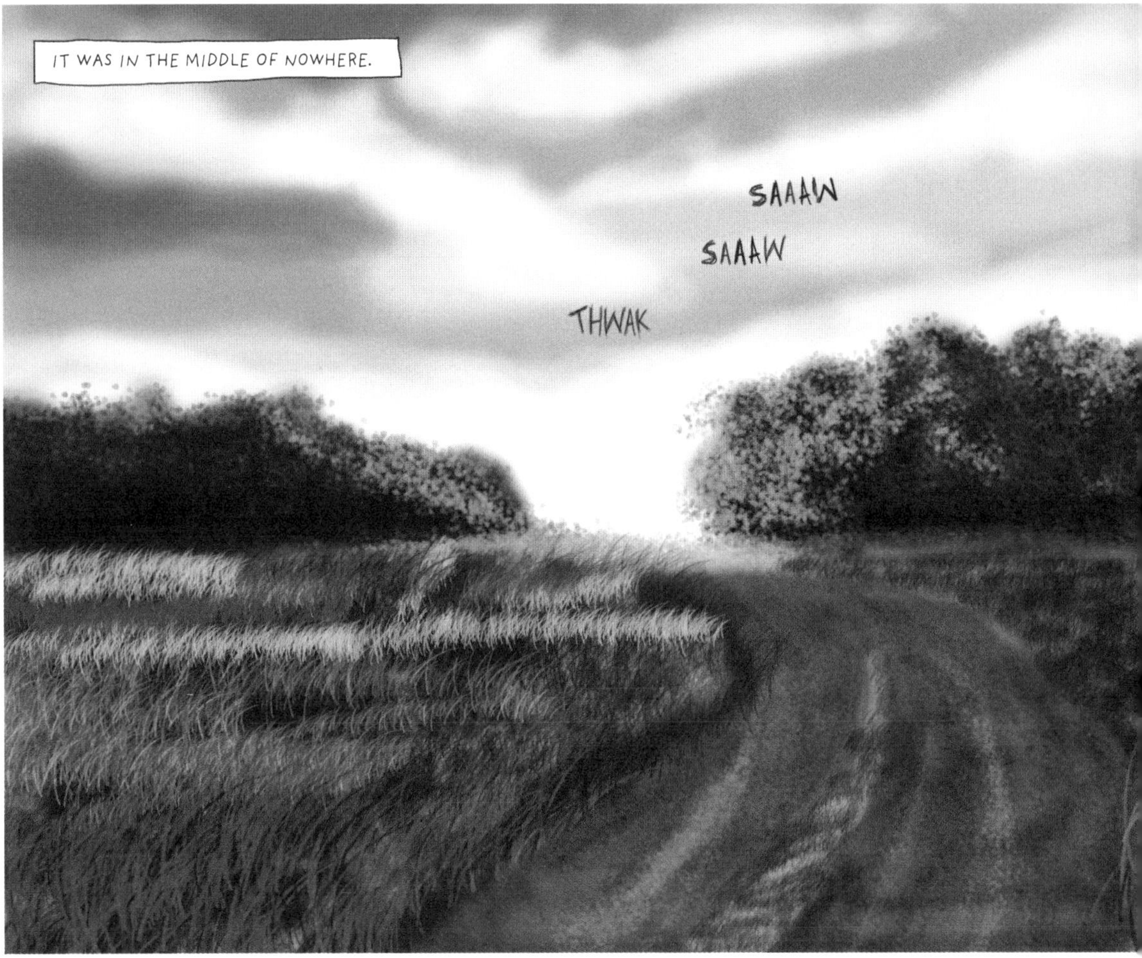
IT WAS IN THE MIDDLE OF NOWHERE.
SAAAW
SAAAW
THWAK

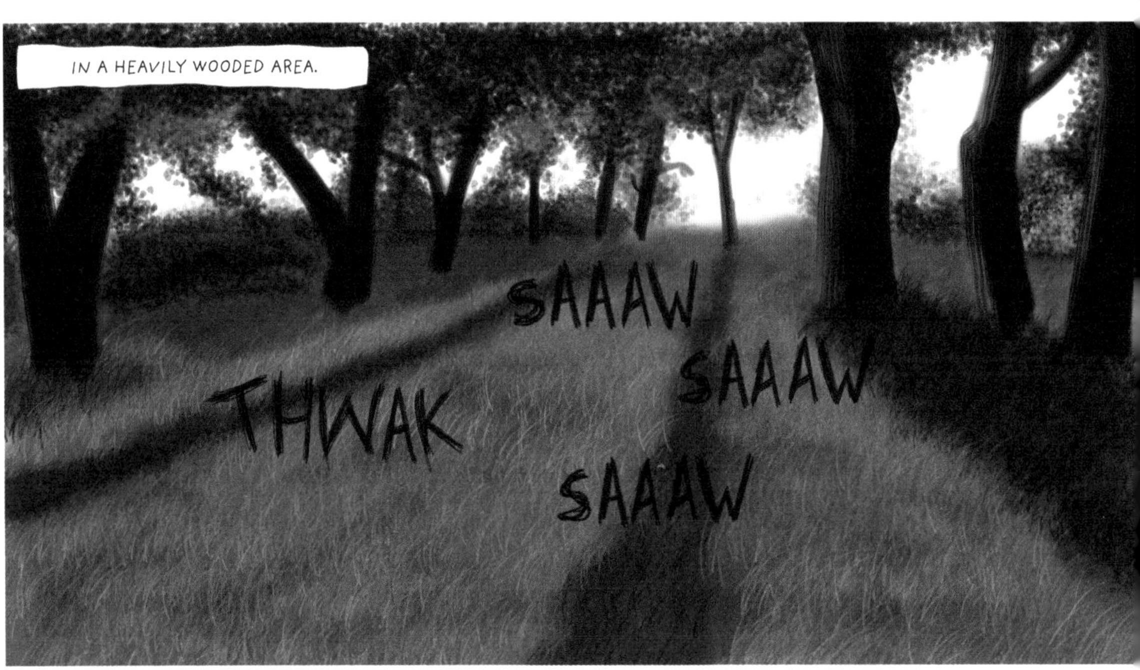
IN A HEAVILY WOODED AREA.
SAAAW
SAAAW
THWAK
SAAAW

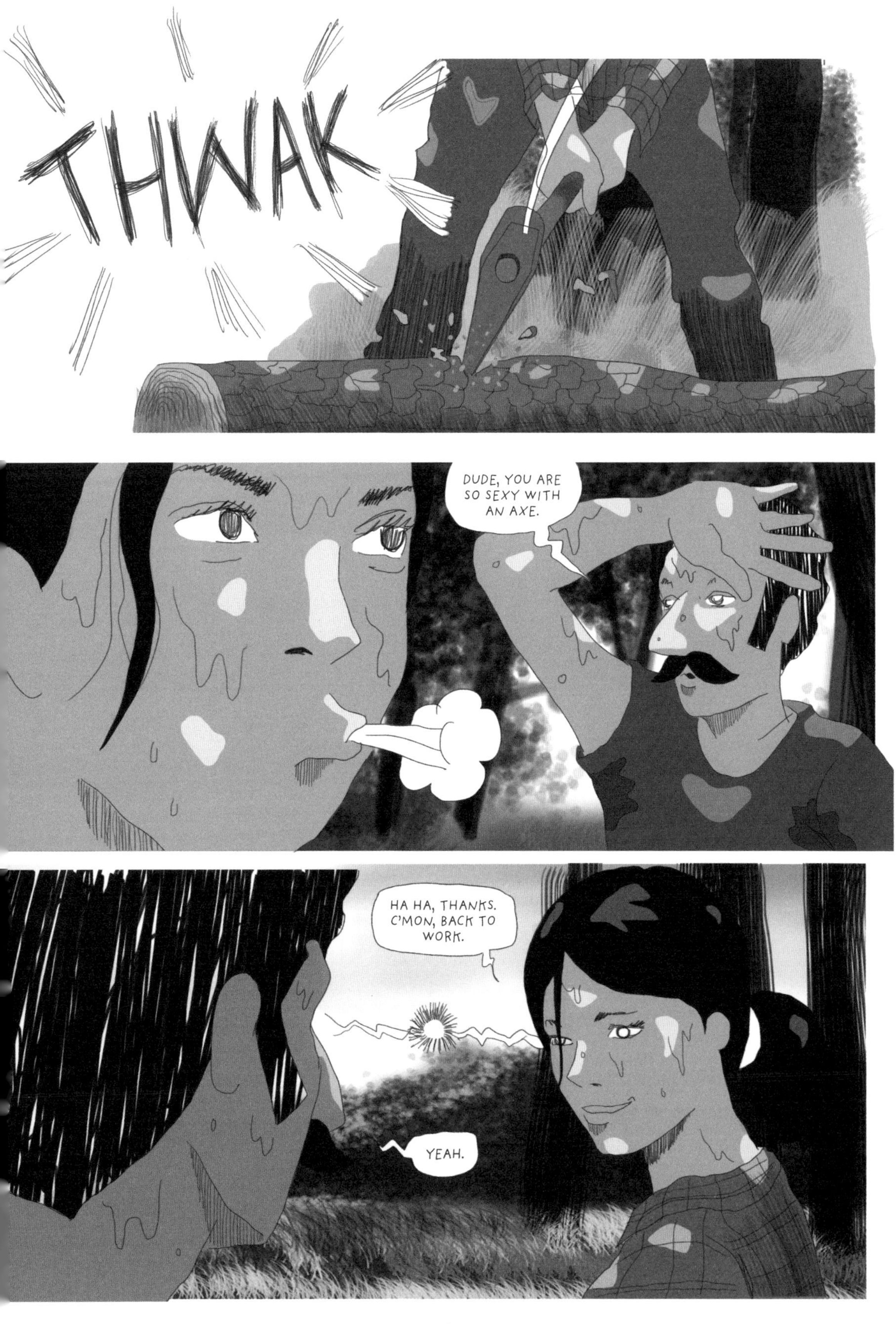
THWAK
DUDE, YOU ARE SO SEXY WITH AN AXE.
HA HA, THANKS. C'MON, BACK TO WORK.
YEAH.

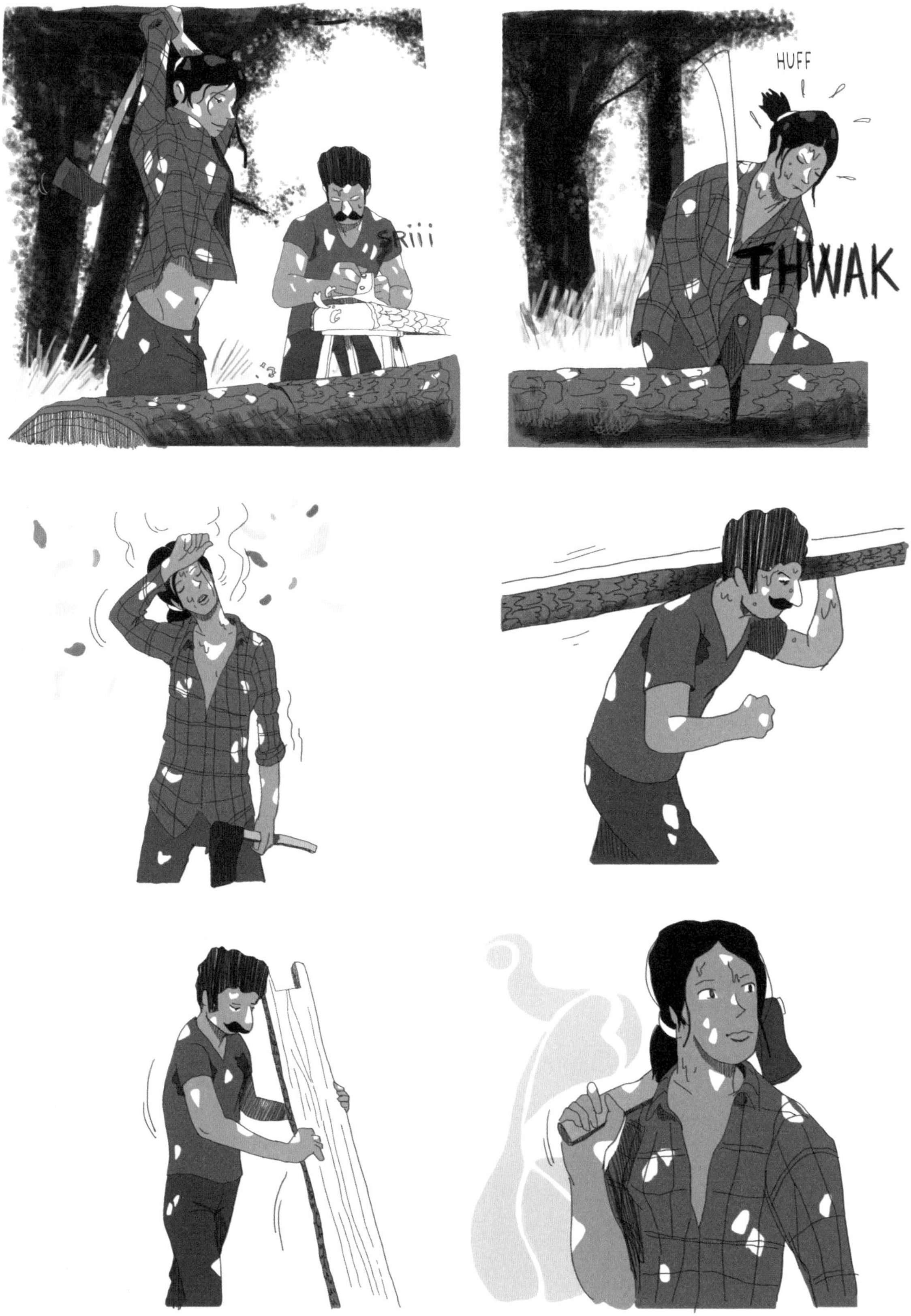
SRiii
HUFF
THWAK

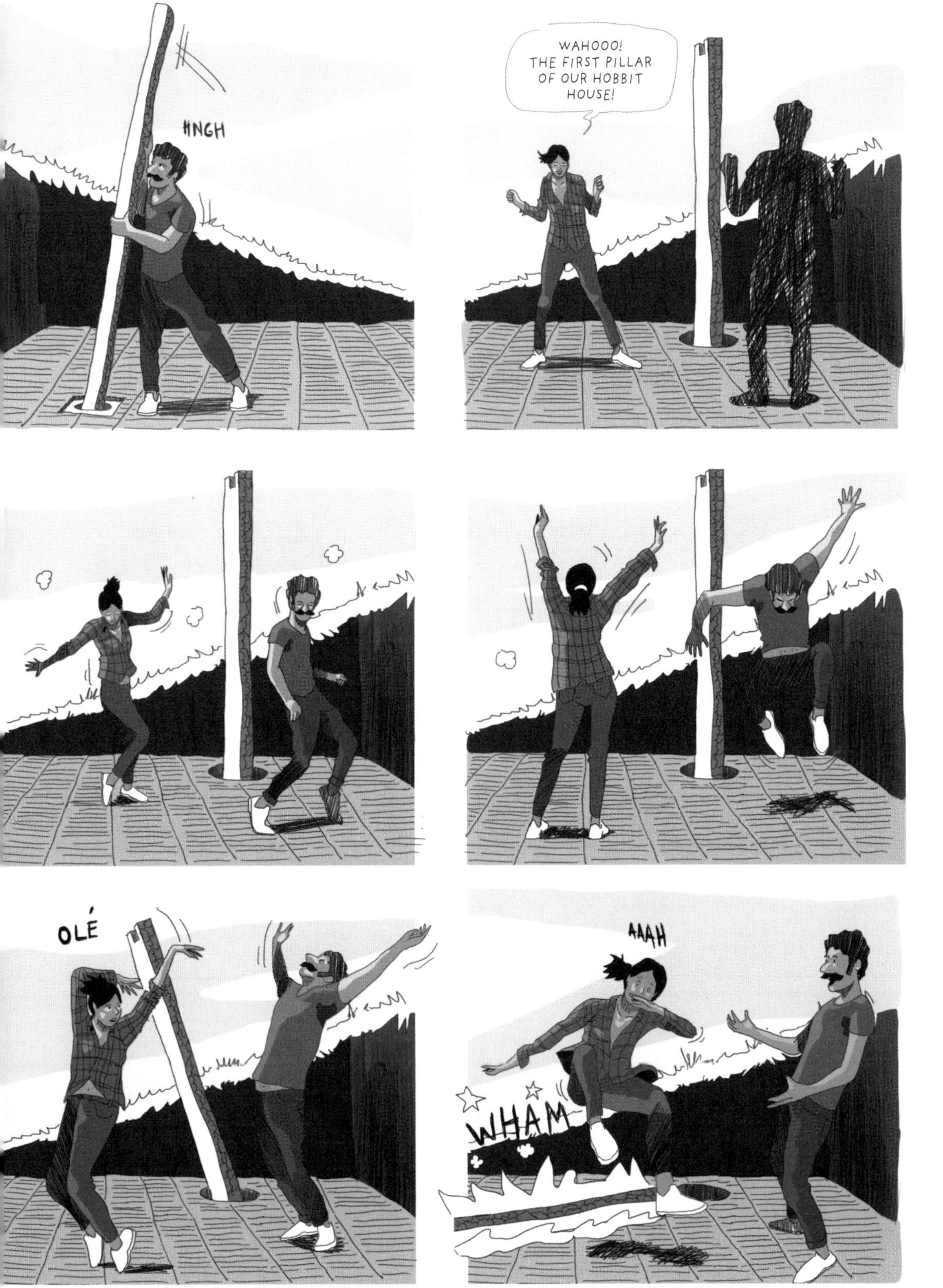
HNGH
WAHOOO! THE FIRST PILLAR OF OUR HOBBIT HOUSE!
OLÉ
AAAH
WHAM

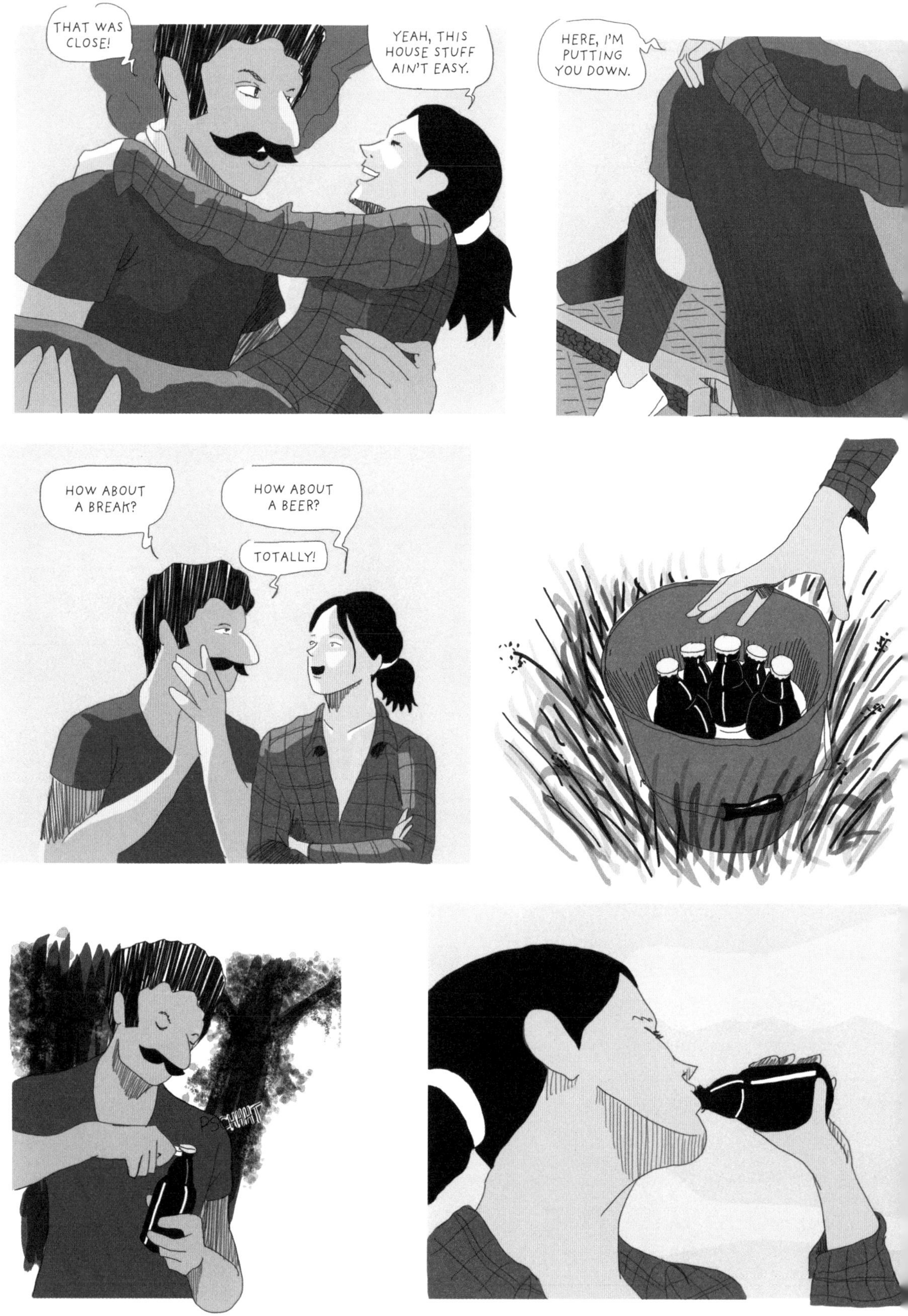
THAT WAS CLOSE!
YEAH, THIS HOUSE STUFF AIN'T EASY.
HERE, I'M PUTTING YOU DOWN.
HOW ABOUT A BREAK?
HOW ABOUT A BEER?
TOTALLY!
PSCHHT

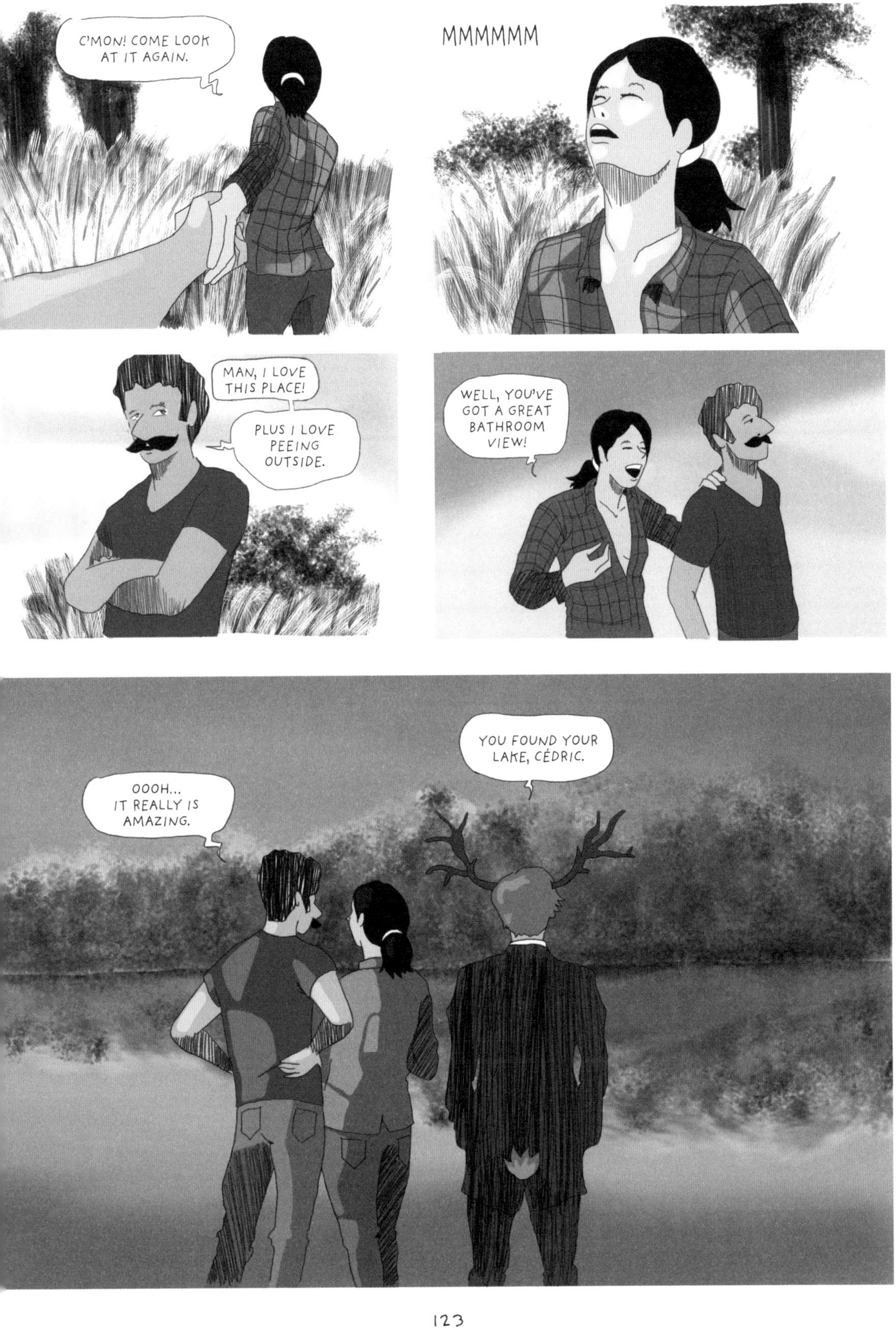
C'MON! COME LOOK AT IT AGAIN.
MMMMMM
MAN, I LOVE THIS PLACE!
PLUS I LOVE PEEING OUTSIDE.
WELL, YOU'VE GOT A GREAT BATHROOM VIEW!
OOOH... IT REALLY IS AMAZING.
YOU FOUND YOUR LAKE, CÉDRIC.

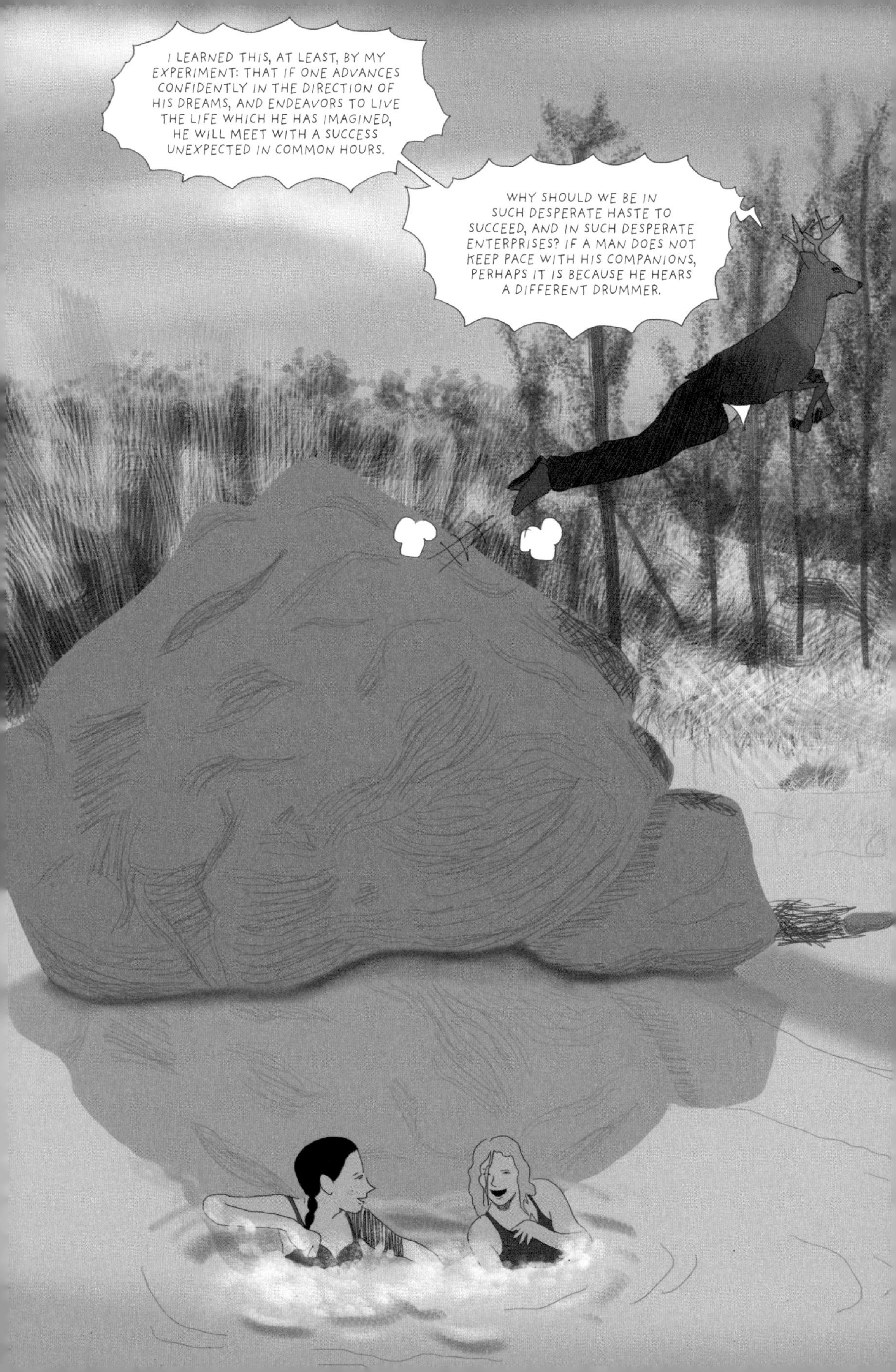
I LEARNED THIS, AT LEAST, BY MY EXPERIMENT: THAT IF ONE ADVANCES CONFIDENTLY IN THE DIRECTION OF HIS DREAMS, AND ENDEAVORS TO LIVE THE LIFE WHICH HE HAS IMAGINED, HE WILL MEET WITH A SUCCESS UNEXPECTED IN COMMON HOURS.
WHY SHOULD WE BE IN SUCH DESPERATE HASTE TO SUCCEED, AND IN SUCH DESPERATE ENTERPRISES? IF A MAN DOES NOT KEEP PACE WITH HIS COMPANIONS, PERHAPS IT IS BECAUSE HE HEARS A DIFFERENT DRUMMER.

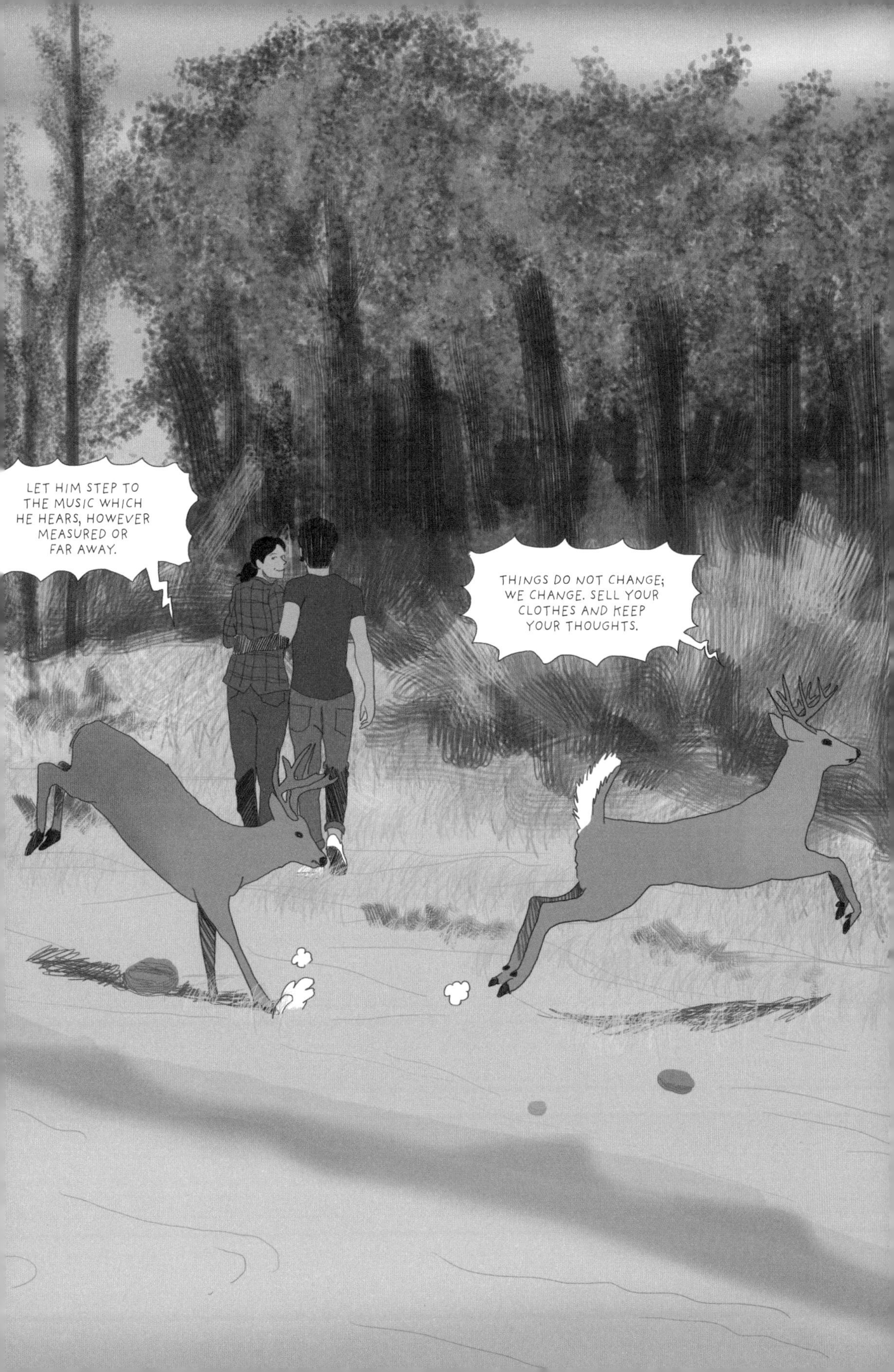
LET HIM STEP TO THE MUSIC WHICH HE HEARS, HOWEVER MEASURED OR FAR AWAY.
THINGS DO NOT CHANGE; WE CHANGE. SELL YOUR CLOTHES AND KEEP YOUR THOUGHTS.

IN MEMORY OF JACQUES TASSIN,
A THOREAU IN HIS SOUL

GRATITUDE AND THANKS GO TO NICOLAS FINET AND
THOMAS BOUT, LÉA, AND MANON FOR THEIR TRUST AND WORK.
TO BETTIE, FOR HER EYE, HER INSPIRATION, AND HER MADNESS IN
LIFE. UNCONDITIONAL LOVE FOR MY DAUGHTERS FOR THEIR IDEAS
AND THEIR ENTHUSIASM. TO MY MOTHER, MY FAMILY, AND MY
FRIENDS FOR THEIR UNWAVERING SUPPORT OF THIS BOOK.

AND ABOVE ALL, TO YOU, MY READERS — A BIG THANK YOU.

ABOUT THE AUTHOR

CÉDRIC TALING IS A PAINTER AND ILLUSTRATOR. HE HAS WORKED
AS A SCREENWRITER FOR CANAL+ ID AND AS AN ANIMATOR FOR
CINEMA AND TELEVISION. HIS PAINTINGS, WHICH ARE INSPIRED BY
COMICS ART, BLEND AMERICAN AND JAPANESE GRAPHIC INFLUENCES.
HE PRODUCED HIS FIRST SOLO EXHIBITION IN 2007 AND, IN 2014,
CO-FOUNDED THE CONTEMPORARY ART CENTRE LA TRAVERSE
D'ALFORTVILLE. *THOREAU AND ME* IS HIS DEBUT GRAPHIC NOVEL.